ABJECT BODIES IN THE GOSPEL OF MARK

The Bible in the Modern World, 45

ABJECT BODIES
IN THE GOSPEL OF MARK

Manuel Villalobos Mendoza

SHEFFIELD PHOENIX PRESS

2017

Copyright © Sheffield Phoenix Press, 2012, 2017

First published in hardback, 2012
First published in paperback, 2017

Published by Sheffield Phoenix Press
Department of Biblical Studies, University of Sheffield
45 Victoria Street
Sheffield S3 7QB

www.sheffieldphoenix.com

A CIP catalogue record for this book
is available from the British Library

Typeset by the HK Scriptorium
Printed by Lightning Source

ISBN 978-1-907534-54-6 (hardback)
ISBN 978-1-910928-27-1 (paperback)

ISSN 1747-9630

CONTENTS

ACKNOWLEDGMENTS

Words are inadequate to express my gratitude to all those people who have been part of this book. I have been blessed to work with scholars whose passion for God's Word is not just for show in the classrooms but instead reflects their deeply rooted commitment to justice. Dr Osvaldo Vena, of Garrett Evangelical Theological Seminary, passionately and fully engaged my hermeneutical approach to the biblical text, even when I did not know how to embrace my *muchos lados* of exclusion. He has been not only my teacher and mentor but also a friend, whose words in times of loneliness, despair, and anxiety provided peace and comfort to my body. His office indeed became a "holy ground" where the Eucharistic, and the traditional Argentinian mate created bonds of friendship, solidarity, and hope for a more inclusive society. Gracias, por haberle robado tiempo a su diáfana musa para escribir el 'blurb' de este libro. Usted como fiel 'partera' no me ha abandonado en los momentos de este 'alumbramiento' (ahora solo falta celebrar). Gracias, y espero que nuestros caminos, voces y escritos se vuelvan a unir en algún otro proyecto.

I am grateful also to Dr Lallene Rector of Garrett Evangelical Theological Seminary for kindly agreeing to be part of my committee. At a time when I was still searching for my 'hermeneutical approach', she exposed me to other voices and other bodies that had been living in *otros lados* of exclusion due to the (ab)use of the Bible. She helped me to realize that indeed the biblical text is always open to interpretation.

My gratitude goes also to Dr Ken Stone of Chicago Theological Seminary without whose insight and wisdom my dissertation—and now book—would not have been possible. Dr. Stone introduced me not just to Judith Butler but also to other theorists who helped me find my own voice in biblical interpretation. His seminar on Judith Butler not only provoked my own 'gender trouble' but also helped me to understand why some bodies matter more than others. He patiently witnessed my metamorphosis from being skeptical of Judith Butler to becoming a fervent devotee of Butler's notions of the precariousness and vulnerability of the body. I admire and respect his scholarly work, particularly for having opened a path to the Bible on behalf of the LGBTQ community here on *este lado* del Río Grande.

Quiero darle las gracias al Dr Timothy Sandoval, por solidarizarse y caminar conmigo. Gracias por tu generosidad en editar, dialogar y cuestionar algunos de mis argumentos. El Dr Ricardo López Rosas, biblista extraordinario, corrigió acentos, descubrió errores, y pacientemente me leyó, escuchó, una y otra vez algunas de las ideas aquí plasmadas, cuando estas sólo existían en mi imaginación. Gracias Ricardo por tu tiempo y compasión con este desterrado hijo de la madre Eva.

Quiero darle las gracias, a todas las personas que son parte de la Escuela Bíblica Claretiana de Chicago, cuyas historias y experiencias me han enseñado más de lo que he aprendido en la Universidad. Gracias, por su entrega, dedicación y por seguir trabajando por una comunidad más inclusiva y justa. I am particularly grateful to Fr Carl Quebedeaux for welcoming me into the religious community at a time when no other religious community or diocese would take me for being *del mítico 'otro lado'*. Gracias, Carl, por ser un buen hermano de comunidad, y el mejor amigo del Camino que he tenido.

I would like to give special thanks to the Hispanic Theological Initiative for providing me with a skillful editor. Ulrike Guthrie made this book possible, readable, and understandable, for she could see what I meant to convey despite my poor English language skills. This dissertation has benefitted tremendously from Uli's 'gifted eyes'. I want to express my gratitude also to the anonymous and generous reader from Sheffield Phoenix Press whose positive comments still resound like music to my ears.

Le doy las gracias a mi familia, especialmente a mi madre, Luz Mendoza, que sin haber estudiado la Biblia en libros, me la enseñado en la 'praxis'. Gracias especialmente a mis cuatro hermanas—Graciela, Raquel, Rosita y Ana—que a pesar de haber sido marginadas, excluidas y privadas de una —vida vivible— por el simple hecho de 'ser mujeres' han sabido encontrar fortaleza para continuar en la lucha diaria. Gracias por cuidarme, y por ser mi voz cuando no podía hablar. ¡De rodillas me tienen!

Last but not least, the poet Federico Garcia Lorca in his 'Ode to Walt Whitman', let his accusing voice be heard:

Against you, perverts of the cities,
Of swollen flesh and filthy thought,
Mothers of mud. Harpies.
Sleepless foes of Love that gives garlands of happiness.

I also let my voice be heard, not against you, but for you and with you; and I ask you for forgiveness, not in the name of the church (because she does not understand these things) but in Jesus' name, the beloved and abject Son of God. For you and with you, the abject, abused, excluded and crucified body of God is revealing God's solidarity and unconditional love for all. For you and with you, by whatever name you are called:

Jotos de México,
Faggots of North America,
Pájaros de Cuba,
Huecos de Guatemala,
Pirobos de Colombia,
Patos de Venezuela,
Zamel de Marruecos,
Queers from around the world!

All who have entered in a new covenant with the 'God of the rainbow' (Gen 9:12-13). For you and with you, I, a sinful man, ask for forgiveness and dedicate my work.

INTRODUCTION

Reading and gazing upon another male's body are always risky and dangerous, especially if such a body is believed to be that of God's Son. One of my earliest memories of gazing upon Jesus' body took place one Good Friday in a remote village in Mexico. Each Good Friday, the black Christ, or *Señor de Esquipulitas* as we called him, is exposed for veneration. My Aunt Pella, who was the unofficial 'pastor' of the church, every year would remove Jesus' black body from the cross to clean him and prepare him for the liturgy. My aunt as a priestess of a different deity would allow us to take a good look at the inert wooden body, a body that instead of moving us to compassion provoked fear and repulsion on discovering that Jesus' decayed body was transformable! She would follow the same ritual: First she would remove from his head the crown of thorns. After we had heard her sermon about how our sins had killed him, she would remove the black wig (à la Cher). Then, with great care she would detach the arms from the rest of the body. When our black Jesus was only a torso, she would ask us to take Jesus' arms and nails to the sacristy and clean those disabled arms there. She would not allow us to come out from the sacristy until she called us. Once we had meticulously cleaned Jesus' arms, she would perform an enabling ritual upon Jesus' broken and vulnerable body.

One particular Good Friday I was moved by curiosity to see the entire ritual of Jesus' transformation. I decided to hide in an old closet. With great anxiety and holding my breath, I attentively peered through the slightly open door. My avid eyes did not miss a single action that my Aunt Pella performed upon Jesus' torso. In silence, with prayers, sprinkling holy water, and with great devotion she would clean each remaining part of Jesus' body. The stripping of Jesus' loincloth was the climax of her forbidden ritual. Finally, the secret of what was behind Jesus' loincloth was revealed to me: he had no penis!

That particular Good Friday has stayed with me not just because Jesus' lack of genitalia but also because later in the day and in front of the whole congregation the priest made me feel that I was 'different' and that because of that I did not belong in the community of believers. What happened was this: After hearing with devotion Mark's passion narrative, we blindly followed the priest's exhortations to show our love to Jesus' broken and vulnerable body. The priest divided us according to our 'gender'. All the boys were lined up on the priest's right side and the girls were lined up on the priest's left side. Between them was an invisible but obvious abyss that no one could cross or transgress from either side. In silence, each girl and boy in turn approached and kissed some part of Jesus' disabled body. When I approached *Señor de Esquipulitas,* without hesitation I kissed him on the mouth. The irritated priest 'situated' me in my 'place' by saying: 'What are you doing? Are you *del otro lado,* Are you from the other side?' Immediately by instinct, I knew that being *del otro lado* was something that I should fear and avoid, even though I did not know why.[1]

Why Mark?

I use this story to introduce my book because it touches on some of the main elements that I will investigate in this project, such the (un)doing of gender, the notion of masculinity, the vulnerability, abjectness, and precariousness of the body, the power of gazing upon other male bodies, and the subversion and transgression of boundaries. I will show how these elements are present in some of the characters that Mark's depicts in his passion narrative. I quite deliberately chose to study Mark's passion narrative because this Gospel has been part of my life since my childhood. It was not till recently that I realized that Mark through his Gospel had in my childhood and youth become my imaginary friend, a friend I particularly needed when people pejoratively identified me as being *del otro lado* and *mano quebrada* or *mano caída,* 'limp-wristed'.

Sometime later to my great surprise I learned that Mark or his Gospel was remembered among the fathers of the church as a kind of *mano quebrada,* when they write: 'Mark declared, who is called "stump-fingered" (colobodactylus) because he had short fingers in comparison to the size of the rest of his body.'[2] The *Anti-Marcionite Prologue* and the *Evangeliorum prologi vetustissimi* describe Mark as being *colobodactylus* ('stumpy-fingered'), a description used by Hippolytus in the third century.[3] Clayton Croy argues

---

1. I have been using some of these stories elsewhere (Manuel Villalobos, 'Bodies *del otro lado*: Finding Life and Hope in the Borderland: Gloria Anzaldúa, The Ethiopian Eunuch of Acts 8:26-40, *y Yo*', in Teresa J. Hornsby and Ken Stone (eds.), *Bible Trouble: Queer Reading at the Boundaries of Biblical Scholarship* [Atlanta: Society of Biblical Literature, 2011], pp. 191-221).

2. Kurt Aland, *Synopsis quattuor Evangeliorum: Locis parallelis Evangeliorum apocryphorum et patrum adhibitis edidit* (Stuttgart: Deutsche Bibelgesellschaft, 1996), p. 548.

3. Hippolytus *Refutation of All Heresies* 7.30.1. J.L. North ('Marcos ho kolobodaktylos: Hippolytus Elenchus vii.30', *JTS* 28 [1977], pp. 498-527 [498]) notices that this particular word appears nowhere else in the whole of Greek literature.

that the word is a compound of *koloboō* ('to dock, mutilate, shorten') and *daktylos* ('finger'), so the etymology would seem to suggest a meaning like 'stump-fingered'.[4] Some scholars suggest that *kolobodaktylos* is a double entendre, and refers not only to the appearance of Mark's actual fingers, but to him being a 'shirker' and to his Gospel as being merely a 'torso',[5] not a complete body.

Mark, with its abrupt ending at 16.8, is indeed only a torso. The fathers of the church could not accept that the author of Mark would have chosen 'to finish' his work at 16.8. Yet as it stands, the body of the Gospel is indeed unfinished, incomplete, imperfect and mutilated. The other Gospels provide what is missing in Mark, that is, they provide its legs and feet. These are the resurrection appearances, or narratives. Without these, Mark is for many a broken body (Mark 14.22): no head (that is, no birth narratives) and no legs (no resurrection narratives). By being complete, the other Gospels betray Mark's deformed creation. They cannot bear the stigma of dealing with a deformed body. In a certain way, Mark's mutilation situates him in *el otro lado*. 'Mark has suffered almost total eclipse in Christian awareness by its three longer fellows (Matthew, Luke, and John).'[6] In a religion that demands one have a complete and whole body to approach the living God (Lev. 21.16-23), Mark's mutilation was probably the reason why, of all the Gospels, it has been the most deliberately neglected since the patristic period.[7] Mark as the 'scariest gospel'[8] has prompted scholars to perform 'surgery' on Mark's torso. Brendan Byrne reminds us, 'A century and a half ago, in scholarly circles at least, the second Gospel underwent notable rehabilitation.'[9] Unfortunately, scholars at the time apparently had not realized that people who had been left behind or neglected, those who had been called *mano quebrada* or *del otro lado* might develop what Gloria Anzaldúa

---

4. N. Clayton Croy, *The Mutilation of Mark's Gospel* (Nashville, TN: Abingdon Press, 2003), p. 64.

5. It is not my intention to resolve the riddle of whether colobodactylus refers to Mark or to his Gospel. See Burnett Hillman Streeter, *The Four Gospels: A Study of Origins* (New York: Macmillan, 1925), pp. 336-37. Also, Edgar J. Goodspeed, 'The Original Conclusion of the Gospel of Mark', *American Journal of Theology* (1905), pp. 484-90.

6. Brendan Byrne, *A Costly Freedom: Theological Reading of Mark's Gospel* (Collegeville, MN: Liturgical Press, 2008), p. ix.

7. See Brenda Deen Schildgen, *Power and Prejudice: The Reception of the Gospel of Mark* (Detroit: Wayne State University Press, 1999).

8. Byrne, *A Costly Freedom*, p. x.

9. Brendan Byrne, 'The Scariest Gospel' (accessed September 2009); online at http://www.americamagazine.org/content/article.cfm?article_id=4816.

called *la facultad,* which is the capacity to see beyond surface phenomena to the submerged deeper realities.[10]

According to Anzaldúa, those who are pushed out of the tribe for being different are likely to become more sensitized as a result (when not brutalized into insensitivity). Those who do not feel psychologically or physically safe in the world are more apt to develop this sense. Those who are pounced on the most have that capacity the strongest: the females, the homosexuals of all races, the dark skinned, the outcast, the persecuted, the marginalized, the foreign.[11] There is no doubt that Mark's Gospel is 'different' and that for centuries it has shared Cinderella's fate in being the overlooked one.[12] That Mark shares *la facultad,* I recognize in the way that he depicts his characters during the passion narrative. Mark the 'stumpy-fingered one', using this *facultad,* depicts some bodies (un)doing their gender and transgressing all kinds of boundaries.

For instance, Jesus breaks the rules of purity by entering the house of Simon the Leper (Mk 14.3-9); the unnamed woman confuses gender roles by entering male territory and performing a role that does not belong to her (Mk 13.3-19); Judas crosses the boundaries of friendship by betraying Jesus (Mk 14.10); an unnamed man subverts the genders of being male and female by bearing a pitcher of water (Mk 14.12-16); Jesus confuses the meaning of his body by identifying with the broken bread and his blood with the wine that is shed for many (Mk 14.22-25); a young man crosses the boundaries of discipleship: instead of following Jesus, he flees naked in the middle of the night (Mk 14.51-52); Peter transgresses the boundaries of fidelity—by sitting with Jesus' opponents (Mk 14.54) and by openly denying him (Mk 14.66-72); a little slave girl subverts gender roles—by being in male territory and by usurping the role of the High Priest by accusing Peter (Mk 14.66-72); Barabbas—the son of Abba— passes for something that he is not (Mk 15.6-11); the crowd exchanges the true Son of Abba for a murderous man (Mk 15.6-11); Jesus is momentarily forced to 'suspend' his 'identity' in order to pass for a king (Mk 15.17-19); Simon of Cyrene confuses his role by doing Simon Peter's job of bearing the cross (Mk 15.21); the centurion passes for a believer while he is still associated with Roman power (Mk 15.39); and some women subvert their roles by being faithfully present at the moment of Jesus' death (Mk 15.40-41).

---

10. Gloria Anzaldúa, *Borderland/La Frontera: The New Mestiza* (San Francisco: Aunt Lute, 3rd edn, 2007), p. 60.

11. Anzaldúa, *Borderland,* p. 60.

12. Byrne, *A Costly Freedom,* p. ix.

Methodology

One of the privileges of being educated here in the United States is to witness the great variety of methodologies and hermeneutics of biblical interpretation used to bring hope and liberation to some minority groups. Through my classes here in the United States I have been exposed to many interpretive approaches, and the work of a vast range of biblical scholars and theologians has left a tremendous mark on the way that I approach the biblical text. I celebrate and applaud the way in which our African American brothers and sisters find their own voice and have unmasked the Eurocentric interpretation of the Bible. And how can I forget our white middle-class sisters who are still struggling against the androcentric interpretations of the Bible that have legitimized all kind of abuses against women? Actually, it was here in the United States at Catholic Theological Union that I was first challenged to read the Bible with feminist eyes. I am also impressed by postcolonial interpretation, which teaches us that we, the descendants of colonized countries, are still suffering the marks of subjugation. I give thanks for all those Latinos/as who have incorporated the experience of the community into their theological discourse as well as into their biblical interpretation. The gay, lesbian, bisexual and transgender (hereafter GLBT) scholars here in the United States have emerged to denounce and unmask the oppression that GLBT persons have suffered by the misinterpretation of a few 'texts of terror'.[13] These scholars have found their own voices: they have faces, they have claimed the sacredness of their bodies, and they who once were marginalized and despised for their sexual orientation have started the process of celebrating God's unconditional grace. All these dissident voices have illuminated my understanding of the Bible. Together they create the perfect melodies to perform their hymns and to chant their manifestos. Yet despite this magnificent rendition, there are still some notes missing, still some voices that are not being heard, still some manifestos that are not read nor chanted. There continue to be more interpretations that need to come out of the shadows of death.

It is in this context where I situate myself as one *del otro lado*. Therefore, my hermeneutic will be called accordingly *del otro lado*. I am consciously avoiding the terms Latino and Hispanic because of the ambiguity that both terms convey.[14] Moreover, those terms do not define me, and are still some-

---

13. I am borrowing this phrase from Phyllis Trible, *Texts of Terror: Literary-Feminist Readings of Biblical Narratives* (Philadelphia: Fortress Press, 1984).

14. See Fernando Segovia, 'Toward Latino/a American Biblical Criticism: Latin(o/a)ness as Problematic', in Randall C. Bailey *et al.* (eds.), *They Were in One Place? Toward Minority Biblical Criticism* (Leiden: Brill, 2009), pp. 193-223.

how 'vague' and alien to my own experience. I am a *Mexicano del otro y de este lado*. Both sides of El Rio Grande dwell in my body and struggle for autonomy. My hermeneutic *del otro lado* is inspired from Latin America hermeneutics: *Vida-Texto-Vida*, 'Life-Text-Life'. Scholars familiar with the way in which *comunidades eclesiales de base*, 'base ecclesial communities', read the Bible will be able to see the influence of my interpretation. In my *comunidades eclesiales de base*, every time that we approach the Bible we begin with our own experiences, stories, struggles and hopes. Then we open the Bible with the confidence that our precarious and vulnerable life will find meaning by reinterpreting, appropriating and recontextualizing our biblical text. With the help of the Bible, we discover a new experience of God and a new vision of the powerful and liberating action of the Word of God in our lives. Finally, we return to our lives in which we are challenged to put into *praxis* our beliefs as a way to transform our society.

I am not using a particular method of interpretation; rather, my hermeneutics of *el otro lado* relies heavily on the insight of Judith Butler. For a while, I was thinking of using as my underlying theorist the insights of Gloria Anzaldúa. However, Butler's understanding of the vulnerability and precarious nature of the body, of how some bodies become human and others do not, proves more helpful for this project. Nevertheless Anzaldúa's insights concerning *la facultad*, *nepantla* and borderland will be evident throughout this project. Scholars familiar with the work of Judith Butler would agree with me that she is not easy to read. She brings into the conversation a plethora of philosophers and theories without explaining who or what they are. Butler's own prose style has become notorious for its obscurity, allusiveness and incoherence.[15] In this project, instead of reading some philosophers through the lens of Butler, I have decided to go *ad fontes*, for example to Julia Kristeva's concept of the abject, Emanuel Levinas's understanding of the face, and Michel Foucault's understanding of power.

How am I going to use Butler's lenses in a *biblical* interpretation of Mark's passion narrative? In this project I will follow other scholars who have used contemporary philosophers to engage with our biblical text, including Judith Butler's notion of gender, performativity and sex.[16] There-

---

15. Sara Salih, *Judith Butler* (New York: Routledge, 2002), p.145.

16. See Halvor Moxnes, 'Jesus in Gender Trouble', *Cross Currents* 54.3 (2004), pp. 31-46. See also the several articles in Ellen T. Armour and Susan M. St. Ville, (eds.), *Bodily Citations: Religion and Judith Butler* (New York: Columbia University Press, 2006). Moreover, see also Ken Stone, 'Bibles That Matter: Biblical Theology and Queer Performativity', *BTB* 38 (2008), pp. 1-20; Karen Trimble Alliaume, *Re(as)sembling Christ: Feminist Christology, Identity Politics, and the Imagination of Christian Community* (PhD diss., Duke University, 1999); David Jobling *et al.* (eds.), *The Postmodern Bible Reader* (Oxford: Blackwell, 2001); and Daniel Boyarin, *A Radical Jew: Paul and the Politics of Identity* (Berkeley: University of California Press, 1994).

fore, this monograph is not about Judith Butler per se, particularly since I am neither a philosopher nor an authority on Butler's philosophical approach. I am still processing and digesting 'the thick soup of Butler's prose',[17] which I hope will one day be more fully assimilated and digested in order to sustain me in my battle to understand why some bodies matter more than others. Who decides which bodies matter and which do not? Who might count as a human? How is a person deemed more or less human? What is our responsibility toward *other* bodies? Of course, drawing on Butler's work has limited usefulness since she herself has neither interpreted Mark's passion narrative nor any other biblical texts. However, she has challenged us by saying, 'To know how to live, one had to know how to read, and one had to be able to develop an interpretation of what one reads.'[18] And this is precisely what I am intending to do in my reading and interpretation of Mark's passion narrative. In this book I am thus not analyzing a Butlerian interpretation of Mark's passion narrative, but as a biblical apprentice I am reading and gazing upon some bodies that appear in Mark's passion narrative, and in so doing am taking seriously certain aspects of Butler's insights such us gender, abjectness, the precariousness and vulnerability of the body, and the responsibility that we have toward the other.

The bodies that I choose to focus on in this book, bodies such as the unnamed woman (Mk 14.3-9), the slave girl (Mk 14.66-72), the unnamed man who carried a jar of water (Mk 14.51-52) and Simon the Leper (Mk 14.3-9), have attended Butler's invitation of (un)doing their gender. I will demonstrate that these bodies, which had been marked as 'man' and 'woman' by their society and religious system, are disrupting and transgressing their assigned gender roles because of their scandalous performances. Their words and actions demonstrate that gender can be constructed differently. They corroborate Butler's idea that gender is a fluid variable that shifts and changes in different contexts and at different times. By (un)doing their gender, these bodies show how the dominant discourse on gender and sexuality has been and can be resisted, transgressed, contested and subverted by acts of performance. I open this study by confessing that gazing upon Jesus' body has not been easy task. However, in this book I have dared once again to gaze upon Jesus' broken and vulnerable body through other lenses. Applying Butler's concepts of abjection, vulnerability and precariousness to Jesus' own body has brought new nuances to my own understanding of Jesus' death and crucifixion.

17. Martha C. Nussbaum, 'The Professor of Parody: The Hip Defeatism of Judith Butler', *The New Republic* 220.4 (1999), pp. 38-45 (38).
18. Judith Butler, "Afterword', in Ellen T. Armour and Susan M. St. Ville, (eds.), *Bodily Citations: Religion and Judith Butler* (New York: Columbia University Press, 2006), p. 278.

This work is primarily concerned with how Mark present events, and how he depicts some of his characters in the passion narrative, but I do not attempt further assessment of textual historicity here. Because of the necessarily limited scope of this book, I do not discuss the many other attractive bodies that might have been included in such a study, bodies such as the young man who runs away naked in the middle of the night (Mk 14.51-52), the figure of Barabbas (Mk 15.6-15), and Simon of Cyrene (Mk 15.21-24), to mention only a few. This project has piqued my curiosity to return at another time and examine diligently those bodies that seem to be passing for something that they are not, as Butler would say.

Chapter 1: I Confess ... That my Body
Has muchos lados / Many Angles of Exclusion

My hermeneutics begins with the experience of the people who read and interpret the biblical text. Therefore, in this first chapter I disclose the ambiguity and ambivalence of being *en el otro lado*. Through this chapter I intend to let my readers know from where I am reading and interpreting the biblical text so that my readers are able to understand the struggles and hopes that I bring to the biblical text. They thus understand that I represent many *lados* of exclusion, and that it is not always easiest or most true to embrace a single angle and read the biblical text from that particular angle. I will explore how the process of being situated *en el otro lado* is not something that was accomplished once and for all, but rather is something that must be enacted over and over again by culture and religion. I will point out that it is not just my sexual orientation that enters into the picture when interpreting the biblical text, but that issues of race, language, marginality, segregation, power and religious belief also play a pivotal role in my own understanding of my body and the Bible.

In this first chapter, I use Octavio Paz's understanding of *La Chingada*—the fucked one—to explain how we as Mexicans are products of rape. According to Paz, we have a tremendous problem of identity as a consequence of colonization, and this is evident in our sense of inferiority in the light of U.S. culture. Paz explains how the word *chingar* has multiple meanings for the Mexican people, ranging from failure to violation, the latter being perhaps the meaning that best reveals their inferiority complexes. For Paz, *La Chingada* 'is the Mother. Not a Mother of flesh and blood but a mythical figure.... *La Chingada* is the mother who has suffered—metaphorically or actually—the corrosive and defaming action implicit in the verb that gives her her name.'[19] In this chapter I will proudly embrace *La Chingada*

---

19. Octavio Paz, *The Labyrinth of Solitude: Life and Thought in Mexico* (trans. Lysander Kemp; New York: Grove Press, 1961), p. 75.

as my forgotten and neglected mother whose presence has accompanied me since my birth. This concept of *La Chingada* and her innumerable symbolic meanings will be helpful at several points in this project, especially when analyzing the figures of Judas, Jesus and the Roman centurion.

Chapter 2: Marimachas,[20] descaradas,[21] malcriadas[22] y hociconas / *The Dykes, the Shameless, the Ill-bred and the Loudmouths*

> One is not born a woman, but becomes one (Simone de Beauvoir). Strictly speaking, 'women' cannot be said to exist (Julia Kristeva). Women do not have sex (Luce Irigaray). The deployment of sexuality … established this notion of sex (Michel Foucault). The category of sex is the political category that founds society as heterosexual (Monique Wittig).[23]

In her most influential book, *Gender Trouble*, Butler opens with these five quotations that embrace various themes that she subsequently develops. The first two cast doubt on the idea of wo/man[24] as an essential category; the third contests the link between wo/men and sex; and the last two seek to problematize the 'naturalness' of sex.[25] Despite the amount of inspiration and insights that Butler draws from these theorists regarding the notion of 'wo/man', 'fe/male', 'sex/uality', 'desire', 'gender' and the 'body', however, Butler rejects their final theoretical positions—and all for the same reason: that is, for their reliance on certain prediscursive or naturalistic assumptions.[26] For Butler, all these concepts are discursively constituted. Take for instance the notion of 'gender', which marks a body as being wo/man. According to Butler, the notion of gender is neither natural nor innate, but rather is a social construct that serves particular purposes and

20. *Marimacha* is a combination of the name *María* and the word *macho*, which is an adjective used to describe manliness. In the word *Marimacha*, the *macho* component is feminized with the 'a' ending instead of the 'o'. Of course the word *marimacha* is slang for 'lesbian'. The word *hocico* means snout and is a derogatory term that indicates some sort of ugliness. This term is used almost exclusively against loud-mouthed women who 'protest too much'.

21. *Descarada* literally means 'without face or barefaced'.

22. *Malcriada* is word used when a woman talk backs to a male figure or when she is opinionated.

23. Judith Butler, *Gender Trouble: Feminism and the Subversion of Identity* (New York: Routledge, 2006), p. 1.

24. I am borrowing this deconstruction of the word 'woman' from Elisabeth Schüssler Fiorenza. See for instance her book *Jesus: Miriam's Child, Sophia's Prophet: Critical Issues in Feminist Christology* (New York: Continuum, 1994).

25. Moya Lloyd, *Judith Butler. From Norms to Politics* (Cambridge: Polity Press, 2007), p. 30.

26. Lloyd, *Judith Butler*, p. 30.

institutions. Yet gender is not just a social construct but also a kind of 'performance'. It is throughout the continuous act of repetition and performance that a 'body' becomes a 'man' or a 'woman', because 'gender is always a doing'.[27] If being 'man' or 'woman' is neither natural nor divine in origin, then these categories can be troubled, problematized, destabilized and subverted. This is so because these categories, as Butler points out, tend to be instruments of regulatory regimes, whether as the normalizing categories of oppression structures, or as the rallying points for a liberatory contestation of that very oppression.[28] Once Butler unmasks the false appearance of 'stable gender identity' through the notion of performance, she calls for 'gender trouble'. For Butler, 'gender itself becomes a free-floating artifice, with the consequence that *man* and *masculine* might just as easily signify a female body as a male one, and a *woman* and *feminine* a male body as easily as female one' [italics in the original].[29]

In this chapter I will examine two wo/men that have 'responded' to Butler's invitation of troubling their gender. The first woman that I analyze is the unnamed woman who anoints Jesus' head (Mk 14.2-12). I will show how this woman, by entering a public space and performing her ritual of love over Jesus' head, transgressed her assigned gender. Her undoing of gender is evident when the male disciple harshly attempts to put her in her proper place. The second woman that I will study is the 'little' girl who 'accused' Peter of being a follower of Jesus (Mk 14.66-72). Mark depicts this little slave girl as being in a very dangerous place. She is in 'men's territory', talking with them and acting like a man. This little slave girl not only undoes her gender, but there is no male who reacts against her. These two wo/men, who have been gendered, or marked as 'women', use their bodies to transgress all kinds of boundaries. Their performance, words and actions demonstrate that gender can be constructed differently. So these groups of wo/men provide an opening for subversive action. They corroborate Butler's idea that gender is a fluid variable that shifts and changes in different contexts, and at different times.

Chapter 3: No somos machos pero somos muchos /
We Are Not macho *but We Are Many*

There is a saying in Mexico that goes like this: *No somos machos pero somos muchos,* 'We are not *machos* but we are many.' The saying is a way for peo-

27. Butler, *Gender Trouble*, p. 34.
28. Judith Butler, 'Imitation and Gender Insubordination', in Henry Abelove, Michèle Aina Barale, and David M. Halperin (eds.), *The Lesbian and Gay Studies Reader* (New York: Routledge, 1993), pp. 307-20 (308).
29. Butler, *Gender Trouble*, p. 9.

ple to (un)do their gender in a public space and to destabilize their assigned gender roles by behaving like a wo/man. Yet hetero/sexual men also use this saying, usually either when ridiculing someone or as a way of proving their manliness among themselves. *Jotos*[30] are often accused of being *descarados,* for instead of feeling ashamed of their *joterías*[31] they celebrate it—with pride and arrogance and in public. Often I hear compassionate and well-intentioned hetero/sexual people saying: *Yo no tengo nada con lo que ellos hagan en su vida privada, pero en la calle que se comporten como 'hombres',* 'I do not have anything against whatever they might do in their private lives, but on the street they should behave like "men".' Some *'joto*-friendly' hetero/sexuals in a more intimate setting even go so far as to ask: *¿Quién es el 'hombre' y quién la 'mujer'?,* 'Who is the man and who is the woman?—meaning, who is the one who penetrates and who is the one who is penetrated?' In short, even ostensibly liberated people feel the need to assign stereotyped gender roles or gendered behaviors to others. Butler's theory of performativity responds to the notion that there is an abiding substance that makes a 'man' or a 'woman'. We saw above that for Butler gender is not something one is, but rather something one does, an act, or more precisely, a sequence of acts, a verb rather than noun, a 'doing' rather that a 'being'.[32] Butler succinctly argues that from birth we are labeled or understood as gendered beings and we are constantly gendered or attributed a gender throughout our lives in a variety of ways and situations. Our being a man or a woman is always constrained by cultural norms, taboos, social convention, religious assumptions and even laws. Indeed, 'There are punishments for not doing gender right: a man in Maine walks down the street in a dress, walking the way that women are supposed to walk; next day his body is found dead in a ravine.'[33] Lloyd echoes Butler's notion of gendering, concluding that some categories, such as 'straight' and 'queer', are not fixed categories and that such categories do not represent a particular group of subjects. For her, one *is* never straight *or* queer, merely in the condition of 'doing' straightness or queerness. She affirms, 'There is, thus, no single modality of embodiment that stands for straight-ness or queer-ness. Rather there is openness, fluidity, flux; an endless possibility of de-termination and re-citation (with "re" understood both as repetition and as a different citation).'[34]

30. Mexican slang for a faggot.
31. The deeds, performance, behavior, and words of a *joto.*
32. Salih, *Judith Butler*, p. 62.
33. Judith Butler, 'Gendering the Body: Beauvoir's Philosophical Contribution', in Ann Garry, Marilyn Pearsall (eds.), *Women. Knowledge, and Reality: Explorations in Feminist Philosophy* (Boston: Unwin Hyman, 1989), pp. 253-62 (256).
34. Moya Lloyd, 'Performativity, Parody, Politics', *Theory Culture and Society* 16 (1999), pp. 195-213 (197).

In this third chapter I gaze upon two 'men' who are 'not doing their gender right'. The first man is Simon the Leper (Mk 14.2-9), whose inflicted body makes him *del otro lado,* unable to prove his masculinity. The second body that I investigate is the unnamed man who carries his pitcher of water on a Jerusalem street (Mk 14.12-16). By performing this unmanly task this man is deemed effeminate, unable to show any strength. For unknown reasons, Mark depicts these two men with some overtones of effeminacy. These men fail their gender in some way by not always measuring up to the cultural norm and expectations of what a 'real man' is and does. Anthropologists have helped us to understand that masculinity is not easily defined because of the fact that it could mean different things to different cultures at different times. Moreover, masculinity is not some-thing that is given but rather something that one must achieve. Manhood is never something that can be taken for granted. A male must constantly, obsessively and anxiously demonstrate that he indeed is a man. 'The state of being a "real man" or "true man" [is] uncertain or precarious, a prize to be won or wrested through struggle.'[35] Therefore, manliness, virility, masculinity, and the honor and privileges that such categories entail are scrupulously examined. 'Masculinity was a matter of constant public self-presentation; it was always under negotiation, always at the risk of losing male honour or increasing it.'[36] In this chapter, I show that these two men depicted in Mark's Gospel are somehow unperturbed by being considered effeminate or by assuming effeminate roles. Although they have the opportunity to negotiate their masculinity and prove that they are real men, they are not anxious to do so. These men, by performing and using their bodies in a womanly (and ridiculed way), challenge the rule of what constitutes being 'man'. Indeed, these weak, vulnerable, womanish, slavish and disfranchised men seem to be an integral part of Jesus' new household.

Chapter 4: Jesus' Abject, Precarious and Vulnerable Body

Readers of Judith Butler have, it seems, almost compulsively focused on her understanding and construction of gender as well as the notion of per-formativity to the exclusion of some of her other ideas. The few biblical scholars and theologians who have used Butler's theories have similarly drawn only on these aspects of her work. I myself have been seduced by

35. David D. Gilmore, *Manhood in the Making: Cultural Concepts of Masculinity* (New Heaven: Yale University Press, 1990), p. 1.

36. Moisés Mayordomo Marin, 'Construction of Masculinity in Antiquity and Early Christianity', in *Lectio Difficilior* 2 (2006) (accessed 9 August 2009); online at http://www.lectio.unibe.ch/06_2/marin_construction.htm.

Butler's understanding of gender, wo/man, sexuality, masculinity and performativity, as will be obvious in Chapters 2 and 3. Unfortunately, the focus on these key concepts has overshadowed some of Butler's revolutionary, provocative and meaningful ideas of the precariousness and vulnerability of the body. In approaching such questions, Butler creatively adapts Kristeva's idea of abjection. Butler uses the term 'abject' to describe the 'unlivable and uninhabitable zones of social life' populated by those 'who do not enjoy the status of the subject, but whose living under the sign of the "unlivable" is required to circumscribe the domain of the subject'.[37] Butler takes the abject bodies as the *punctum dolens* to examine how the materiality of the body is controlled, normalized, labeled, organized and ready to be classified as human or inhuman by the elite culture. In *Bodies That Matter* Butler invites us not just to examine how bodies are constructed and with what purpose, but also how and why certain bodies are 'not constructed'.[38] For Butler, abjection is not restricted to sex and gender but pertains to all kind of bodies whose lives are not considered to be 'lives' and whose materiality is not understood to 'matter'.

In this chapter I explore how the abjection, precariousness and vulnerability of Jesus' body reaches its climax during his last meal, his betrayal by Judas and the trial before the Sanhedrin. Mark has framed Jesus' final hours in Jerusalem as being surrounded by all kinds of ambiguity. It is in the context of a meal that Jesus identifies his body—which was meant to be intact, whole and complete—with the broken and perishable bread that is given freely to all. By doing this, Jesus becomes an abject being whose deeds and actions break down the meaning of subject and object, self and other, life and death. So in this chapter, after analyzing the so-called Eucharistic words of Jesus, I show how Judas's betrayal of Jesus will unleash all kinds of violence toward Jesus' vulnerable and precarious body. And here Butler is helpful again, for she suggests that it is never possible to access— or know— the full reality of the entity called the body. Any attempt to think, talk or write about it requires the use of language.[39] Through the mediation or use of language the body is given a certain kind of existence, but language can by the same token also deny and injure the body. I show how Judas, by hailing Jesus with the solemn pronouncement of the title 'Rabbi', in effect 'gives up' or hands over Jesus' body, sells it and seals Jesus' fate by his murderous language. In Butler's reading of Levinas's ethics, the 'face of the other' becomes for Butler the fundamental ethical experience that grounds one's humanity by way of the other's vulnerability to death. In

---

37. Judith Butler, *Bodies That Matter: On the Discursive Limits of Sex* (New York: Routledge, 1993), p. 3.
38. Butler, *Bodies That Matter*, p. 16.
39. Lloyd, *Judith*, p. 74.

this chapter, I show how the religious authorities (high priests, scribes, and Pharisees) did not recognize in Jesus' 'face' God's voice, which utters, 'You shall not kill.'

Chapter 5: La muerte de un hijo de la Chingada[40] /
The Death of a Son of a Bitch

I opened this study by confessing that gazing upon Jesus' body provoked in me all kinds of feelings and anxieties. In this chapter, I gaze once again upon Jesus' vulnerable and precarious body to show how he was 'sexually penetrated' through the 'gaze' of other, manlier men. I will show how for the Greco-Roman culture as well as the Palestinian culture, there was power, submission, control and penetration in the act of gazing. In those cultures men assured their manliness and authority through the dynamic of the gaze. In the dialectic of 'gazing', males exhibited power and dominion over women, slaves and effeminate men. And women, slaves and effeminate men showed vulnerability and submission to the one who gazed upon them. In this chapter, I show how Jesus was gazed upon by other, manlier men during his trial, crucifixion and death. I will use once again Paz's understanding of *la Chingada* in order to explain the relationship between Jesus and the Roman soldiers. For Paz, *chingar* is a masculine verb and *chingada* is a passive noun. The idea that the masculine principle violates while the feminine suffers the act of aggression becomes a perspective of life for the Mexican of Paz's description: 'To the Mexican there are only two possibilities in life: either he inflicts the action implied by the *chingar* on others, or else he suffers them himself at the hands of others.'[41] It has become a value of Mexican society to prize the masculine role of the active *chingón* and denigrate the feminine *chingada*.[42] I show how Jesus became *la Chingada* or *el chingao*, and the Roman soldiers become *los chingones*. According to Paz, we as Mexicans understand life as a perpetual struggle and division between the haves and the have-nots, between the *macho* and the *effeminate*, between the strong and the weak, between *chingones* and *chingados*. I will show how Jesus' death is understood according to those realities as well. In the end, Jesus died perceived as a *chingao* by all—the Romans, the religious authorities, some of his followers and even by his absent God.

40. The death of 'a fucked one'.
41. Paz, *Labyrinth of Solitude*, p. 78.
42. Sandra Messinger Cypess, *La Malinche in Mexican Literature: From History to Myth* (Austin: University of Texas Press, 1991), p. 95.

Epistolary Epilogue: First Letter of Manuel Villalobos Mendoza
to the Markan Community

One of the principles in my hermeneutic of *Vida-Texto-Vida*, 'Life-Text-Life', is to recontextualize the biblical text in the life of the community. In this epilogue, I return to my experience and the struggles and hopes of my community by writing a letter to Mark and the Markan community. I more or less use the epistolary genre of the Greco-Roman world to let Mark know, in an apocalyptic kind of way, who we are, where we are, what is troubling us, what we can do, what time it is and for what we hope.

The idea of writing a letter to Mark was quite complicated. On one occasion, I made a comment in my Bible group about how we often fail Mark's Gospel by not going back to Galilee but by preferring to stay in Jerusalem and Rome. When I added the comment 'If only Mark knew what we had done to his Gospel', Lupita, a very active member of the group, immediately responded: *Escríbele una carta y cuéntale todo,* 'Write him a letter and tell him everything.' I laughed at her comment, but she was quite serious. For a few weeks Lupita's idea would not let me go. Then, I remembered that we in Latin America have taken the Bible quite personally without waiting for the invitation of our North American brothers and sisters.[43] And what could be more personal than writing a letter to Mark, I thought? I emailed my mentor, Dr Vena, and asked him about this issue, and he emailed back saying, *La idea de terminar con una carta a Marcos completa el círculo hermenéutico y me parece muy creativo,* 'The idea of finishing with a letter to Mark completes the hermeneutical circle and seems to me to be very creative.'[44] With my mentor's approval I decided to write my letter to Mark.

In the process of writing the letter to Mark, many memories of my encounter with Mark's Gospel come back to me. For instance, it was the Mexican Markan scholar Carlos Bravo's book *Jesús, hombre en conflicto: El relato de Marcos en América Latina*[45] that introduced me to Mark's radical Gospel. With the intention of offering the good news of Mark's Gospel to a broader audience, Bravo reworked his book with the title *Galilea año 30: Para leer el Evangelio de Marcos.*[46] In this last book, Bravo took on Mark's personality and wrote as if he were Mark. By passing for something that he was not, Bravo indeed brought good news to all of us who were struggling between death and life in our martyrized Latin America. Moreover, by nar-

---

43. Janice Capel Anderson and Jeffrey L. Staley (eds.), *Taking It Personally: Autobiographical Biblical Criticism* (Atlanta: Scholar Press, 1995).

44. Osvaldo Vena, E-mail communication, 26 January 2010.

45. Carlos Bravo, *Jesús, hombre en conflicto: El Relato de Marcos en América Latina* (Mexico City: Centro de Reflexión Teológica, 2nd edn, 1986).

46. Carlos Bravo, *Galilea año 30: Para leer el Evangelio de Marcos* (Córdoba: Ediciones el Almendro 1991).

rating the entire Gospel in the first person, Bravo transgresses the usual and accepted way of reading, writing and interpreting the biblical text. Although my creativity does not compare with Bravo's, his insights in interpreting Mark's Gospel relieved my anxieties about talking and writing personally to Mark. Additionally, my Colombian friend Agustín Monroy brought to my attention that the biblical scholar Elsa Tamez had already written a letter using the epistolary genre of the Greco-Roman world.[47] He graciously send me Tamez's letter, which had been delivered to all the theologians who were in Sâo Paulo, Brazil. In her letter, Tamez is the one in charge of reading publically the letter that Priscila—the apostle and friend of Paul—had written to them. When I read Priscila's/Tamez's letter, I realized that the idea of writing a letter to Mark was not so crazy after all. Although my letter to Mark is the inverse of Tamez's letter, because I am not the recipient of Mark's letter but rather the sender, Tamez's letter gave me the courage to transgress the conventional way of writing and finishing a book. Writing this letter was for me a kind of cathartic experience in which I expressed all my frustrations, anxieties, troubles and hopes for a better future for me, for my community and for the whole of God's creation.

Perhaps you are asking yourself whether you, the reader, really need to know all of this information about me? Perhaps not. However, 'if I try to give an account of myself, if I try to make myself recognizable and understandable, then I might begin with a narrative account of my life'.[48] By giving an account of myself, I invite you to cross to my *otros lados,* which has been marked by exclusion, negation and segregation. I invite you to witness how my reading of particular biblical texts *del otro lado* has started the painful process of recovering my voice, my body and my experience of God. I invite you to observe that by reading and interpreting the biblical text from *otros lados* the Word of God once again becomes sacred and full of life for all those people who have suffered at the hands of bibliolatrous interpretations. With this in mind, I invite you to be part of my story by reading and hearing my confession.

---

47. Elsa Tamez, 'Epístola de Priscila a los hermanos y hermanas reunidos en Sâo Paulo Brasil' (paper presented at Conferencia Sobre Cristianismo en América Latina y el Caribe: Trayectorias, Diagnóstico y Perspectivas. Sâo Paulo, Brazil, 29 July 2003).

48. Judith Butler, *Giving an Account of Oneself* (New York: Fordham University Press, 2005), p. 37.

1

I Confess . . . That my Body
Has *muchos lados* / Many Angles of Exclusion

In Subjectivity and Truth, Michel Foucault comments that confession is 'to declare aloud and intelligibly the truth of oneself'.[1] When scholars publicly establish their social location in their writings, it is usually a way of confessing the particularity of their viewpoint—their origin and ethnicity, their social class and political convictions, their age and gender, and so forth. Yet I wonder, do we, by the very act of confessing our social location, have the right to talk about other people's experience? Or are we using the suffering, the exploitation and marginalization of *the other* to promote our own agenda? For instance, some biblical scholars write and talk with such passion about the poor when they are living in the comfort of the empire. Their books have become indeed *libros liberadores con pastas opresivas*, 'liberating books with oppressive covers', as the Mexican theologian Alberto Anguiano called them.[2] Even the poor people who witness incongruity between the writing and the scholar's style of life often exclaim, *Dios me libre de mis liberadores*, 'God delivers me from my liberators.'

Foucault suggests that our modern, secular society has ingrained elements of Christian, and especially Catholic, tradition which he broadly describes as 'pastoral power'. Akin to priests or pastors, he suggests, a certain sector or class of people has assumed the power to 'guide' and cultivate others ethically. As with the Christian notion of the pastor, says Foucault, the assumption is that such a man has particular insight into the people to whom he ministers, and that application of this knowledge to the person is the means by which that particular man [woman] is not only helped but also,

---

1. Michel Foucault, *The Politics of Truth* (ed. Sylvère Lotringer; intro. John Rajchman; trans. Lysa Hochroth and Catherine Porter; Los Angeles: Semiotext(e), 1997), p. 173.

2. By this, he means that monetary reward is involved in the publishing industry. Alberto Anguiano, Email correspondence.

more sinisterly, controlled.[3] Analogously, when biblical scholars exercise their power in interpreting the biblical text on behalf of marginalized people whose voices are absent in academia, these scholars are assuming that they are the ones with authority and power to guide the community, and that this particular community of faith becomes 'informed' and 'represented' by the academics' interpretation of this community to the academic world.

Yet confession surely assumes that the one confessing is fully implicated in the life, struggles, despairs and hope of the one(s) whom s/he intends to represent, otherwise that confession is spurious and illegitimate. Jeffrey L. Staley validly argues that the possibility that our writing might re-victimize the voiceless and powerless raises serious ethical issues.[4] Judith Butler also warns that one gives an account of oneself always to another, whether that other is conjured or actually exists. Because the act of confessing to others implies an ethical relation between the one who confesses and the one who hears the confession, Butler continues, 'this other establishes the scene of address as a more primary ethical relation than a reflexive effort to give an account of oneself'.[5] Here is where I see a problem in scholars' confessions of location and particularly of solidarity to those not represented—in this case, in the biblical field: often the ones confessing are not really impli-cated in the lives of the communities with which they associate themselves, whether that be the poor, or any kind of *other*. It is absolutely wrong and arrogant to coopt another's being. It is equally wrong to assume that oth-ers have no means of their own to describe their situation and therefore to describe and prescribe it for them, as happens so often in unequal power relations. People create their own myths and stories, and these give them identity in a foreign land.

Ser y estar en el otro lado

Some Latinos scholars have argued 'that U.S. Latinos/as have become invisible people, subaltern people. They have been left out of the master narratives; their voices and stories are silenced and covered.'[6] Despite this awareness of exclusion, Latino/a scholars have themselves not incorporated

3. Judith Butler, *Undoing Gender* (New York: Routledge, 2004), p. 161.

4. Jeffrey L. Staley, 'What Is Critical about Autobiographical (Biblical) Criticism?' in Ingrid Rosa Kitzberger (ed.), *Autobiographical Biblical Criticism: Between Text and Self* (Leiden: Deo, 2002), pp. 12-33 (18).

5. Butler, *Giving an Account*, p. 21.

6. Hjamil A. Martinez-Vazquez, 'Dis-covering the Silences. A Postcolonial Critique of U.S. Religious Historiography', in Benjamin Valentin (ed.), *New Horizons in His-panic/Latino(a) Theology* (Cleveland: Pilgrim Press, 2003), pp. 50-78 (73).

into their own biblical interpretation the experience of GLBT.[7] Although, I have been involved in the continuous struggles for justice for some GLBT people, I do not pretend to talk or represent the experience of other GLBT Latinos/as who are out there struggling in a homophobic culture and its institutions. My coming out through my writings is for the purpose of coping with my own struggles of living as a *Mexicano del otro lado*. Yet now that I am in a 'privileged position' of writing publicly about my own experience, a crowd of voices tells me I don't have the right. I recognize my elementary teacher's voice deriding me because, *eres un indio, no sabes ni hablar*, 'you are an *indio*, you do not know even how to talk.' Even more painful, I recognize God's voice (as my grandmother used to call the priest) proclaiming with authority that *gente que es del otro lado merece morir*, 'people from the other side deserve to die.'

Yet here I am, a *Mexicano del otro lado*, confessing and reclaiming some of the experiences that have influenced the way that I see not just the biblical text but my own body, the world and God. Biblical scholars have in recent decades recovered their 'personal voice in biblical interpretation'.[8] Autobiographical criticism timidly has appeared in biblical scholarship to announce that neither text nor reader is subject or object but rather that together they enter into a continuous dialogue of interpretation.[9] It is this that I hope to do with the texts under discussion in this book. In autobiographical criticism, the body as an essential aspect of self and identity is

7. James B. Nickoloff ('Sexuality: A Queer Omission in U.S. Latino/a Theology', *Journal of Hispanic Latino Thoelogy* 10.3 [2003], pp. 31-51) correctly criticizes this intentional omission by a theology that pretends to be 'inclusive'. However, there are a few scholars who see the importance of including the experience of GLBT persons into theological reflection. For instance, Miguel A. De La Torre and Edwin David Aponte, *Introducing Latino/a Theologies* (Maryknoll, NY: Orbis Books, 2001), p. 158, argue that 'a conversation is beginning to occur among Latino/a theologians on the issue of homosexuality'. Luís N. Rivera Pagán ('El Sida: desafío a la conciencia Cristiana', in *Los sueños del Ciervo: Perspectivas teológicas desde el Caribe* [San Juan: Programa de educación y teología del concilio evangélico de Puerto Rico; Quito: Ediciones Clai, 1995], pp. 53-68 [66]) points out: 'Uno de los signos claves en la defensa actual de las libertades civiles es el reclamo de los homosexuales a que se respete su igualdad en derechos humanos sin que ello oblitere su diferencia en orientación *erótica*, su alteridad.' In relation to the Bible and homosexuality, see Miguel A. De La Torre, *Reading the Bible from the Margins* (Maryknoll, NY: Orbis Books, 2002), pp. 96-102, as being sensitive to the homosexual person. Also Carla E. Roland Guzman, 'Sexuality', in Edwin David Aponte and Miguel A. De La Torre (eds.), *Handbook of Latina/o Theologies* (Saint Louis: Chalice Press, 2006), pp. 257-64.

8. Ingrid Rosa Kitzberger (ed.) *The Personal Voice in Biblical Interpretation* (New York: Routledge, 1999).

9. See the several articles in Kitzberger (ed.), *Autobiographical Biblical Criticism.*

seriously taken into account in the interpretative process.[10] For this reason, I begin here with my body as a way to communicate my struggles in interpreting the biblical text.

From a young age, I thought I had been born into the wrong place with the wrong people and at the wrong time. I did not fit in with the men around me, because I did not like to do the things that males were 'supposed' to do. I did not fit into my small village, a sense others constantly confirmed by mockingly asking, *¿¡Qué vas a hacer cuando seas grande si no sabes hacer nada!?,* 'What are you going to do when you grow up, you good-for-nothing?' In this phalocentric environment where wo/men and children were subjected totally to the authority of the (heterosexual) male, I quickly realized that my village was not the place for me. I felt exiled from my own gender, my own people and my own culture. Part of that alienating culture was my religion. Though at night I would hear my mother's prayer, *Dios te salve. A ti llamamos, los desterrados hijos de Eva; a ti suspiramos, gimiendo y llorando en este valle de lágrimas,* 'To thee do we cry, exiles, sons of Eve. To thee do we sigh, moaning and weeping in this valley of tears.' I could not tell my own mother that I was experiencing a kind of exile in my own family, village and culture. That exile was one I experienced even in and with my own body. As Jean-Luc Nancy argues, *De ahí que no se trate de estar 'en el exilio interior de sí mismo', sino ser sí mismo el exilio,* 'Hence it has to do not with being in the interior exile from oneself but rather to oneself the exile.'[11] Since then, my body has become the place of my own exile; my experience and desires had been so alienated from my life that sometimes I do not even recognize myself. In order to survive in a homophobic culture and religion, I learned how to camouflage my feelings and desires, especially when other males described me and 'situated' me as one *del otro lado.*

I narrated in the introduction how my earliest recollection of being *del otro lado* happened while hearing Mark's passion narrative. However, the process of *ser y estar en el otro lado* is possible only through the continuous act of repetition. According to Judith Butler, neither materiality nor sex is given, but rather, the materiality of sex is constructed through a ritualized reception of norms. She argues that performativity is a kind of 'citational practice' by which sexed and gendered subjects are continuously constituted.[12] In the same vein, my *ser y estar del otro lado* is not something that was situated and accomplished once for all. *Ser y estar en el otro lado* was the

---

10. See Ingrid Rosa Kitzberger, 'Pre-liminaries', in *Autobiographical Biblical Criticism*, pp. 1-11.

11. Jean-Luc Nancy, 'La existencia exiliada', *Archipiélago: Cuadernos de Crítica de la Cultura* 26-27 (1996), pp. 34-40 (38).

12. Butler, *Bodies That Matter*, p. x.

result of continuous repetition by other people, the community, the law and religion. Once the priest dared to call me *del otro lado,* he opened a door to injurious language against my body with the intention of denying my existence. According to Butler, the one who utters hate speech is responsible for the manner in which such speech is repeated, for reinvigorating such speech, for reestablishing contexts of hate and injury.[13] When the priest situated me as one *del otro lado,* he as a representative of the church inaugurated all the hegemonic discourse that the Catholic Church would use against people like me. Through his injurious speech, immediately I became not just *the other*, but also the sinner, the evil one, the sick one, the pervert, the immoral one, the inverted one, the transgressor and the grotesque one. Furthermore, the injurious speech that the priest used against me not only condemned me to be *the other* and to live en *el otro lado*, but also legitimated and indirectly blessed the words of my choir colleague who taunted me after worship with the words, *El Moreno es del otro lado, es del otro lado.*

Why had my classmates and friends not situated me as being *del otro lado* before? How did they know that I was *del otro lado* when I myself did not yet know what exactly *del otro lado* meant? Who might know what *del otro lado* means and be willing to tell me? In my curiosity to find out, I asked my mother. She was surprised at my question, and with great compassion she told me that people *del otro lado* were 'special'; and she became silent. She could not hide her fear, and a few months later, I knew why. It was during harvest time that I witnessed how some male members of my villages raped and beat a young man for being *del otro lado.* Immediately I reported this incident to my parents. My mother became pale and my dad said to me: *A esos les gusta que les golpien,* 'those ones like to be beaten.' I thought that by reporting this incident to my dad, who at the time was the chief of the village with power to implement the law, something would be done about this incident. Soon I realized that our society's law and customs are not applied to people *del otro lado*. I did not have the nerve to confess to my dad that the priest, as well as my classmates, had taunted me by saying I was *del otro lado.* Though of course I did not want either to be beaten or to be situated *en el otro lado,* this incident helped me to realize that I was not the only one *del otro lado* and that there were others to whom I could talk about it.

Initially I thought that some males from my village beat the guy and called him *del otro lado* because he lived on the other side of the Rio Lerma. And so when my older brother one day told me, *Yo creo que tú también eres del otro lado,* 'I believe that you are also *del otro lado,'* I reminded him that we did not live on the *other side* of the river, so how could I be *del*

13. Judith Butler, *Excitable Speech: A Politics of the Performative* (New York: Routledge, 1997), p. 27.

otro lado? Even then he did not clarify exactly what *del otro lado* meant. But once again his silence told me that we were not on the *same side*. Being *del otro lado* evoked emptiness in my heart; it was like walking under a sky without stars, where no one knew exactly what to do with me. In my desire to know and meet a person *del otro lado,* one day I crossed the river searching for the young man who had been raped and beaten, hoping that he would explain to me how to live the life *del otro lado.* When I arrived at his house, I found him lashed to a weeping willow tree by his neck. There were no words between us, only a mystical silence. His tears and body were sufficient to tell me there was no place for the likes of us in our small village. As if this realization were not enough, my brother appeared from the middle of nowhere at that very moment and harangued me saying, *Dios los hace y el Diablo los junta,* which literally means, 'God creates them and the Devil puts them together,' probably the equivalent of the English-language saying 'birds of a feather flock together.' My brother made me swear that I would never cross to the *otro lado* and I would never talk with a person *del otro lado*, warning me that otherwise I would burn in hell. From that day on *Dios y el Diablo* were present in each moment of my life, if anything fighting more for my body than my soul. On the one hand, I would hear my mother telling me how special I was, how I was born when no one expected me, that I was a miracle of God. On the other hand, my brother and the priest never stopped reminding me that as one *del otro lado,* I belonged to hell and deserved to die.

A few months after my 'crossing' to *el otro lado del Rio Lerma*, I heard my dad telling my older brother that the raped and beaten guy had 'abandoned' his family and crossed the Rio Grande illegally to *el Norte.* If for the Greeks, the Ethiopians and their lands were paradise, where, 'the rams grow their horns quickly. Three times a year their flock gives birth, and there no lord would ever go wanting, nor would his shepherd, for cheese or meat, nor for the sweet milk either, but always the sheep yield a continuous supply for their sucklings' (Homer, *Odyssey* 4.84), for us people *del otro lado del Rio Grande, el Norte* is a similar symbol, not just of abundance but also of refuge.

Because of the economic and political situation, most of the males from my village cross to the *otro lado,* or as my mother says, *se van pal' Norte,* 'They go to el Norte'. For months at a time my village becomes a no-man's land; only women, children, and old men remain. Once when I confessed to my grandmother Mina that as soon as I grew up, I would go likewise to el Norte, she warned me, *el Norte se come a los hombres,* 'the North devours men'. Later on, my mother told me that my grandfather Octavio, during the *bracero* program, had crossed the Rio Grande, that he was 'lost' to the family for almost twenty-five years, and that consequently, my grandmother had to raise my dad by herself. At that moment, I understood my grandmother's saying, *Pobre de Mexico, tan lejos de Dios y tan cerca de los*

Estados Unidos, 'Poor Mexico, so far from God and so close to the United States.' I could not explain to her that my crossing to *el Norte* would have a different purpose and goal. I did not want to cross el Rio Grande in order to achieve the American Dream but to find peace and safety with other bodies *del otro lado.*

In my innocence, I believed that in *el Norte*, people *del otro lado* lived in peace and harmony. El Norte became something sacred, appealing, and desirable. El Norte was like the lost paradise. After all, the beaten guy had escaped to *el otro lado,* hadn't he? Of course, no one knew for sure if he was alive or dead. In the village, no one talked about him, for his very existence brought misfortune and shame to his family, his younger brother told me. A couple of years ago, I met the 'beaten guy' in Anaheim, California, and he confessed to me that he had been dead to his family and village since the day his dad told him, *Prefiero un hijo muerto, que un hijo del otro lado,* 'I prefer a dead son to a son who is del otro lado.' In Mexico, like any other part of the world, the crime, violence and aggression against people *del otro lado* is real, and we experience it every day. Why such aggression? Because we people *del otro lado* have not yet been deemed human. On one of the few occasions when I went to a certain city in the state of Guanajuato, I read in a public restroom, *Se prohibe la entrada a animales y homosexuales*, 'Entrance forbidden to animals and homosexuals.' At the time I thought that a homosexual was a kind of aggressive animal, capable of inflicting contagion on humans. Then I understood that this word was used to describe people *del otro lado.* 'Homosexual' was another word to fear, another word with the power to negate my existence.

In a homophobic culture, animals and homosexuals belong to the same category of nonhumans. Butler helpfully explains that the terms by which we are recognized as human are socially articulated and changeable. And sometimes the very term that confers humanness on some individuals are those that deprive certain other individuals of the possibility of achieving that status, producing a differential between the human and the less-than-human.[14] Perhaps it was my continued desire to attain human status that helped me to cross to *el otro lado del Río Grande.* Since early in my childhood the mythical idea of *el Norte* had chased me like a ghost, until finally a decade ago, the spirit of adventure took me to Tijuana, where Manu Chao greeted me with his song:

Welcome to Tijuana.
Tequila, sexo y marihuana
Welcome to Tijuana.

---

14. Butler, *Undoing Gender*, p. 2.

Con el coyote no hay aduana, with the smugglers there is no customs.[15] Unfortunately, el Norte soon disappointed me and revealed *otros lados* of exclusion, marginalization, segregation, exploitation and dehumanization. I realized that people *del otro lado* are condemned to be like Cain, forever roaming without a country to call our own, fearing for our lives all the time, hiding our bodies from God's face, and always looking for the nonexistence *del otro lado*.

My Body Houses Abjection

Scholars often become apprehensive when someone does not declare fairly quickly their social location. I remember a Latina theologian advising me on one of my papers. She asked why I did not 'come out' immediately by confessing that I am gay and that it is from this perspective that I will read the text? I wish it were that easy. But there are *otros lados* that must be taken into consideration in my biblical interpretation. For me, it would be relatively easy to declare or to come out by plainly confessing 'I am gay' and read the biblical text through my 'gay eyes'. But, due to the complexity of the vocabulary and what 'gay' and 'homosexual' entail nowadays, I am not sure if I am gay or homosexual anymore! In order to illuminate this insight, allow me to use a joke.

A young man, after several days of meditation, decided to confess to his dad that he was gay. In a solemn and ritualistic way, he said to him, 'Dad, I would like to reveal the secret of my life: I am gay.' Unperturbed, his dad replied, 'Let us see. Do you study at Yale or Harvard University?' Confused, the young man replied, 'No, I study in a community college.' His dad continued, 'Do you live in a luxury apartment or penthouse?' 'No,' he answered, 'I live in a mobile home on the south side of the city.' 'Do you drive a Lincoln or a BMW?' 'No, I use public transportation.' 'Do you have a Swiss bank account?' 'No, I am barely surviving on my salary.' Then the father said to him, 'You are not gay; you are an ordinary faggot.' In Spanish, the joke ends, 'You are not a gay, you are *pobre, puto y pendejo*.' In the joke, the young man cannot aspire to be classified as gay because his body bears the stigma of poverty. His misery and ordinariness do not fulfill the conditions to have a livable life. According to Butler, when we ask what makes a life livable, we are asking about certain normative conditions that must be fulfilled for life to become life.[16] The place where someone is born and their economic situation determines whether their life is livable or not. These economic factors also make someone an ordinary 'faggot' or '*pobre, puto y*

---

15. Manu Chao is a singer and political activist. This song is taken from his CD *Clandestino*, original released on 6 October 1998.

16. Butler, *Undoing Gender*, p. 226.

pendejo' for pretending to pass for something that they are not. In Mexico, if a gay is born into a wealthy family, he is described as someone who is refined, delicate and with good taste. However, if someone is born into poverty he is identified as being *pobre, puto y pendejo*, with bad manners. In the same way, my body is a more complex entity than these categories of being gay can encapsulate. *Ser y estar en el otro lado* cannot be reduced to my sexual orientation. There are other factors that deny my humanity.

In Mexico, people *del otro lado* have been called a great variety of terms. We can count more than a hundred ways to describe, situate and negate the existence of those people who fail to qualify as humans.[17] In the Christian tradition, one has typically not named the 'dreadful sin' (*peccatum illud horribile, inter Christianos non nominandum*), probably for fear that naming the sin might extend some measure of human dignity to the sinner. There are probably no other words that are so burdened with meaning in Mexico than the words that describe a person *del otro lado*. Most of those injurious terms used against people *del otro lado* are as follows: María *(marica, maricón, mariquita)*, evil (*shotos, choto*), animals that live among excrement (*mayate*), animals that approach fire and perish in it (*mariposa, mariposón*),[18] lack of courage (*culero, puto, puñal, putazo, putón, putiflais*), crooked or devious *(desviado, invertido, amanerado, torcido)*, limp wristed (*mano quebrada, cacha granizo, quiebra la muñeca, mano caída*), referring to a place (*de ambiente, del otro lado, del otro Laredo, del otro bando*). We could go on. The point is that this endless list of adjectives conveys one and the same thing: a person *del otro lado,* in Paz's words, is an abject, degraded being.[19]

One of the powerful and provocative ways in which Butler contests the normative violence that such a mass of bodies has suffered at the hands of the heteronormative ideology is through the notion of abjection—a concept she adapts from Kristeva. According to Kristeva, society, culture and religion are founded on the expulsion of the other, the impure, the unclean, the repulsive and the improper.[20] Butler uses the term 'abjection' to refer to those legions of bodies who are not subjects and are deemed 'unlivable'. Lloyd correctly argues that abjection is a matter of ontology. 'Alongside those subjects who can "lay claim to ontology" because they *count* or *qual-*

17. In order to see all the words the people used against a person *del otro lado,* go to Fernando Flores, '101 formas de llamar a un homosexual' (accessed on 1 June 2009). Online at http://anodis.com/nota/4092.asp.

18. See Federico Garza Carvajal, *Butterflies Will Burn: Prosecuting Sodomites in Early Modern Spain and Mexico* (Austin: University of Texas Press, 2003), pp. 62-63.

19. Paz, *Labyrinth of Solitude*, p. 39.

20. Julia Kristeva, *Powers of Horror: An Essay on Abjection* (trans. Leon S. Roudiez; New York: Columbia University Press, 1982), p. 4.

ify as real', there are those who 'do *not* have claim to ontology' and who are, in some sense, unreal.[21] As an 'abject degraded being', my existence had been both challenged and denied on several fronts. My body houses abjection in several rooms, and these must be taken into account in how I approach the Bible. It is not just my *ser y estar del otro lado* that enters into the game of negotiating my body; issues of race, language, marginality, segregation, power and religious belief also play a pivotal role in my own understanding of my body and the Bible.

As a matter of fact, memories of poverty, exclusion, abuse of religion and misinterpretation of the Bible by the people of my village are more vivid in my imagination than my being *del otro lado*. I still remember my entire village gathering together during the harvest time and separating *las primicias*, 'first fruits/tithes', of the harvest to be blessed by the priest. In a special ceremony, the priest would read to us a text like the following,[22] 'When you have entered the land the LORD your God is giving you as an inheritance and have taken possession of it and settled in it, take some of the first fruits of all that you produce from the soil of the land the LORD your God is giving you and put them in a basket. Then go to the place the LORD your God will choose as a dwelling for God's Name and say to the priest in office at the time, "I declare today to the LORD your God that I have come to the land the LORD swore to our forefathers [foremothers] to give us"' (Deut. 26.1-3). There was no need for the priest to exhort us to be generous, for we were all already extremely generous toward the obese priest who was, in my grandmother's words: *lleno de vida*, 'full of life'. After the sermon, the priest would bless the crops, and he would collect the first fruits of the mother earth. Often his golden pickup truck would get stuck in the mud, and we would push it with pleasure in order to touch a 'truck'. The golden truck became our golden calf that called all her devotees to worship. This idolatrous liturgy of touching, feeling and admiring a golden pickup truck would awaken our desires and ambitions between the one who has and the one who has not. My uncle would say, *Si quieres una camioneta conviértete en cura,* 'If you want a pickup truck became a priest.' Other times, the golden truck/calf would not be able to accommodate all 'the priest's blessings', and because of the geographical situation of my house, he would leave them with us with the warning that *Dios ve todo*, 'God sees everything,' probably fearing that we might rob him.

---

21. Lloyd, *Judith Butler*, p. 75.

22. In this experience, I am relying totally on my mother's memory. I asked her if she remembered the biblical text that the priest used to read during the blessing of '*las primicias*'. She informed me that the biblical reading has to do with the blessing of the land, and the fruits. Thus, I am assuming that it was probably Deut. 26.1-3.

Typically, a few months after our generosity to the priest/god, our own food supplies would have dwindled to such a point that we were forced to go to the priest to ask him for some seeds in order to cultivate our earth. He would write down our names in what he called *el libro del perdón,* 'the book of forgiveness.' From that moment, our Bible would become *el libro del perdón.* Sunday after Sunday in the holy house of God, he would read aloud all the names of those parishioners who were incapable of repaying their debts to him. In order to avoid embarrassment, many parishioners would understandably not go to mass. We were so dehumanized that we did not distinguish between the Bible and *el libro del perdón,* between God's blessing and the priest's rapacious and voracious stomach. My grandmother was right in describing him as being *lleno de vida,* in comparison with the precariousness of our bodies, which were marked by poverty and malnutrition. The poverty, exploitation and subjugation that we suffered at the hands of the priest left us in a very vulnerable place. We were living our slave/master dialectic *à la Mexicana*, with the same deadly results.

G.W.F. Hegel argues that self-consciousness occurs only through another. This process of self-recognition in another is not simple, because these two self-conscious beings must first engage in mortal combat before one can enslave the other. He uses the image of master/slave, in which the master is recognized but the slave is not. The slave works; yet it is the master who enjoys the fruits of that labor.[23] Butler describes the confrontation between master and slave as a struggle to the death, for 'only through the death of the Other will the initial self-consciousness retrieve its claim to autonomy'.[24] We recognized our village priest not just as *the other*, but as one *lleno de vida*. However, he did not recognize us as the *other*. By negating our very humanity, the priest became autonomous, independent and self-sufficient. Instead of being a devotee of the living God, he became a devotee of the golden truck/calf. We, on the other hand, year after year became more enslaved—to him, dependent on his blessings, his religion, and his idolatrous god. We, as the slaves, were busy working the land, and through our connectedness to the land found our very identity. On the other hand, the priest/master frittered away his time and spirit in fruitless liturgies. This death/life relationship made us abject beings unable to qualify as bodies that matter, or, as Butler would say, devoid of 'ways of living that count as "life", lives worth protecting, lives worth saving, lives worth grieving'.[25]

---

23. See G.W.F. Hegel, *Phenomenology of Spirit* (trans. A.V. Miller; Oxford: Oxford University Press, 1979).

24. Judith Butler, *Subjects of Desires: Hegelian Reflection in Twentieth-Century France* (New York: Columbia University, 1999), p. 49.

25. Butler, *Bodies That Matter,* p. 16.

I might forgive the priest and his evil desires for power, but I cannot forgive him for making us feel unworthy in relation to God. He denied us not just our existence but also the existence of the living God. I cannot forgive him for his betrayal of the gospel, his betrayal of Jesus' good news. I cannot forgive him for making us believe that we were poor because *Dios así lo quiere*, 'It is God's will.' He reduced us to mere objects without any possibility of becoming subjects of transformation. He was more concerned about keeping immaculate his golden truck/calf than seeing in our suffering and dirty bodies Jesus' face. Butler reminds us that in the slave/master relationship, the slave is a constant producer, whereas the master is simply a consumer. For the master, then, nothing endures except perhaps his own consuming activity, his own endless desire.[26] This described perfectly the figure of the priest who so badly needed the fruits of our labor in order to be full of life. People who did not show gratitude to God by donating willingly, the priest called ungrateful *hijos de la Chingada.*

Eres un hijo de la Chingada mal agradecido[27]

Scholars remind me often that I am now in a privileged position because I am a priest, and thus, an 'educated' person. By doing this, they are extending me some recognition, but at the same time, they are forcing me to embrace the power that is bestowed on me through my priesthood and education. According to Foucault, 'Where there is power, there is resistance, and yet, or rather consequently, this resistance is never in a position of exteriority in relation to power.'[28] This power/resistance relationship is part of my daily negotiation. My body becomes the battlefield where these two realities fight for autonomy and recognition. If we follow Foucault in the relationship between power and resistance, we can argue that one has the faculty either to exercise power or to resist it. Honestly, I am not sure if the simple act of being both a priest and an educated person puts me in a privileged position. What if I decide not to exercise such power? What if I resist instead of exercise such power? Foucault's axiom seems to conclude that there has to be some exercise of power in the first place for someone to be able to resist it. This seems to be my case: the institution of the church has exercised her power and I have often exercised my resistance within it. Moreover, Foucault argues that resistance comes first and then power: 'So resistance comes first, and resistance remains superior to the other forces of the proc-

26. Butler, *The Psychic Life of Power* (Stanford, CA: Stanford University Press, 1997), p. 39.

27. You are an ungrateful *hijo de la Chingada!*

28. Michel Foucault, *History of Sexuality, I* (trans. Robert Hurley; London: Penguin, 1990), p. 95.

ess; power relations are obliged to change with the resistance. So I think that resistance is the main word, the keyword, in this dynamic.'[29] I do not want to be naïve and deny that very often the relationship between power and resistance is blurred. I often succumb and claim my privileges of being both priest and educated. However, I often resist exercising my power and privileges.

The professor who on several occasions had remarked on my privileged position because of my priesthood and education did not allow me to confess my ambiguous feelings regarding my power and privilege. I confess that I do have power; knowledge is always a form of power, as Foucault told us. 'Knowledge linked to power not only assumes the authority of "the truth" but has the power to make itself true.'[30] But the exercise of my privileges and power is a continuous negotiation. Butler has argued extensively that no one becomes a subject without first becoming subjected or undergoing subjectivation.[31] For someone outside of the Catholic Church, it is quite complicated to understand this kind of hate/love, master/slave, subject/object relationship that I negotiate every day in order to become a subject through subordination. In order to have power and be capable to resist the institution, I need to be considered human first. My desire to survive or 'to be' makes me claim, as Butler does, 'I would rather exist in subordination than not exist. . . .'[32] Once I exist, the privileges of exercising power and resistance emerge as a possibility, not as a necessity. How can I exercise my power and privileges in such a vulnerable situation?

My power and privileges are limited, frugal, and could easily be taken away if I do not play according to the rules of the game. I have power and privileges as long as I am a docile person, a normalized body. I have power as long as I do not publicly disclose my sexual orientation. I have power as long as I do not denounce the double moral life that is lived regarding celibacy. I have power as long as I do not criticize in any way the teachings of the church regarding sexual issues. I have power as long as I do not question the hierarchical church. I have power and privilege as long as I do not advertise that we have often betrayed Jesus' Gospel. And above all, I have power, privilege, promotion and position when I deny my sexual orientation and hate myself for being *del otro lado*. Of course I am mercilessly segregated and excluded when I transgress those norms.

---

29. Michel Foucault, 'Sex, Power and the Politics of Identity', in Paul Rabinow (ed.), *Ethics: Subjectivity and Truth* (trans. R. Hurley; New York: New York Press, 1997), pp. 163-73 (167).
30. Michel Foucault, *Discipline and Punishment* (London: Tavistock, 1977), p. 27.
31. Butler, *The Psychic Life of Power*, p. 11.
32. Butler, *Psychic Life of Power*, p. 7.

Butler argues, 'There is a certain departure from the human that takes place in order to start the process of remaking the human. I may feel that without some recognizability I cannot live. But I may also feel that the terms by which I am recognized make life unlivable.'[33] The teachings of the church, as well as her norms, theological discourse and interpretation of the Bible have made my life unlivable on several fronts. However, it is inside the institution that I can exercise my resistance. It is in this kind of negation from which critique emerges, 'where critique is understood as an interrogation of the terms by which life is constrained in order to open up the possibility of different modes of living; in other words, not to celebrate difference as such but to establish more inclusive conditions for sheltering and maintaining life that resists models of assimilation'.[34] Unfortunately, when I critique the institution, I become an outsider, a traitor.

People do not understand how I can be such a 'monster' toward the Mother Church that has 'given me everything'! They start by naming the formation that I received, and the opportunity to study the Bible. When I reply to my accusers that the church has not given me anything, but rather that in an act of justice the church is returning to me something that belonged to me, my family and my people in the first place, they cannot believe my arrogance and irony. We as priests have often been educated into being unconditional defenders of the institution rather than of Jesus' gospel. Often we follow the teachings of Rome more closely than we do the Good News that arose in Galilee. Often we are blinded from recognizing the mistakes, suffering and dehumanization that God's creation has suffered at the hands of the church. My grandfather Jesús, for instance, lost his land for fighting in favor of the hierarchical church during *Los Cristeros* war.[35] When he returned home, his land had been seized, and he was landless. When my grandfather got drunk, he would curse the church for having sacrificed thousands of innocent lives. He used to say, *Mientras nosotros luchábamos contra el Gobierno, los Obispos cenaban con ellos,* 'while we were fighting against the government, the bishops would have dinner with them.' I am glad that my grandfather is not alive to see how Mother Church has compensated their sufferings by canonizing many Cristeros. I often joke with people who claim that I should be more grateful to the church by saying that by accepting education and the opportunity to study I am helping the institution in her conversion. The church has an opportunity to show repentance for exploit-

33. Butler, *Undoing Gender*, p. 4.
34. Butler, *Undoing Gender*, p. 4.
35. The Cristeros War occurred in response to the anti-Catholic laws of Mexican president Plutarco Elías Calles. The struggle between the church and the state resulted in armed conflict during the years 1926 to 1929.

ing and impoverishing my family. In the end, of course, they cannot explain how I can be such an ungrateful *hijo de la Chingada.*

Probably there is no more aggressive term in Mexico than being called *hijo de la Chingada.* How can someone become *hijo de la Chingada*? What is the *Chingada*? We saw how for Paz *la Chingada* represents the woman who had been forcibly penetrated, violated or deceived. The *hijo de la Chingada* is the offspring of violation, abduction or deceit. Paz even associates *la Chingada* with the traumatic consequence of the conquest. 'If the Chingada is a representation of the violated Mother, it is appropriate to associate her with the Conquest, which was also a violation, not only in the historical sense but also in the very flesh of Indian women.'[36] In this context, the priest who accused me of being *hijo de la Chingada* was right. I had been *hijo de la Chingada* since my mother, sisters, grandmother and great grandmother were fucked by the Spaniards with the blessing of the church. Is being a *hijo de la Chingada* an option for me? I was born of *la Chingada* and I will die in *la Chingada.* Both life and death are part of *la Chingada.* As Carlos Fuentes says, *Nacidos de la Chingada, muertos en la Chingada, vivo por pura chingadera: vientre y mortaja, escondidos en la Chingada,* 'Born of fucking, dead from fucking, living fucked: pregnant belly and winding sheet, hidden in the word'.[37] I am a bastard *hijo de la Chingada,* born of an illegitimate breed, with an orphan *logos* (voice). Without knowing it, I have all the time been *la Chingada's* favorite son. According to Paz, the verb *chingar* denotes violence, an emergence from oneself to penetrate another by force. It also means to injure, to lacerate, to violate—bodies, souls, objects—and to destroy.[38] I wonder who is the most *hijo de la Chingada*? Is it the one who has suffered the violence or the one who has done the violence toward the Indian woman and people *del otro lado*? I wonder how a passive, opened, violated, penetrated and wounded *hijo de la Chingada* might have power and privilege? Assuming that as a *hijo de la Chingada* I have power and privilege, from where did I get it?

I am sure that my understanding of power/resistance would not convince everybody. I hope at least to demonstrate that my power/resistance comes not from being a priest or educated but rather from the people that I serve. The church institution often forgets that the Son of Humanity did not come 'to be served, but to serve, and to give his life as a ransom for many" (Mk 10.45). Instead, the institution boastfully claims that she is not a democratic institution, and we who are part of this institution know exactly what the church means. How do I understand power and privilege? In order to

36. Paz, *Labyrinth of Solitude,* p. 86.

37. Carlos Fuentes, *The Death of Artemio Cruz* (trans Sam Hileman; New York: Farrar, Straus & Giroux, 1964), p. 138.

38. Paz, *Labyrinth of Solitude,* p. 77.

answer this question, I will draw on Foucault's understanding of power. It is easier to comprehend what power is not, in Foucault's perception, than what it is. According to Foucault, power is not a substance, structure, institution or personality characteristic. It 'is not something that is acquired, seized, or shared, something that one holds onto or allows to slip away'.[39] It is amazing that Foucault's understanding of power might be more in tune with Jesus' gospel than the institution that was commissioned by Jesus to serve the vulnerable ones.

When I claim the power of being a priest and being educated, I become distant from the people that I intend to serve. Foucault reminds us that power exists everywhere and comes from everywhere, and that it is always in relation to an other. Power finds its goal in caring for an other, sharing one's knowledge and being open to learn from the other. According to Foucault, 'power reaches into the very grain of individuals, touches their bodies and inserts itself into their actions and attitudes, their discourses, learning processes and everyday lives'.[40] Power is something that we exercise every day. 'Power comes from below; that is, there is no binary and all-encompassing opposition between rulers and ruled at the root of power relations.'[41] For me power really comes from below, from the humble people who attend my Bible groups and find in the Bible a source of hope. My power resides not in the knowledge that I possess about the Bible, but rather in the creativity to relate the biblical text to their lives, stories and tragedies. Scholars who have used autobiographical biblical criticism correctly argue, 'The more personal you get in your writing, the more crucial become the ethical and political questions.'[42] My reading and understanding of the Bible are powerful and meaningful as long as I am fully implicated in the lives of those people who struggle for justice. Without this, my reading and understanding become vain and spurious. With this in mind, I invite you to gaze on the unnamed woman who anointed Jesus' head (Mk 14.1-9) and the slave girl who put Peter on trial (Mk 14.66-72) from *otros lados* of interpretation.

39. Foucault, *History,* p. 94.
40. Michel Foucault, *Power/Knowledge: Selected Interviews and Other Writings, 1972-1977* (New York: Pantheon, 1972), p. 39.
41. Foucault, *History*, p. 94.
42. Staley "What Is Critical about Autobiographical (Biblical) Criticism?, p. 17.

2

MARIMACHAS, DESCARADAS, MALCRIADAS Y HOCICONAS /
THE DYKES, THE SHAMELESS, THE ILL-BRED
AND THE LOUDMOUTHS

*The Unnamed Woman Who Anointed Jesus
and my Neighbor Pola*

There was a woman who lived by herself next to our home. She was baptized as *Apolinar* (a masculine name). Actually, it is very common in my village to meet women with masculine names. I used to think such naming was simply part of the tradition, but now I am sure it is a form of domination. There was something extraordinary about Apolinar, or Pola, as we called her. A few examples will illustrate what I mean. According to my mother, when Pola's sister passed away one summer night, Pola did not cry or show any emotion toward Antonia (Pola's sister). Indeed, my mother commented that Pola 'behaved not like a woman but like a man'. Furthermore, Pola never got married but lived her life very independent of the rest of the community. She was, for example, the only one who did not give *las primicias* (tithes) to the priest. Moreover, every morning I saw her riding her donkey and working her land 'just as any man' would do. The women from my village commented that Pola's voice was strong and direct, and easily recognizable among other voices. She typically attended the village men's public meetings in order to discuss issues related to her land. The men could not explain why she did not stay at home like the rest of the women, but no one dared to confront her because she was a very opinionated woman, a real *marimacha y hocicona*, they would say.

Being *marimacha y hocicona* was apparently the price that Pola had to pay. Her 'manly' behavior was seen as a threat to the masculinity of the males, who started the rumor that Pola was *manflora*[1] *mitad y mitad*, 'half and half',[2] neither woman nor man but a deviation from 'nature'. One day

1. A slang expression for 'lesbian'.
2. Gloria Anzaldúa also reports this myth (*Borderlands/La Frontera*, p. 41). 'There was a *muchacha* who lived near my house. *La gente del pueblo* talked about her being *una de las otras*, "one of the others". They said that for six months she was a woman

the males gathered together to deliberate about Pola's future—of course without inviting her to participate. They decided that Pola must resign from working her land and stay at home like the rest of the women. Although Pola spoke out, her voice was silenced with a brutal punch to her face. 'Finally someone has the courage to put Pola in her place', someone from the crowd said. Not a single person spoke on behalf of Pola; she could find no solidarity among all those men who felt aggravated by her behavior. *La dejaron como a Cristo llena de sangre,* 'They left her like a Christ full of blood,' the women commented. In Pola's absence and without her approval, the men decided that from that moment on Pola's land would be passed to Jesús, whose nickname was *el huérfano,* or orphan. He agreed to sustain Pola until her death, which came soon after, for, following the men's decision, Pola became sick and passed away in the company of some women. *Se murió de pura tristeza,* 'she died of sadness', my oldest sister would remark. This was the first time of many times that I heard my mother comment, *Es muy difícil ser mujer,* 'It is very difficult being a woman.'

Every time that I read the story of the unnamed woman who anointed Jesus' head, Pola's life and death come to mind. Despite the different times, cultures and historical situations in which these women lived, I find many similarities between them. Just like Pola, the unnamed woman whom Mark presents to us is totally disconnected from conventional first-century family ties. We do not know for sure whether or not she was married. We can speculate that there was a male figure, such as an elder brother, watching over her, but we do not know that for sure, either. This unnamed woman does not utter a single word in the entire narrative. However, by the way in which she used her body, she could be classified as a *marimacha y hocicona.* By entering into a male's space and performing her ritual of recognition over Jesus' head, this unnamed woman is undoing her gender. She is challenging the male disciples to understand that categories of social identity such as *femininity* and *masculinity are unstable and always open to reinterpretation.* Butler argues that the terms 'masculine' and 'feminine' are notoriously changeable; there are social histories for each term; their meanings change radically depending on geopolitical boundaries and cultural constraints on who is imagining whom, and for what purpose.[3]

By performing certain activities and uttering certain words outside of their 'dominion', both women are remaking their assigned gender roles. They confirm Butler's notion that 'terms of gender designation are thus

who had a vagina that bled once a month, and that for the other six months she was a man, had a penis and she peed standing up. They called her half and half, *mita' y mita',* neither one nor the other but a strange doubling, a deviation of nature that horrified, a work of nature inverted.'

3. Butler, *Undoing Gender,* p. 10.

never settled once for all but are constantly in the process of being remade'.[4] The boldness of the unnamed woman is something that Jesus' male disciples respond to strongly and negatively. Fortunately for her, Jesus the Galilean was there to recognize her as a worthy disciple.

Because of the similarities that I see between the life of the unnamed woman and that of Pola, I would like to baptize this unnamed woman with the name of Pola in memory of the one that I knew. By this very act of naming her, I would like to extend her some recognition. Being *marimacha y hocicono* situates these women in a very subversive arena. For Anzaldúa, a *marimacha* is a woman who is very assertive. 'That is what they used to call dykes, *marimachas,* half-and-halfs. You were different, you were queer, not normal, you were *marimacha.*'[5] These *marimachas,* as I understand, have little to do with their sexual orientation. Their struggles were against discrimination, the gender division of labor, violence, injustice, and having their voices silenced.

Pola la descarada *Who Anointed Jesus*

Mark introduces his passion narrative by changing the scenery from Jerusalem to Bethany, an action that could be interpreted as a sign that God's presence is no longer in the Temple. It is not the first time that God's glory has left the Temple (Ezek. 10.18-19; 11.22-23); in fact, every time that Jerusalem/the Temple fails God's poor we hear the voice of the prophets announcing doom against the Temple of God. Each time that the Israelites do not change their lives and actions to conform to God's way, but rather find security in 'the Temple of God, the Temple of God, the Temple of God' (Jer. 7.4) they perish. So in this story we see Jesus and his disciples moving from the Mount of Olives to Bethany, where Simon the Leper lives. It is striking that a polluted home with an excluded body is the setting of what is probably the most extravagant act of love that Jesus received in his miserable life. Without being invited,[6] Jesus has come to a house of dubious reputation. This corroborates the idea that Jesus' meals are not simply formalities, customs or banal rituals. He eats easily in public spaces, with people that others prefer to avoid. He accepts hospitality in homes that a pious Jewish man would probably not enter. Jesus' way of eating was scandalous for the priests, Pharisees and elite people. Scholars have claimed that Jesus could

---

4. Butler, *Undoing Gender*, p. 10.

5. Gloria Anzaldúa, 'Interviews with Gloria Anzaldúa by Karin Ika'(accessed 19 July 2009) (online at http://www.auntlute.com/www.auntlute.com/auntlute.com/ GloriaAnzalduaInterview.htm).

6. Lk. 7.36 and 39 explicitly affirm that the Pharisee invited Jesus to dine with him.

be crucified for participating in meals the way he did.[7] It is no surprise that Jesus' sentence of death is reported in the context of a meal (Mk 14.1-2).

Unexpectedly, a body that the culture and social norms have marked and gendered as a woman, in Mark's story appears in a public space performing an extravagant act of love. This biblical Pola is entering dangerous territory, where she might encounter violence and aggression for transgressing the boundaries of her gender. Butler argues that women are the product of the juridical system that regulates their political (and religious) life in purely negative terms—that is, through limitation, prohibition, regulation, control and even protection. But the bodies regulated by the juridical, political and religious systems are, by virtue of being subjected to them, formed, defined and reproduced in accordance with the requirements of those systems.[8] In spite of this, Mark gives us a Pola who is not restricted to those regimes of control. She moves from one place to another without being restricted either by Jesus or Simon. The religious and political system that is supposed to form, define and control an obedient, decent, modest and prudent daughter of Israel has failed totally with Pola. Her crossing and her performance have converted her into a *descarada*, 'barefaced' woman.

This woman in Mark's account finds parallels in my own experience. In my village, when women talked aloud among themselves, or dressed in what were considered (by men) an indecent way, or even worse when they talked with a man on the street, they were considered to be *descaradas*. A person described as *descarada* is someone who talks or acts without decency, modesty, honesty or shame. The word is composed of the prefix *des*, 'without', and *cara*, 'face';[9] so literally *descarada* would mean *sin cara*, 'barefaced'. However, this word conveys not just the meaning of being shameless or indecent, but also of being a slut or a whore. Some Chicana feminists provocatively have reclaimed the word *descarada* to describe 'a woman who removes her mask of silence and is not ashamed to speak her mind and reject oppressive conditions by empowering themselves and other women'.[10] It is in this latter sense that I consider Pola to be a *descarada* because she has removed the mask of oppression and with her body is talking a subversive language. Pola as a *descarada* is not afraid to be vulnerable before Jesus; indeed, it is through her vulnerability, brokenness and exposure to Jesus that she finds recognition as a human being. In the

7. See Robert J. Karris, *Luke: Artist and Theologian* (New York: Paulist Press, 1985), pp. 47-78.

8. Butler, *Gender Trouble*, p. 3.

9. Rufino José Cuervo, *Diccionario de construcción y régimen de la lengua Castellana tomo II* (Santafé de Bogotá: Instituto Caro y Cuervo, 1994), p. 991.

10. Anita Tijerina Revilla, 'Muxerista Pedagogy: Raza Womyn Teaching Social Justice through Student Activism', *High School Journal* 87.4 (2004), pp. 80-94 (90).

interpretation that Butler makes of the Italian philosopher Adriana Cava-
rero, she argues that we as human beings need to be *exposed* to one another
in order to find our lost humanity. 'I exist in an important sense for you, and
by virtue of you. If I have lost the conditions of address, if I have no "you"
to address, then I have lost "myself".'[11] Pola refused to be anonymous and
silent; her being exposed demanded not just of Jesus but of all members of
the community the full recognition and visibility of her deeds.

Pola *la descarada* is free to appear and disappear without being invited
and without asking permission. Mark does not depict her as being connected to any male figures, and it seems that she does not need the approval
of any male body to perform her ritual of love. She easily sums up what
Paz called *la mala mujer*, 'bad woman'. The *mala* is hard and impious and
independent like the *macho*.[12] Even though philosophers and ordinary people in Jesus' time would exclude women both for their lack of intelligence
and for their unwillingness to be seduced by men, Pola knew how to use
her body as a way to communicate and disrupt the androcentric space in
which she found herself. She is not just transgressing the proper boundaries of being male and female, she is also reading Jesus' body in a way in
which to that point no one had read it. By being *descarada* herself, Pola
exposed not only her own but also Jesus' body to the entire community.
Pola and Jesus thus become bound through an ethic of *descaro*. This ethic
of *descaramiento* requires vulnerability and total responsibility toward the
one who is *descarado/a* or exposed. 'The uniqueness of the other is exposed
to me, but mine is also exposed to her. This does not mean we are the same,
but only that we are bound to one another by what differentiates us, namely,
our singularity.'[13] From now on, all the disciples who wish to recognize
Jesus must emulate Pola *la descarada's* behavior. Pola's *descaramiento* has
once and for all made visible and readable Jesus' body. She has revealed
the enigmatic identity of Jesus and has confirmed that Jesus is also a *descarado*! 'What appears as a gesture of victory is, in fact, a gesture which
acknowledges "defeat". It is not elevation but humiliation, not dominion but
death, which is represented in her extravagant action.'[14]

Jesus as a *descarado* accepts a woman as a disciple. And through this new
descaramiento he has confused the proper roles of being male and female.
Pola has crossed borders and genders, and through her *descaramiento* she
has dislocated some identities. This blurring of boundaries causes anxiety
among some male disciples, but for Jesus and for Pola *la descarada,* a new

11. Butler, *Giving an Account,* p. 32.
12. Paz, *Labyrinth of Solitude,* p. 39.
13. Butler, *Undoing Gender,* p. 34
14. Theodore W. Jennings, *The Insurrection of the Crucified: The 'Gospel of Mark'
as Theological Manifesto* (Chicago: Exploration Press, 2003), p. 240.

way of being human emerges. Although some scholars argue that 'Mark's story is designed not for the eye but for the ear',[15] because of the vivid way in which Mark depicts Pola *la descarada*, we can imagine how she moved, how she anointed Jesus. We can even feel the anxiety, terror and discomfort that Pola provoked among the guests. If 'Mark's Gospel was designed not for the eye but for the ear we would miss a great opportunity to read the unwritten body language which is exchanged between Pola, Jesus, and Simon's guests. Jesus and Pola have not uttered a single word, their exposable bodies and *descaramiento* behavior become their weapon against the ones who have controlled, normalized, organized, labeled and institutionalized them as "inhuman, beyond the human, and less than human".'[16] Pola *la descarada* has caused such scandal among Jesus' own disciples that one of Jesus' intimate disciples decided to leave and betray him. After her performance, Judas Iscariot himself transgressed the boundaries of friendship by deciding to betray Jesus (Mk 14.10-11, 17-21).

Pola anointed Jesus' head in a way similar to the way a king was anointed: 'She has poured the perfume on my body beforehand, for its burial' (14.8b). Jesus is reclaiming his entire body, which soon would be abused, broken and killed. I welcome Teresa Hornsby's insight that the woman's silence and namelessness are not necessarily signs of passivity or powerlessness.[17] However, here Pola is neither silent nor passive. Her scandalous message is readable, and her body, as Butler would assert, has become a 'site of contest, a cause for anxiety'[18] for the male guests. Jesus does not challenge Pola's disruptive behavior, even though some disciples react strongly in response to Pola's action. Mark has left us in suspense by not providing much information regarding the disciples who suddenly show concern for the poor. We are not certain who they are. Are they Jesus' disciples? Are they Simon's guests? At this moment, it is unnecessary to reveal the identity of these angered bodies. Their ambition and desire for power would give them away. For now let us be satisfied with the information that Mark gives us, without investigating it further. It is obvious that these bodies that Mark has marked with the masculine pronoun τίνες resist being *descarados* like Jesus and Pola.

15. Sharyn Dowd and Elizabeth Struthers Malbon, 'The Significance of Jesus' Death in Mark: Narrative Context and Authorial Audience', *JBL* 125 (2006), pp. 271-97 (273).

16. Butler, *Undoing Gender*, p. 30.

17. Teresa J. Hornsby, 'The Annoying Woman: Biblical Scholarship after Judith Butler', in Ellen T. Armour and Susan M. St. Ville (eds.), *Bodily Citations: Religion and Judith Butler* (New York: Columbia University Press, 2006), pp. 71-89 (81).

18. Judith Butler, 'Subject of Sex/Gender/Desire', in Anne Phillips (ed.), *Feminism & Politics* (New York: Oxford University Press, 1998), pp. 273-91 (275).

'Some of those present were saying indignantly to one another, "Why this waste of perfume? It could have been sold for more than a year's wages and the money given to the poor." And they rebuked her harshly' (14.4-5). These males started to talk to one another as if nobody else existed around them. By ignoring the bodies of Jesus and Pola, these male bodies distance themselves from them. They are disclaiming any responsibility toward those *descarados/as* who do not act according to accustomed law, institution and gender. We affirmed above that for Butler, gender is a 'doing', a constant activity that produces a gendered body. When we endeavor to become a particular gender, we aim, by and a large, to approximate the historical and cultural norms that define what the gender ought to be: how it should look, walk, talk, sit and so forth. As such, our becoming is always constrained by cultural norms, taboos, conventions and even laws.[19] Whereas the order against Pola was pushing her to restrict herself to the private space, she dared to perform her show in public. Whereas the order to her gender was to be submissive to the male, by her *descaro* she shows superiority by recognizing Jesus as Messiah. The macho male disciples reacted immediately in order to preserve and maintain the gender roles in their proper place. According to Butler, norms, laws and customs that produce gender require repeating, reciting and calling for such practices in order to have effect. In that sense, they are the condition of possibility for gendered subjectivity. Without their repetition, gendered subjects would not exist.[20] Honest, decent, prudent, modest, and honorable males such as Simon's guests would attempt to put Pola in her proper place by repeating and reciting the law against her.

We must keep in mind that Israel's understanding of the body was based on the wholeness and completeness of it. A body was complete and whole when each organ was in its proper place functioning to perfection. The Hebrew word *zākār,* which is translated as 'male', literally could mean the 'male genital member'.[21] On the other hand, the Hebrew word *nĕqēbâ* ('female') could mean also 'orifice bearer'.[22] Therefore, woman's body was seen not just as capable of being penetrated, but also inferior to the male's body because of its lack of a penis. 'By defining the whole body as including a penis, we find that Israel's definition of the body is sexualized. The culture constructed the body ideologically in such way as to exclude women. All bodies were measured against the ideal, and the ideal

---

19. Lloyd, *Judith Butler*, p. 39.

20. Lloyd, *Judith Butler*, p. 65.

21. See R.E. Clements, '*zākār*', *TDOT,* IV, pp. 82-87.

22. Daniel Boyarin, 'Are There Any Jews in "The History of Sexuality"', *Journal of the History of Sexuality* 5 (1995), pp. 333-55 (345).

was defined as a male'.[23] Without a penis women were not complete, and somehow they were mutilated. 'The possession of a penis and testicles was the *sine qua non* of morality and virtue. Those who did not possess them "naturally" suffered from moral weakness and were incapable of "virtuous" behavior.'[24] In this context, the male disciples would find in Pola's lack of a penis the perfect way to punish her for usurping a gender that did not belong to her, and passing for someone that she was not.

Being the Phallus or Having the Phallus

Pola's anointing of Jesus inaugurated an ethic of *descaramiento,* a way of revealing who is in and who might be out, who belongs to Jesus and who does not. Once Pola became a *descarada,* she revealed not just Jesus' identity, she also unmasked the evil intentions of the male disciples who are not ready to give up the honor and privileges that the androcentric and phallocentric culture had ascribed to their bodies simply for having the phallus. For the French psychoanalyst Jacques Marie Émile Lacan the phallus is not the 'flesh member' but a signifier of the body. He argues that the phallus is the privileged signifier, that is, that which originates or generates significations:

> The Phallus is not a fantasy, if what is understood by that is an imaginary effect. Nor is it an object (part, internal, good, bad etc....) in so far as this term tends to accentuate the reality involved in a relationship. It is even less the organ, penis or clitoris, which it symbolizes. And it is not by accident that Freud took his reference for it from the simulacrum which it represented for the Ancients. For the phallus is a signifier.[25]

The phallus is therefore what makes meaning possible, always conjoined with desire. Through the dialectic of demand and desire, man *has* the phallus, while woman *is* the phallus. The equation is simple: the male disciples *have* the phallus, and Pola *is* the phallus.

Butler's critique of this position is that Lacan sustains the hegemonic imaginary that privileges a *machista* and heteronormative regime in his thesis of the phallus as privileged signifier. According to Butler, if the phallus is more than a symbol, then it could just as well be symbolized by any other body part, and those who neither 'have' nor 'are' the phallus may 'reterrito-

23. Jon L. Berquist, *Controlling Corporeality: The Body and the Household in Ancient Israel* (London: Rutgers University Press, 2002), p. 36.

24. David Hester, 'Eunuchs and the Postgender Jesus: Matthew 19.12 and Transgressive Sexualities', *JSNT* 28.1 (2005), pp. 13-40 (19).

25. Jacques Lacan, *Feminine Sexuality: Jacques Lacan and the École Freudienne* (ed. Juliet Mitchell and Jacqueline Rose; trans. Jacqueline Rose; New York: W.W. Norton, 1982), p. 79.

rialize' this symbol in subversive ways.[26] Butler demands that the phallus itself must enter in a perpetual process of 'being signified and resignified'.[27] It can, therefore, be resignified and its meaning can change. The resignification and change that might attend the phallus allow Butler to remove 'it' from the exclusively male domain and to collapse the distinction between 'being' and 'having': 'in fact, *no one* "has" the phallus, since it is a symbol, and disconnecting phallus from penis means that it may be redeployed by those who don't have penises'.[28] In this context, Pola as a *marimacha* is exercising her power of being and having the phallus, both at the same time. Sara Salih argues that women can both 'have' and 'be' the phallus. However, wo/men can suffer from 'penis envy and castration'.[29] This dynamic can be observed in the encounter that Pola had with the male disciples. They suffer from both castration anxiety and penis envy or, as Butler would put it, 'phallus envy'.[30]

One of the many privileges of possessing or having the phallus is the power to interpret the law. When men *have* the phallus, they have the power of the law, the law assists them, and the law reinforces and confirms that they are the ones who have the phallus. However, the men who have the phallus are in constant fear of losing their power, of being castrated and deprived of their privileges. In Mk 14.5, the male disciples who 'physically' 'possess the phallus' would attempt to exercise their power to punish Pola for her *descaro*. These males become ἀγανακτέω (indignant, incensed, offended and irate) at Pola's performance. 'The objection is not to her gender but to her extravagance.'[31] The verb ἀγανακτέω appears three times in the Gospel of Mark. In 10.14, Mark uses ἀγανακτέω to describe Jesus' indignation at his disciples who rebuked the children who were following him. In the same chapter, we encounter the same verb to describe the indignation of the ten male disciples at the uncontrollable ambitions of James and John, who were asking Jesus to be seated one at his right hand and the other on his left (Mk 10.41). Finally, Mark describes again 'some' males who witnessed the woman's act in indignation. What is the problem with Jesus' male disciples?[32] The answer seems to be easy: his disciples have the power to determine who belongs where and who might exercise such power in

26. Sara Salih, *Judith Butler* (New York: Routledge, 2005), p. 85.

27. Butler, *Bodies That Matter,* p. 89.

28. Salih, *Judith Butler*, p. 85.

29. Salih, *Judith Butler*, p. 86.

30. Butler, *Bodies That Matter*, p. 85.

31. M. Eugene Boring, *Mark: A Commentary* (Louisville, KY: Westminster John Knox Press, 2006), p. 382.

32. The crux is what Mark understands by 'disciple' and what he understands by the 'Twelve'. Several Markan texts may be read as though the two groups are identical (2.15, 23; 6.1, 35; 7.2; 8.4, 27, 33-34; 9.14, 18, 28; 10.13; 12.43;14.32; and 16.7).

the community, to decide what bodies are worthy of exercising such power and what bodies are meant to be subjected to them, to decide who has the phallus and who is the phallus. I noted above that Mark does not identify the 'someone' with Jesus' disciples; however, because that indignation and desire for power were part of their reality, it is difficult to resist the temptation of not calling them to 'trial'.

The way the male disciples exercise their privilege of having the phallus is through the absent bodies of the poor. They will use the body of the poor as a way to assure that they still have the power to interpret the law that demands solidarity with the poor during the Passover feast. Needless to say, the disciples' concern for the poor is not real. 'The perfume can be sold for more than three hundred denarii and the money given to the poor' (Mk 14.5). The disciples, who in some previous encounters with the poor showed little concern for them (6.31-44; 8.1-9), now become advocates of the poor, the voice of the voiceless. In the first multiplication of the bread, the disciples are the ones who explicitly demand that Jesus 'send them away, so that they may go into the surrounding farms and villages and may buy themselves something to eat' (Mk 6.35). In these previous feeding stories bread was not sufficient for all those hungry bodies. On one occasion the disciples 'forgot' to bring bread with them (Mk 8.14-21), and Jesus had to teach them a lesson in mathematics so that they might understand the symbolism of the multiplication of bread. Although Mark does not portray the disciples' protest against Pola as an insincere act, I find it difficult to believe it to be anything but that.

I stated above that those males who have the phallus also had the power to interpret the law. Here, the male disciples, in order to prove their manliness, are exercising their privilege of re-interpreting Deut. 15.7-11, which advocates being generous to the poor during the Passover celebrations. There is a confusion of roles: the male disciples are usurping Jesus' authority to reinterpret the law. The poor are called into existence through the linguistic discourse (or interpretation) of the male disciples, but their bodies serve only the purpose of the ones who called them or named them. In other words, the male disciples' perpetual anxiety about being emasculated finds security and stability through the power of exercising and interpreting the law. By naming the poor, the male disciples find their masculinity secure and stable. They realize that they still have power!

However, Jesus said, 'Let her alone' (14.6). It is the first time that Jesus utters a word in this narrative! Mark opens this episode by describing that the powerful and elite bodies (chief priests and the scribes) utter a sentence against Jesus and decide to kill him. In Mk 14.1 Jesus does not have a voice; he is reduced to a mere object of conversation. However, here the voice of Jesus is heard in a very straightforward way in order to recognize Pola *la descarada's* performance. Butler argues that recognition among bodies takes place through communication, a communication that can be verbal but is not necessarily so.[33] The ethic of *descaramiento* does not need written rubrics to form the new community. Pola's *descaramiento* has denounced the erroneous idea of the male disciples' claiming power and privilege for having the physical phallus. It is through service to and recognition of the other that Jesus' disciples become 'powerful', not through physical attributes nor physical location (sitting at Jesus' right or left hand). In one sense, Pola has put the male disciples in their proper place. I showed above how Jesus became a *descarado* once Pola revealed his identity by anointing him. Here, Jesus *el descarado* is not anxious about exercising the power of having the phallus, but rather challenges his male disciples to be engaged and fully implicated in the life and experience of the other.

The body is never an isolated event; it is through the body that gender and sexuality become exposed to others, implicated in social processes, inscribed by cultural norms, and apprehended in their social meanings.[34] Jesus' own body is fully implicated in Pola's body. Any physical aggression or injurious speech against Pola has serious consequences on Jesus' own body. By defending and accepting Pola's transgression of boundaries, Jesus is legitimating not just her act but her body as a true disciple. The body of Pola *la descarada* and Jesus' body have entered into an ethic of solidarity. Someone might not see anything extraordinary in the ethic of solidarity between Jesus and Pola, since the Talmud calls for 'all Israel to be responsible for one another' (*Shebu'ot* 39a). That means in essence that all Israel is bound together, and that what affects one Jew affects the entire community. 'Not so a woman, however. The principle that "all Israel are responsible for each other" does not apply to women.'[35] Jesus and Pola are bound together not just legally but also emotionally, historically and culturally. By defending Pola's performance, Jesus is making her body intelligible, readable, possible and visible for all ages.

Analogically speaking, we can argue that Jesus somehow is prefiguring the 'giving up' of his own body. Here Jesus is giving us an anticipation of his 'Eucharistic meal'. Jesus, who has been in full solidarity with the poor, the outcast and sinners, is presenting Pola's body to the entire world as a symbol of God's justice. 'Wherever the gospel is proclaimed to the whole world, what this woman has done will also be told in remembrance of her' (Mk 14.9). 'The text gives us a mysterious woman. Her character, as Butler might suggest of all "women", should remain without definition, without

33. Butler, *Undoing Gender*, p. 132.
34. Butler, *Undoing Gender*, p. 20.
35. Eliezer Berkovits, *Jewish Women in Time and Torah* (New Jersey: Ktav Publishing House, 1990), p. 6.

limits, discursive.'[36] Pola's body has been institutionalized in much the
same way that some communities would later institutionalize Jesus' Eucharistic body. It is striking that neither Mark nor Matthew portrays Jesus as
saying, 'Do this in remembrance of me (1 Cor. 11.24; Lk. 22.19), but in
remembrance of her.' The true disciples of Jesus must act and must emulate
Pola's performance of her 'good works' and do everything in 'remembrance
of her'. Butler asserts that very often stories do not capture the body to
which they refer. 'To be a body is, in some sense, to be deprived of having
full recollection of one's life. There is a history to my body of which I can
have no recollection.'[37] It is obvious that Pola's body, as Mark presents it
to us, is not fully narratable. Her body and performance have been lost in
translation and interpretation. The constant fear of being castrated by *otras
Polas* who exercise their power in service of the broken ones is still real.
We had excluded Pola's body from our tables, and we have not entered yet
in the ethic of *descaramiento* as she did.

Jesus' Understanding of the Poor

Jesus' plain declaration, 'You will always have the poor with you', has
unleashed all kinds of interpretations, and most scholars tend to justify
Jesus' unclear words. What would happen if we take Jesus' words literally? No doubt this idea could cause anxiety among some readers, and I
might be accused of 'seeing' or, in this case, 'hearing' something that Jesus
did not mean to imply. Did Jesus really care for the bodies of the poor? Of
course he did! Besides, many passages of the Hebrew Bible show God's
preferential option for the poor.[38] However, Butler's idea of being 'human'
has caused me to reflect again about the privilege of being 'poor'. According to Butler, 'To be oppressed means that you already exist as a subject of
some kind, you are there as the visible and oppressed other for the master
subject, as possible or potential subject, but to be unreal is something else
again.'[39] Butler argues that there are some 'bodies' that do not even have
the 'privilege' of being oppressed because they are neither real nor intel-

36. Hornsby, 'The Annoying Woman', in *Bodily Citations,* p. 82.
37. Butler, *Giving an Account,* p. 38.
38. During the early period of ancient 'Israel' as a nation, ethical guidelines in
favor of the poor were provided. Exodus 22–23 instructed the people to provide for
strangers, widows, orphans and the poor. Property is protected, a warning given against
favoritism, and a system of 'gleaning' established to help prevent starvation. Equal justice for the poor in court is constantly reiterated (Exod. 23.6; Ps. 72.14; Amos 5.10-15).
Leviticus 25.8-43 describes the institution of the 'Year of Jubilee', and Deuteronomy 15
describes the requirement that all debts were to be cancelled every seven years.
39. Butler, *Undoing Gender,* p. 30.

ligible. 'To be oppressed you must first become intelligible.'[40] In the first chapter, I demonstrated how the voracious priest failed to see Jesus' face in our impoverished bodies. Although we recognized him as the *other, lleno de vida,* he negated our very existence. Of course from time to time he would be invited to the city to talk about his experience with the poor. I wonder what would happened if we were to interpret Jesus' words in a Butlerian way. We might find out that Jesus is not just caring for the poor but also extending and legitimating their negated humanity to all of those bodies who have been confined to 'the shadowy regions of ontology'.[41]

When Jesus affirms, 'You will always have the poor with you', it is like calling them into existence—what Butler would define as living a viable life. Through the created power of language, Jesus is naming the poor, acknowledging their existence and recognizing their dignity. For Jesus, the poor are in a constant process of 'recovering' their humanity because being human does not occur in a single event. By affirming that there will always be poor among us, Jesus is denouncing the orchestration of power that has confined some bodies to a deplorable state of inhumanity. 'Jesus is not simply the presence of God among the marginalized: more than that Jesus represents a truly marginalized God.'[42] To take care of the poor is to enter in a continuous ethic of *descaramiento.* Taking care of the poor is not reduced to providing bread once for all, but on the contrary is about providing possibilities for them to be recognized as humans. Butler asserts that when somebody is described and categorized as impossibility, it is because the laws of culture and language are not yet in somebody's favor.[43] However, Jesus is giving some recognition, not merely to the poor, but also to Pola *la descarada.* He is allowing those norms by which recognition takes place to work in favor of those unintelligible and liminal people whom Mark presents through his Gospel. Jesus as a *descarado* is changing the norm concerning which bodies count as human and which bodies do not. Those bodies that before did not matter are now the ones that find legitimation, recognition and intelligibility.

Butler affirms that violence against those who are already not quite alive, those who are living in a state of suspension between life and death, leaves a mark that is not a mark.[44] Jesus did not resolve the poverty of his time. Nor

---

40. Butler, *Undoing Gender,* p. 30.
41. Butler used this phrase in an interview to refer to the abject body. See Irene Costera Meijer and Baukje Prins, 'How Bodies Come to Matter: An Interview with Judith Butler', *Signs* 23 (1998), pp. 275-86.
42. Marcella Althaus-Reid, 'Mark', in Deryn Guest *et al.* (eds.), *The Queer Bible Commentary* (London: SCM Press, 2006), p. 523.
43. Butler, *Undoing Gender,* p. 30.
44. Butler, *Undoing Gender,* p. 25.

did he become the 'voice of the voiceless bodies'. However, he announced to, or left a 'mark of hope' in, all those bodies that were counted as less than human, whose lives were constantly threatened by death, not only by poverty but also by their gender. At the same time, in this narrative Jesus is denouncing his disciples' false concern for the poor. They had failed to recognize the body of Pola as human and worthy of being counted as part of Jesus' new family. Jesus' true disciples must take some moral responsibility toward the nobodies if they want to be part of Jesus' alternative household. Here the disciples are just judging her without entering into relationship with her or acknowledging her good deeds. Butler reminds us that prior to judging an other, we must be in some relation to him or her.[45] These relations must show our true humanity. If the disciples cannot take any responsibility toward Pola who is right in front of them, how are they supposed to become the advocates of the poor in general?

Jesus is not so naïve as to believe that he can explain exactly the process or metamorphosis by which a body is deemed human. 'Becoming human is not a simple task, and it is not always clear when or if one arrives. To be human seems to mean being in a predicament that one cannot solve.'[46] Nonetheless, Jesus and Pola *la descarada* had already resolved their predicament. They found out that it is by serving one another that one serves God perfectly. The male disciples are now the ones who need to resolve their predicament of giving up the privilege of possessing the phallus or not. Jesus' demands are not confined to giving money to the poor, but rather to being able and willing, without hesitation, to give up *everything* (manliness, honor, privilege of having a phallus, etc.) with generosity. Discipleship in Mark's Gospel demands a very radical rupture with the traditional notion of being fe/male and human that the Greco-Roman culture promoted. *Seguir a Jesús en Marcos, implica asumir una vida exigente y rigurosa, cuyos gestos inaugurales incluyen la renuncia a varias prácticas normales en la sociedad mediterránea antigua,* 'Following Jesus in Mark's Gospel implies assuming an exigent and rigorous life, whose characteristics include renouncing certain normal practices of ancient Mediterranean society.'[47] The renunciation of some disciples in the Markan community will be evident in the next chapter when we study the man who carries his jar of water on the streets of Jerusalem (Mk 14.13-16). For now we can say in conclusion that the disciples cannot advocate for the poor on the one hand and despise Pola *la descarada* on the other. By acknowledging Pola's humanity, they are indeed taking care of the poor. Of course, some male disciples could not bear the

---

45. Butler, *Giving an Account*, p. 45.
46. Butler, *Giving an Account*, p. 103.
47. Leif E. Vaage, 'En otra casa: El discipulado en Marcos como ascetismo doméstico', *Estudios Bíblicos* 63 (2005), pp. 21-42 (39).

stigma of being counted as *descarados*. Other male disciples must learn how to become *descarados*. Such is the case of Simon Peter, who in the end was transformed by the slave girl.

Murder and Redemption at las lumbradas, *'Fire'*

I still remember the cold winter that I had to endure in my village. Our adobe house, which was always in need of serious repair, did not shelter us well from the cold. In order to keep ourselves warm on cold mornings, we children would make a fire out in the open. To make a *lumbrada*, 'fire', was a kind of ritual passage of survival and 'manhood'. Making a particularly big *lumbrada* and keeping the *lumbrada* going longer than others could was always a source of pride. Being the youngest of four sister and two brothers, I thought that my sisters did not like making *lumbradas* because they were already too old for such things. Besides, my sisters were already busy in keeping the fire going in other ways that would enslave them for life. For example, early in the morning, my sisters would be kneading dough to make our corn tortillas. Our humble adobe kitchen would become a legitimate jail for my *campesinas* sisters who would maintain an immaculate kitchen. In recalling my experience with *lumbradas,* I do not remember any girls attending such rituals. It was a kind of male club where girls were not allowed. The ritual of making our *lumbradas* was very well established. Moisés, my oldest brother, would select our fire location where it was sheltered and protected from the wind, and far away from our goats and cows. Guillermo, my other brother, would build up the wood, beginning with small pieces of wood; and then he would add larger pieces as the fire got going. My duty was to collect all kinds of wood. Then my brother Moisés would select the driest tinder to ignite the fire. While warming ourselves, we would discuss 'important issues', such as who would take breakfast to our dad, who was already working in the field, who would take care of the goats and who would stay and help dad.

There were also *otras lumbradas,* which were made at night on the street rather than at someone's home. These public *lumbradas* were only for adult males and were typically made only for special occasions, such as during Our Lady of Guadalupe's Novena, at Christmas and New Year's Eve, and so on. At these *lumbradas,* the adult males often would get drunk and typically talked about 'male things', as my dad put it. These *lumbradas* were dangerous sites to be, my mother would warn us. One night, returning from my uncle's house in the middle of the village, instead of taking the direct route to our house, we made a big detour to get to our place. When my youngest sister asked mother why we were taking the long way to get home, she replied, *Había unos hombres calentándose y probablemente ya estén borrachos,* 'There were some men warming themselves at *las lumbradas* and probably they are already drunk.' Besides, she continued, *No es apropiado para la mujeres ni para los niños pasar por donde hay puros hombres*, 'It is not proper for either women or children to pass where only men are.' I was suspicious of my mother's obsessive 'prudence', but morning would prove that she was right and I was wrong, when we learned that a woman called Rebeca had been killed by her husband.

It happened during the night when Rebeca's husband was 'keeping warm' and drinking with other males in *la lumbrada* in front of Rebeca's house. Rebeca went out looking for her husband and called him to come home because one of her kids was sick. Immediately, the other males started joking with Juan (Rebeca's husband) saying: *Pinche maricón, ya sabemos quién manda en tu casa/'Pinche maricón*, We know who rules in your home.' Among the males who were part of the *lumbrada* was Rebeca's own brother, who challenged his brother-in-law by saying: *Si Rebeca la hocicona de mierda, fuera mi esposa, le doy una chinga para que sepa quién es el hombre*, 'If Rebeca— the big mouth, the one full of shit—were my wife I would beat her to let her know who is the man.' Thus shamed, Juan left la *lumbrada* and began beating Rebeca mercilessly till she died. Later on we found out that Rebeca was also pregnant! This homicide caused fear and anxiety in the entire village, especially among women. Juan argued that he was defending his honor, that he did not have any choice, otherwise his friends would think that he was a *maricón*. The police let Juan go free, saying that Rebeca should not have gone out of her home in the first place. The men interpreted this incident as a lesson for all women to learn not to be *hociconas y malcriadas*. They must be quiet and never dare to call upon their men in public while they are socializing in *la lumbrada* with their *amigos*.

This kind of violence against women at night in a public space such as *las lumbradas* is not restricted to village life. Even in Mexico City murders like this happened. Anthropologist Marta Lamas succinctly reports, 'That the street at night is a place of masculine power is a belief still so naturalized in urban Mexico culture that women who (inappropriately) occupy that place become responsible for any consequences that result from their action.'[48] This is exemplified by the case of Claudia Rodríguez Ferrando, a mother of five, who on her way home was attacked by a male. She fought her aggressor as well as she could and ended up wounding him. The man died hours later due to the lack of medical attention. Nonetheless, Judge Gustavo Aquiles Gasca denied the woman her legal recourse, blaming Ms.

---

48. Marta Lamas, 'By Night, a Street Night, "Public' Women of the Night on the Streets of Mexico City', in Rosario Montoya *et al.* (eds.), *Gender Places: Feminist Anthropologies of Latin America* (New York: Palgrave Macmillan, 2002), pp. 237-54 (238).

Rodríguez for the death of her aggressor. The judge argued that 'that was not a time [*esas no eran horas*] for a decent woman to be out on the street'.[49] For Héctor Carrillo, the association of sex and sexuality with darkness, fire and night is symbolic of sex's transgressive nature.[50] Night, fire, and 'public space' are a fatal combination for women. For this reason I find very unusual the depiction that Mark gives of the slave girl who brings Peter to trial (Mk 14.66-72).

Rebequita la malcriada

Families in Mexico have obsessively strived to educate their children as *bien criados,* 'well bred, well brought-up'. One who is *bien criado/a* must show respect, modesty and fidelity to one's parents and to elderly people. However, *criado/a* also means slave, and it is probably this last connotation that has chased us like a ghost since the conquest. We have been educated to total *servilismo,* 'servitude', always showing blind obedience to a superior, never questioning anything and always ready to serve other's needs. For women, this has been their tragic destiny—always sacrificing themselves by serving men. Small wonder, for during my years in seminary I would hear day after day, *El que obedece nunca se equivoca,* 'The one who obeys is never mistaken.' Being a slave is what society and religion require and promote: 'Pray, pay and obey!' It is what religion demands for being a 'good' Christian. By contrast, the one who misbehaves, the one who is opinionated, the one who talks back to one's parents is described as *malcriado/a* and *hocicón.* People who resist being enslaved end up dead, as happened with Rebeca, who was accused of being *hocicona y malcriada.* By patriarchal definitions *hocicona* means that a woman talks too much, but Chicana women have re-appropriated this term: 'An *hocicona* is a woman who speaks out against male oppression.'[51] A *malcriada* is a woman accused of misbehaving or not abiding by the rules she was raised to follow. Moreover, our Chicana sisters would argue 'that a *malcriada* is a woman who defies patriarchal prescriptions of "proper" women's behavior'.[52] I think that the little slave girl who put Peter on trial (Mk 14.66-72) is a real *malcriada y hocicona* for not playing by the rules.

In his passion narrative, Mark 'gathers together onto the stage all the characters in his political drama: Roman and Jewish authorities, the crow, the disciples (in the background), and rebels (represented by Barabbas and

---

49. Lamas, 'By Night', p. 238.

50. Héctor Carrillo, *The Night Is Young: Sexuality in Mexico in the Time of AIDS* (Chicago: University of Chicago, 2002), p. x

51. Tijerina Revilla, 'Muxerista Pedagogy', p. 90.

52. Tijerina Revilla, 'Muxerista Pedagogy', p. 90.

the two social bandits)'.[53] To this list we can add the slave girl who I will baptize as Rebequita,[54] in memory of Rebeca la *hocicona y malcriada* who met her death at the hands of her husband for calling for his help while he was gathered with the menfolk at *la lumbrada*. If we analyze each character who appears in Mark's passion narrative, we discover that they have something in common: they cross and transgress a variety of boundaries—geographical, gender and ethnic—that they are meant to observe. In this section, I will analyze the figures of Simon Peter and Rebequita. Both characters subvert the gender roles assigned to them. Peter and Rebequita *la malcriada y hocicona* are engaged in a kind of 'fatal attraction' for recognition as disciples of Jesus.

In the trial of Peter, there are several ironic elements or behaviors that do not fit in the picture.[55] Some characters are out of place. While Jesus is forced to enter into the high priest's house (14.53), Peter voluntarily enters right into the courtyard of the palace of the high priest (14.66). I find it ironic that Peter, instead of being 'with' Jesus, freely and willingly seeks *koinōnia*, 'fellowship', with Jesus' opponents by sitting with the soldiers to warm himself (14.67). Of course, the soldiers will put him in his proper place. Peter is a Galilean, and they are not (14.70). Perhaps one of the most striking ironic motifs in Peter's trial is the way in which Mark depicts Rebequita. She moves freely from *lumbrada* (inside the house where Jesus is interrogated) to *lumbrada* (outside in the courtyard of the house, where she saw Peter) without any restriction whatsoever. Rebequita has dared to go to *la lumbrada,* where all kinds of men are socializing; and she did not die! From this list of ironic motifs we can see how some characters are usurping other characters' roles. Or are they camouflaging their own role? While Jesus is interrogated by the high priest (14.60), Peter is interrogated by Rebequita *la malcriada* (14.67). Simon Peter as a disciple of Jesus is supposed to know who Jesus is, yet does not, whereas Rebequita, who is not officially a disciple, nevertheless knows and recognizes Jesus straight away (14.67). As we can see, all of these characters are behaving in a very ironic way.

In the next chapter, I will demonstrate how men in the Hellenistic culture secure their masculinity and humanity through the skilled use of rhetoric. For now it is important to know that women and slaves were considered less

53. Ched Myers, *Binding the Strong Man: A Political Reading of Mark's Story of Jesus* (Maryknoll, NY: Orbis Books, 1988), p. 357.
54. Notice that I am using the diminutive of Rebeca because Mark in referring to the slave girl uses *paidiskē*, which is a diminutive of *pais*. In this context *paidiskē* could refer to a little slave girl.
55. See Jerry Camery-Hoggatt, *Irony in Mark's Gospel: Text and Subtext* (Cambridge: Cambridge University Press, 1992).

than human. Scholars have informed us that among first-century Greeks and Romans there was considerable pessimism about children because of their physical smallness, underdevelopment and resulting vulnerability, as well as their apparent ignorance, capriciousness and irrationality, characteristics that were to be overcome through rigorous education and harsh discipline.[56] Plato specifically excludes women, slaves and children from the sphere of reason and humanity, deeming them incapable of reasoning. For Butler, 'This xenophobic exclusion operates through the production of racialized Others, and those whose "natures" are considered less rational by virtue of their appointed task in the process of laboring to reproduce the condition of private life.'[57] From my reading *del otro lado,* it is obvious that Rebequita is triply marginalized; she is a 'woman'; she is a 'little girl'; and she is a slave. She has everything going against her. She is even situated in a dangerous *lumbrada* at night with males where all kinds of danger might occur. Ironically, Mark gave her voice, and she is in constant movement! Mark has already introduced to us Pola *la descarada,* who talked through her body in a public space. Mark is now depicting Rebequita in ways that women usually have not been described through his Gospel. By entering a male's domain, Rebequita is following in the footsteps of Pola *la descarada* in order to challenge other male disciples who need to hear about Jesus.

Note above that Jesus' trial (Mk 14.53-65) and Peter's trial (Mk 14.66-72) are intertwined by the use of irony. Indoors, in the judgment hall, Jesus is on trial. Outside the judgment hall, Peter is also on trial. 'The contrast between the two trial scenes is ironic.'[58] The use of irony revolves around the identity of the characters. In the case of Jesus, his accusers testify falsely against him. In Peter's case, Rebequita, *la malcriada,* speaks the truth about Peter's identity while saying, 'You also were with that Nazarene, Jesus' (Mk 14.67); and later on she would accuse Peter before the bystanders saying, 'This is one of them (Mark 14.69).'As I mentioned above, I find it very compelling that Mark who has depicted women as silent throughout his Gospel,[59] and typically shows them perpetually afraid and terrified (Mk

56. Judith M. Gundry, 'Children in the Gospel of Mark, with Special Attention to Jesus' Blessing of the Children (Mark 10.13-16) and the Purpose of Mark', in Marcia J. Bunge (ed.), *The Child in the Bible* (Grand Rapids: Eerdmans, 2008), pp. 162-63.

57. Butler, *Bodies That Matter*, p. 48.

58. Edwin K. Broadhead, *Mark* (Sheffield: Sheffield Academic Press, 2001), p. 121.

59. Actually Mark gave voice to two women with their respective daughters (the Syrophoenician women and her daughter [Mk 7.24-30] and Herodias and her daughter [Mk 6.14-29]) in the entire narrative. Even here the irony motif is present. Mark seems to contrast both women and their respective behaviors. One is anonymous and situated in the margins or borderland; the other one has a name and is situated in the center with the powerful ones. The Syrophoenician woman seeks life for her daughter; Herodias takes away John's life through her daughter.

5.33; 16.8), for some unknown reason abruptly gives voice to Rebequita, who appears confident, accusing Peter and talking with other males. All the scholars that I have studied portray Rebequita in a negative light. Most of them focus on Peter' denial and pay little attention to Rebequita's words and location. Even feminists who interpret Peter's denial and discover that 'In typical Markan fashion, the anonymous, lowly, and marginal character stands for truth while the high status, powerful character rejects the truth or tells lies',[60] fail to really recognize Rebequita herself. Even worse, feminists who have otherwise brilliantly and exhaustively analyzed the role of women in Mark's Gospel conclude that Rebequita's role 'thus corresponds to that of Satan and the human enemies who test Jesus (1.13; 8.11-13; 10.2; 12.13-17)'.[61] For other feminist scholars, Rebequita's words are considered 'banal' and 'quite mundane' in nature, with power to bring disorder in God's plan: 'The maidservant causes major disorder in the order of God that this gospel has portrayed Jesus setting out to establish, by calling male disciples to follow him.'[62] Because my hermeneutic *del otro lado* intends to read the text in unorthodox ways, I will situate Rebequita in the place that she deserves. I will snatch her from Satan's claws and bring her into Jesus' community. Moreover, I will argue that Rebequita's 'mundane' words, instead of bring disorder in the community, instead bring order and wholeness by reinstating Peter back in Jesus' community.

We can easily recognize irony in Peter's trial, but we would be hard pressed to define it or explain it. After all, irony is about what is not written; it is about silence, and speculation. We must read and interpret the irony between the lines. Therefore, irony requires other techniques of interpretation. Attentiveness to silence—to the importance of what is not said—is a significant part of the enterprise of reading and interpreting our biblical text.[63] Although the etymology of irony is still in debate, scholars trace its origin to Greek comedy, which 'gave the name of *eirōn* to that person who slyly pretended to be less than he really was'.[64] It is from here that our word irony comes. Usually Greek comedy presents a conflict between two characters, the *eirōn* and the *alazōn,* the latter being the 'impostor', the

---

60. Mary Ann Tolbert, "Mark' in Carol A. Newsom and Sharon H. Ringe (eds.), *Women's Bible Commentary* (Louisville, KY: Westminster John Knox Press, 1998), pp. 350-62 (360).

61. Susan Miller, *Women in Mark's Gospel* (New York: T. & T. Clark, 2004), p. 151.

62. Michele A. Connolly, *Disorderly Women and the Order of God: An Australian Feminist Reading of the Gospel of Mark* (PhD diss., Graduate Theological Union, 2008), p. 316.

63. Carolyn J. Sharp, *Irony and Meaning in the Hebrew Bible* (Bloomington: Indiana University Press, 2009), p. 7.

64. Paul D. Duke, *Irony in the Fourth Gospel* (Atlanta: John Knox Press, 1985), p. 8.

'fake', who pretends to pass for the former, the *eirōn*. The comedy ends, of course, in bursting the *alazōn's* bubble, the triumph of the *eirōn*. The audience knew all along which character was the imposter, which the ironic person, and they knew how things would turn out. The comedy lies in watching the imposter being exposed and deflated by the machinations of the ironic person.[65] Unluckily, in Peter's ironic trial we do not know who is who. We are informed about the conflict, but we are not totally aware of the double entendre that Mark intended to communicate to his first audience. Is Mark presenting Peter's plot on two levels of interpretation? Who might be the *eirōn*? Who might be the *alazōn*? Probably Mark, in imitating the conflict of Greek drama, is depicting Peter as *alazōn* and Rebequita as *eirōn*. Or perhaps both Peter and Rebequita could be the *alazōn* and the *eirōn* at the same time. I do not think that anyone is in a position to decipher for sure the identity of these characters. In interpreting ironic biblical text, we often move from speculation to doubt, from doubt to uncertainty, from uncertainty to wonder.

In early Greek comedy, the *alazōn* was the one who boasts, exaggerates and tries to give an impression of superior knowledge and brevity. I cannot help but relate the figure of Simon Peter to the *alazōn*. Peter as *alazōn* could be identified through the Gospel; however, in his arrogance and boastfulness, it becomes obvious at the point when Jesus announces his death: 'You all will fall away' (Mk 14.27). In the face of the imminent danger and violence that is about to surround the community, they all become silent, all except Peter, the *alazōn,* the macho man: 'Even if everyone falls away, it will not be I' (14.29). Jesus, the one who speaks the truth, tries to put Peter in his place, but Peter still has a lot to learn, and he is not yet ready to remove his mask. 'Even if it is necessary for me to die along with you, I will never deny you' (Mk 14.31), he insists. Immediately after Jesus' prediction, Mark prepares the stage on which Peter will show his weakness. Peter had said he was willing to die with Jesus, but in reality he couldn't even stay awake and pray with him for an hour (Mk 14.37). He did not know how to take his words *like a man*. Peter, having the characteristics of the *alazōn,* is exposed or unmasked by Rebequita, who acts as the *eirōn*. We stated above that the etymology of the word *eirōn* is uncertain, though it seems related to *eirein*, 'to say, speak', or perhaps is more closely to the Ionic *eirōmai,* 'to ask questions'.[66] If such is the case, Rebequita fulfills such a requirement to perfection. Not only is she *malcriada* and *hocicona,* but she also fulfills her role as *eirōn* by disclosing Peter's identity and her own as disciples of Jesus.

---

65. Edwin M. Good, *Irony in the Old Testament* (Philadelphia: Westminster Press, 1965), p. 14.
66. Duke, *Irony in the Fourth Gospel,* p. 8.

Throughout Mark's Gospel, Jesus has taught his disciples on several occasions to be like Rebequita, that is, to be servants and slaves. 'Sitting down, Jesus called the Twelve and said, "If anyone wants to be first, he[she] must be the very last, and the servant of all"' (Mk 9.36). Of course, many disciples were moved by desire of power and control, as I pointed out above. We saw in the previous chapter how power can come from 'any-where' and especially from below, always in relation with one another, serv-ing one another and always open to embrace the needs of the other. This is something that the male disciples in Mark did not learn, that power is for service to others and not for building up one's own privilege. On the con-trary, Rebequita as a little slave is doing something great for Peter, as I will show below. Rebequita, as a member of Jesus' community, has understood perfectly Jesus' teaching: 'Whoever wants to become great among you must be your servant, and whoever wants to be first must be slave of all' (Mk 10.43-44). As a true disciple of Jesus, she will bring Peter into existence through her *hocico* language discourse.

Rebequita la hocicona

Miller correctly observes that Rebequita emerges from the crowd of people on her own initiative, as other women have done in the past (ἔρχεται, 14.66; cf. 5.26; 7.25; 12.42; 14.3).[67] This observation puts Rebequita on a different level. Before she utters a word, Mark informs us, she looks closely at Peter (14.67a). The look or gaze that Rebequita gives to Peter is ironic. In all cul-tures, gazing on another male body is always risky and dangerous. In antiq-uity, men were the only ones allowed to gaze on women, and this estab-lished them as the subjects in any context. For their part, by being gazed upon, women became objects. In the dialectic of gazing, males exhibited power and dominion over women, and women showed vulnerability and submission to men. 'This gendered gaze ensures a hierarchical positioning of male and female encoded in terms such as active/passive and subjective/objective.'[68] Mark depicts Rebequita transgressing the boundaries of the 'gendered social system'. By describing Rebequita gazing upon Peter, Mark is subverting the dominant gender hierarchy. Here, I am not so much inter-ested in describing the dialect of gazing upon other bodies, a topic I develop at greater length in Chapter 5. However, I cannot help but notice how Mark subordinated the manly Peter to the gaze of Rebequita.

In the first encounter that Rebequita had with Peter, Mark uses two verbs (participles) of seeing (*idousa* ... *emblepsasa*), suggesting first a sighting and

---

67. Miller, *Women in Mark's Gospel*, p. 148.

68. Blake Leyerle, 'John Chrysostom on the Gaze', *Journal of Christian Studies* 1 (1993), pp. 159-74 (159).

then a closer look that leads to a recognition of Peter.[69] As soon as Peter is gazed upon by Rebequita, he intends to leave, but once again Mark informs us that Rebequita 'saw' him again. Probably Rebequita's gazing upon the manly Peter was not appropriate behavior for a slave girl. (Indeed, for this reason each Gospel has its own nuance on the 'gazing motif'. Scholars have observed that 'in all Gospels except Mark the persons who recognize Peter are always different, although the first one is always a maidservant'.[70]) For the sake of the argument, let us briefly examine who else besides Rebequita gazes upon Peter's body. I am struck by the fact that Matthew denies Rebequita the privilege of gazing upon Peter. 'Now Peter was sitting out in the courtyard, and a servant girl came to him. "You also were with Jesus of Galilee', she said' (Mt. 26.69). Matthew, often concerned to preserve the proper gender roles, omits this detail; however, immediately, he informs us that another girl was the one who gazed upon Peter: 'Then he went out to the gateway, where another girl *saw* him and said to the people there, "This fellow was with Jesus of Nazareth" (Mt. 26.71). For our investigation, it is irrelevant who gazed at Peter; what is at stake here is that Peter has been identified with an inferior status. In Luke there are many people who gazed upon Peter. Rebequita gazed upon Peter on one single occasion: 'A servant girl *saw* him seated there in the firelight. She *looked closely at* him and said, "This man was with him"' (Lk. 22.56). After Rebequita's first gaze, other males (ἕτερος) would have the privilege of submitting Peter to their gaze: 'And a little later someone else saw him and said, "You also are one of them." But Peter said, "Man, I am not"' (Lk. 22.58). In Luke, even the humiliated Jesus would gaze upon Peter: 'The Lord turned and looked straight at Peter' (Lk. 22.61). In the Gospel of John, it is a male slave (δοῦλος) who gazes upon Peter's body: 'One of the high priest's servants, a relative of the man whose ear Peter had cut off, challenged him, "Didn't I *see* you with him in the olive grove?"' (Jn 18.26).

As we can see, Mark is the only one who depicted Rebequita gazing constantly upon Peter. I cannot help but think that in so doing Mark has deliberately left an 'ironic mark' for all of us who gaze upon his text. 'When we "feel" as if a certain line or work is ironic it is generally because the author has planted some subtle signal which we may not consciously recognize as such, but which has hooked us nonetheless.'[71] I stated above how Pola's ethic of *descaramiento* can be communicated without words. In a simple gaze, someone can be implicated in the life of the other. In the case of Rebequita and Peter, we do not know exactly what really happened in

---

69. John R. Donahue and Daniel J. Harrington, *The Gospel of Mark* (Collegeville, MN: Liturgical Press, 2002), p. 425.

70. Ulrich Luz, *Matthew 21-28* (Minneapolis: Fortress Press, 2005), p. 453.

71. Duke, *Irony in the Fourth Gospel*, p. 32.

the particular moment, or what the 'looks' of each communicates. There is more meaning behind this unspoken language than we are able to grasp. Do they recognize each other as disciples who were somewhere at the wrong time, with the wrong people, at the wrong place, passing for something that they were not? It is difficult to say. Nonetheless, the light of the *lumbrada* would challenge Peter to enter in the dynamic of *descaramiento.*

The ironic mark that Mark left on Peter's denial is not restricted to the gaze of Rebequita upon Peter, but also there is irony in the symbolism of the fire. After all, it is the light of the *lumbrada* that helped Rebequita to recognize Peter among the other men, and called him out of darkness. Although some scholars have kept Rebequita in perpetual enslavement since 'she is there to keep the fire going and to open the gate' (John 18.16),[72] Mark may have had something different in mind. According to Miller, 'Peter desires to remain hidden, but the light from the fire reveals his identity to the woman and also illuminates his character.'[73] For Montefiore, 'The fire shines upon Peter's face and reveals him.'[74] Neither Miller nor Montefiore explains exactly how the fire illuminates Peter's character. I think it is Rebequita's words, not the fire, that attempt to illuminate Peter's character and face, as I will show below. The light of the *lumbrada* might help Rebequita to recognize Peter among the other men. However, it would be Rebequita's hailing that would bring Peter out of darkness. Furthermore, Miller seems to associate the symbolism of the fire with something evil as she says, 'Our account takes places at night, and darkness is associated with the time of increasing evil.'[75] It is true that fire among all phenomena, as psychoanalyst Gaston Bachelard says, 'is really the only one to which there can be so definitely attributed the opposing values of good and evil. It shines in Paradise. It burns in Hell.'[76] I find Miller's interpretation disturbing and dangerous for having opted to associate Rebequita with Satan, and so I have opted to bring her out of hell. It is true that the night conveys danger, and people might find their deaths at *lumbradas*; but for children of the light, the night could also be a sign of liberation (Exod. 3.24; 13.21; 19.18). Furthermore, *La luz era una manera de designar al Mesías*, 'the light was a way to designate the

72. Luise Schottroff, *Lydia's Impatient Sister: A Feminist Social History of Early Christianity* (trans. Barbara and Martin Rumscheidt; Louisville, KY: Westminster John Knox Press, 1995), p. 83.

73. Miller, *Women in Mark's Gospel*, p. 151.

74. Claude Goldsmid Montefiore, *The Synoptic Gospel, I* (London: Macmillan, 1927), p. 367.

75. Miller, *Women in Mark's Gospel*, p. 151.

76. Gaston Bachelard, *The Psychoanalysis of Fire* (trans. Alan C.M. Ross; preface by Northrop Frye; Boston: Beacon, 1964) p. 7.

Messiah'.[77] Rebequita, as a daughter of the light, would share her insights with her brother Peter. Rebequita's eyes are indeed the 'lamp of her body' and her body had become full of light[78] to bring Peter from darkness to the true light that Jesus had offered them.

For some unknown reason, Matthew is the only one of the four evangelists who omits the *la lumbrada* motif from his Gospel. 'But Peter followed him at a distance, right up to the courtyard of the high priest. He entered and sat down with the guards to see the outcome' (Mt. 26.58). Perhaps he knows that *lumbrada's* symbolism conveys the meaning of social reality,[79] where people might enter in a deep relationship by the very act of warming. In Matthew, Peter does not seem to be cold; he is not warming himself: 'Now Peter was sitting out in the courtyard, and a servant girl came to him. "You also were with Jesus of Galilee", she said' (Mt. 26.69). Contrary to Matthew, Mark twice mentions Peter as warming himself at a fire with other males: 'He sat with the guards and warmed himself at the fire' (Mk 14.54; 14.67). Most scholars correctly argue that Peter has associated himself with those who will range themselves against Jesus, and the treatment he receives from them (enquiry concerning his association with Jesus) is met with a loud and vehement denial.[80] Why does Mark depict Peter as being attracted to fire? Is there any hidden symbolism about fire that we are not able to understand? It is ironic that Peter, as representative of the entire community, remarked to Jesus, 'We have left everything to follow you!' (Mk 10.28); and here in *la lumbrada* he is falling away from Jesus, separating himself from Jesus by the symbolism of the fire. Psychologists inform us that 'fire suggests the desire to change, to speed up the passage of time, to bring all of life to its conclusions, to its hereafter'.[81] The fact that Mark depicts Peter twice at *la lumbrada* intends to show that his alliances had changed. Now Peter is with Jesus' enemies.

> *Aparantemente, pertenece al mismo bando de los presentes; está junto a los que sirven al poder que va a condenar a muerte a Jesús. Marcos insinúa así que, como ellos, Pedro está también al servicio de un poder violent,* Apparently, [Peter] belongs to the same band as those present; [he] is with those who serve the power which would condemn Jesus to death.

77. Juan Mateos and Fernando Camacho, *El Evangelio de Marcos: Análisis lingüístico y comentario exegético III* (Córdoba: Ediciones el Almendro, 2008), p. 574. See Isa. 10.17; Ps. 36.7-9.

78. In order to understand the proverb of 'the eye as a lamp of the body', see the excellent article of Dale C. Allison, 'The Eye Is the Lamp of the Body (Matthew 6.22-23=Luke 11.34-36)', *NTS* 33 (1987), pp. 61-83.

79. Bachelard, *Psychoanalysis of Fire*, p. 10.

80. Geoff R. Webb, *Mark at the Threshold: Applying Bakhtinian Categories to Markan Characterisation* (Leiden: Brill, 2008), p. 210.

81. Bachelard, *Psychoanalysis of Fire,* p. 16.

> In this way Mark insinuates that, like them, Peter is also at the service of
> a violent power.[82]

Mark depicts Peter in a constant process of detachment from Jesus. This detachment somehow originated in another *lumbrada*,[83] when Peter was not able to watch one hour while Jesus was praying (Mk 14.37). Moreover, Peter's disassociation from Jesus continues when he follows Jesus at a distance (Mk 14.54); and finally, Peter's total disconnection from Jesus happens when he publicly denied him by the fire. Mark portrays through the symbolism of fire Peter's desire to shift allegiances and credentials from being with Jesus to being with the soldiers. Peter, by the very act of warming himself at *la lumbrada*, wants to disappear symbolically from Jesus; he wishes, as it were, to be swallowed up by the fire, to leave no trace of his friendship with the one who once called him. Bachelard seems to be correct when affirming that 'Love, death, and fire are united at the same moment'.[84] It would be at *la lumbrada* that Peter must confront his 'inner demons' in order to pass from death to life, from inner darkness to light, from traitor to disciple. *La lumbrada* would prove once again to have magical powers to illuminate and heal any broken heart, to be a site of revelation and transformation. It is in *la lumbrada* that Peter must attend to the call of Rebequita and confess publicly that he is with Jesus the Nazarene! I have argued that, for Butler, we cannot have any knowledge of the body except through discourse. For Butler, the body takes place and is constituted as a body through the repetition and ritualization of language. We are, from our very nature, in some sense 'linguistic beings who require language in order to be'.[85] We observe that prior to Rebequita's hailing of Peter, he does not speak. Has he been ironically transformed from being the *alazōn* into the *eirōn*? Not yet. Peter is not prepared for such conversion. The last time we heard Peter's voice was when he vehemently affirmed that he would never betray Jesus (Mk 14.31). After that, Peter does not know what to say when Jesus rebukes him because he could not watch for one hour (Mk 14.37). Although Mark depicts Peter as the only disciple attempting to follow Jesus, in the end he fails totally just like the rest of the group. Moreover, he is situated in a not-very-manly position: he follows Jesus at a distance (Mk 14.54), just like the women who witnessed Jesus' death (Mk 15.40). After this, Peter, the macho man, the vociferous man, the *alazōn,* becomes silent, mute, fearing for his life, until Rebequita *la hocicona,* the *eirōn,* like a daughter of Sofia, brings

82. Mateos and Camacho, *El Evangelio de Marcos,* p. 575.
83. Mark does not inform us about any *lumbrada,* but because the nights could be cold in Jerusalem, we might speculate that they might kindle a *lumbrada* in Gethsemane to warm themselves.
84. Bachelard, *Psychoanalysis of Fire,* p. 17.
85. Butler, *Excitable Speech,* p. 2.

him to life! When Rebequita states, 'You also were with that Nazarene, Jesus' (Mk 14.67), she is extending recognition to Peter; she is bringing him out of the anonymity in which his lack of courage had hidden him. Feminist scholars, instead of rejoicing with Rebequita *la hocicona* for being outspoken and *malcriada*, have accused her of being a 'stock character' 'who moves around, chatters whether her opinion is sought or not, talks to all and sundry, and destroys a man's reputation and entire life by apparently trite remarks'.[86] Quite the contrary, Rebequita is bringing Peter back to life. Rebequita's words are not intended to condemn or arrest her brother Peter. 'She wants to know whether Peter belongs to Jesus' followers and has the courage to acknowledge it.'[87] Both Peter and Rebequita had engaged in a process of transformation and conversion, and both of them need to confess their allegiance either to Jesus or to Jesus' enemies.

I showed in the first chapter how for Butler no individual becomes a subject without first becoming subjected or undergoing subjectivization through the use of language. For her, it is through the total submission to power that the subject is formed. After Jesus' arrest, Peter does not exist as a subject. Furthermore, Peter is an object of Rebequita's gaze and discourse, as I demonstrated. It is Rebequita who found Peter, who gazed at him attentively and hailed him into existence. In *Psychic Life,* Butler examines Althusser's account of interpellation as an example in which the subject is formed. According to Althusser, the subject is formed when it is interpellated—or hailed—by an authority figure. Thus, the policeman in the street calls out, 'Hey, you there', and the individual, recognizing that he/she is being spoken to, turns to respond to the policeman's voice. In a moment the individual is transformed into a subject.[88] Rebequita, exercising the authority that Jesus bestowed on her for being slave of all (Mk 10.43-44), recognizes Peter as a subject; but he must learn how to be 'with' Jesus and not with Jesus' opponents. A few scholars correctly argue that Rebequita is not interrogating Peter, for she simply states that Peter was with Jesus. 'Being with' Jesus was the fundamental element in the establishment of the Twelve (3.14) and their association with the ministry of Jesus (3.15; 6.7-13).[89] Rebequita *la malcriada* challenges Peter to recognize that he is in the wrong place, that he belongs to Jesus the Nazarene. However, Peter must give up his privileged place of warmth in order that he might have life again with Jesus. Rebequita

86. Connolly, *Disorderly Women and the Order of God,* p. 318.

87. Irene Dannemann, 'The Slave Woman's Challenge to Peter,' in Claudia Janssen *et al.* (eds.), *Transgressors: Toward a Feminist Biblical Theology* (Collegeville, MN: Liturgical Press, 2002), pp. 53-57 (55).

88. Lloyd, *Judith Butler,* p. 98.

89. Francis J. Moloney, *The Gospel of Mark* (Peabody, MA: Hendrickson, 2006), p. 307.

is breathing new life into Peter. Through Rebequita, Jesus is giving him a new chance, a new beginning. Peter must learn the lesson taught by the fire: 'After having gained all through skill, through love or through violence you must give up all, you must annihilate yourself.'[90] Peter must kill his desire for superiority, for being called the 'rock', for being the first among the disciples. He must learn from Rebequita to be a slave, humble and willing to serve something called Kingdom of God. Unfortunately, Peter is not yet ready to 'kill' himself and become subject to Jesus.

As soon as Peter heard Rebequita's true confession, he denied it by saying, 'I don't know or understand what you're talking about.' Immediately afterward he 'went out into the gateway' (Mk 14.68). Rebequita, by hailing Peter, has set the conditions and possibilities that he might become a subject once again, and rejoin the status of being counted as a disciple of Jesus. But Peter's fear of being subordinated to a female slave who is acting in Jesus' name is too much. For Donald Senior, Peter is speaking an ironic truth.[91] In Mark's Gospel, 'knowing' and 'understanding' have the connotation of discipleship. These two words are key elements to understand the faith that disciples must place in Jesus (Mk 4.12; 6.52; 9.6, 32). By knowing Jesus of Nazareth and knowing Peter, Rebequita is challenging him to admit his guilt and his betrayal of his friend Jesus. In attempting to explain why the individual turns when the policeman hails someone, Butler infers that the individual responds to the voice of the law because he/she is guilty of some infraction. Otherwise, why would the policeman be calling out? He/she responds, that is, because their conscience tells them to.[92] This makes perfect sense in Peter's case because he vocally swore to Jesus that he would never deny him (Mk 14.31). However, Peter is suffering a severe case of dementia; he does not know who Jesus is. Peter does not want to remember that in other *lumbrada,* he killed all his alliances with Jesus and gave his fidelity to Jesus' opponents. For Myers, here is another irony that speaks the truth: in what follows, Peter truly does not know who Jesus is (which even the demons knew, 1.24, 34).[93] But Rebequita knows who Jesus is and who Peter is, and as a *malcriada* who would not take no for an answer she would do anything to bring Peter into the community of believers.

Butler points out that 'To be injured by speech is to suffer a loss of context, that is, not to know where you are.'[94] Although Rebequita's speech is not an injurious one, Peter is dislocated. He neither knows who he is nor

90. Bachelard, *Psychoanalysis of Fire, p.*17

91. Donald Senior, *The Passion of Jesus in the Gospel of Mark* (Collegeville, MN: Liturgical Press, 1991), p. 104.

92. Lloyd, *Judith Butler*, p. 98.

93. Myers, *Binding the Strong Man*, p. 377.

94. Butler, *Excitable Speech*, p. 4.

where he is. Poor Peter has problems of identity! Rebequita's statement has put Peter 'out of control', and he decides to 'escape' to a safer place. This change of location also places him in a position where a rapid escape may be possible if events turn against him.[95] However, for the followers of Jesus, there is no such thing as a safe place, or, as Butler would put it, 'But such a place may be no place',[96]—until Peter recognizes his guilt and his being with Jesus. By contrast, Rebequita, as a true disciple of Jesus, puts her life at risk by talking with those standing around: 'This fellow is one of them' (Mk 14.69).

How does Rebequita know that Peter is one of them? Did she see him before with Jesus? Scholars find it unlikely that Rebequita would have been part of the arresting crowd, and therefore the hearing reader can only conclude that her knowledge must come from other encounters.[97] But what other encounters? I believe that Rebequita recognizes Peter as one of them, because she is also one of them! Why do I suppose this? Because Rebequita is not one of those who stand by. They are male, and Rebequita is a female slave. They are in their proper place, and Rebequita is out of place. Mark does not depict Rebequita warming herself along with the soldiers. She does not seek fellowship by sitting down with them. Moreover, Rebequita's behavior is similar to that of Pola *la descarada*. Rebequita as *la mala mujer* is not passive; she comes and goes, and her extreme mobility renders her invulnerable.[98] For this reason I am suggesting that in Rebequita's role, Mark may have hidden another 'secret,' so that they 'may see but not perceive, and may indeed hear but not understand' (Mk 4.12). The difference between Rebequita and Peter is that she knows who she is and where she is, whereas Peter does not know that. Furthermore, she knows that Peter does not belong where he think he does. Scholars realize that Rebequita does not just recognize Peter as an ordinary disciple but as the leader. 'The intensification of the maid's accusation in Mk 14.69 becomes another example of ironic understatement since Peter is not merely one of the disciples, he has been the *leading* one of the band.'[99] Peter has serious responsibilities toward the community. Unfortunately, he not only failed Jesus but also his brothers and sisters whom he was supposed to guide.

'After a little while, those standing near said to Peter, "Surely you are one of them, for you are a Galilean"' (Mk 14.70). Here the irony motif seems to be at its climax. Everyone seems to know who Peter is except Peter himself, who has been earnestly looking for fellowship with the guards (Mk 14.54)

---

95. Moloney, *The Gospel of Mark*, p. 308.
96. Butler, *Excitable Speech*, p. 4.
97. Webb, *Mark at the Threshold*, p. 211.
98. Paz, *Labyrinth of Solitude*, p. 39
99. Webb, *Mark at the Threshold*, p. 211 [italics in original].

and bystanders (Mk 14.70), even attempting to pass as one of them, before now being exposed as a Galilean by the guards. Unluckily for him, Peter is not one of them, and they disclaim any association with him. The guards know that Peter is from Galilee, and they are from Jerusalem. Peter belongs to Jesus and they do not. Mark does not inform us how the soldiers knew that Peter was from Galilee. According to Matthew, they knew because of Peter's accent. 'After a little while, those standing there went up to Peter and said, "Surely you are one of them, for your accent gives you away"' (Mt. 26.73). Here Jesus' opponents tried to identify the clueless Peter as to where he belongs. Donald Senior argues that the charge of being a Galilean refers, on the surface, to the district's dialect that Peter presumably speaks. 'But for the reader of the Gospel a deeper meaning is unavoidable.'[100] Being a Galilean has serious connotations of discipleship for the Markan community. In other circumstances, even the mention of Galilee would help Peter discover his identity. It was in Galilee that everything began, where Jesus with the power of the Spirit began to announce Good News to all (Mk 1.14-15). It was in Galilee that Jesus, for the first time, saw Simon Peter and invited him to be with him (Mk 1.16-20). Galilee is where Jesus had promised to reconcile the scared community after his resurrection (Mk 14.28; 16.7). However, here Peter is not yet ready to recognize his discipleship, and his true first love.

Peter insists in hiding his identity, even when everyone already knows who he is and where he comes from. 'He began to call down curses on himself, and he swore to them, "I don't know this man you're talking about"' (Mk 14.71). Peter had some opportunities throughout this trial to recognize his mistakes, but his continuous negation ends in the last one. 'Yet the language of his third denial is surprisingly strong (14.71): he calls down an anathema, even takes an oath (cf. Herod's oath, 6.23) in insisting than he does not "know" (*ouk oida*) Jesus.'[101] To some scholars, Peter's third negation is not only strangely strong but also unnecessary, since Peter's accusers are servants with minimal authority. 'The fact that his "accusers" before whom Peter must defend himself are servants, indicates, on the other hand, their minimal authority: they are people who take orders from others and, obviously, have no power to condemn anybody.'[102] I wonder what would happen if we take Peter's denial literally?

In the first chapter I demonstrated how the act of confessing implies ethical responsibility toward the one who hears the confession. Peter, by being

100. Senior, *The Passion of Jesus in the Gospel of Mark*, p. 103.
101. Myers, *Binding the Strong Man*, p. 377.
102. Agustín Borrell, *The Good News of Peter's Denial: A Narrative and Rhetorical Reading of Mark 14:54, 66-72* (trans. Sean Conlon; Atlanta: Scholars Press, 1998), p. 117.

totally vulnerable and exposed to the others, has started the process of healing. Here, for the first time, Peter is giving an account of himself because by calling down curses on himself and swearing that he does not know Jesus, he has opened his heart for conversion. According to Butler, when someone calls upon himself/herself injurious names, it is a way to constitute oneself socially. In Butler's words, 'I am led to embrace the terms that injure me because they constitute me socially.'[103] Peter, by speaking of himself with all kinds of injurious language, is reclaiming his existence. He is both embracing his brokenness and opening himself to be admitted into Jesus' community. It is true that at *la lumbradas* people might find violence, death, aggression and destruction, but it is also true that *lumbradas* might provide a perfect time for healing and conversion. After all, the fire is a privileged phenomenon that can explain anything.[104] The *lumbradas* could be the intimate space, where enemies once again become friends, where people who were distant become closer than ever, where strangers become part of one's family, where hospitality to the strangers is offered (Acts 28.2-3).

I demonstrated above how Pola *la descarada* and Jesus became ethically implicated through the act of *descaramiento*. It is striking that Mark left us with Peter's tears. 'And he broke down and wept' (Mk 14.72). Peter is removed from the scene, and we must understand Peter's tears as an act of redemption. In a culture that promotes masculinity over femininity, male over female, citizen over slave, Peter's tears could be interpreted as a sign that he is also a *descarado* who is not afraid to show his emotions. Peter as a *descarado* is ready to enter into a new kind of relationship with Jesus and his brothers and sisters. Peter, who persistently approached *la lumbrada,* had found his love and his doubts dissipated: 'For to love is to escape from doubt, it is to live in the certainty of the heart.'[105] Peter's tears demonstrate that he is no longer concerned with being or having the phallus. In Jesus' community, all kinds of *descarados/as* are welcome. Peter as a *descarado* has understood that Jesus' movement is open even to people like Rebequita and Pola. Peter as *descarado* must accept women's company and words as a symbol of Jesus' *descaramiento*. The last time that Peter is mentioned is when a young man announces that Jesus has been resurrected. He says to the women, 'But go, tell his disciples and Peter, "He is going ahead of you into Galilee"' (Mk 16.7). Peter as a *descarado* must return to his first love, to Galilee, where Jesus would meet him again. Galilee once again would become a symbol of hope for all *descarados/as* who discovered in the Crucified One the Resurrected One!

103. Butler, *Psychic Life of Power*, p. 104.
104. Bachelard, *Psychoanalysis of Fire,* p. 7.
105. Bachelard, *Psychoanalysis of Fire,* p. 106.

Conclusion

In this chapter I introduced two wo/men, whom I called Pola and Rebequita. Both wo/men, by performing certain deeds, uttering certain words and using their bodies in 'men's territory', demonstrated that it is possible to undo assigned gender. By subverting their gender and entering dangerous territory, these women demonstrated their boldness, courage and assertiveness to find life when the law against them was death! In the case of Pola, scholars did not have any trouble accepting that she is portrayed as a prophetic figure whose action expresses Jesus' identity as Messiah and king.[106] I showed that Pola looked so beautiful in comparison with the envious male disciples that they could not hide their anger and violence toward her. Pola walked with pride and boldness, talked with her body like a prophetess, and with her hands performed such a miracle upon Jesus' body that even the Son of God praised her for her beautiful deed. Who cannot fall in love with such a woman? I demonstrated how Pola deliberately and intentionally undid her gender. For this reason she has been a source of inspiration for many wo/men who have found in her *descaramiento* a sense of liberation.

I have been arguing that my hermeneutic is not just *del otro lado* but it is also *descarada,* which is not restricted to the conventional rules of interpretation. I dare to place Rebequita in the place that she deserves. I demonstrated how the irony motif is present in Mk 14.54, 66-72, and I attempted to interpret it accordingly. Scholars have advised us that opportunities are rife for misunderstanding the biblical text ironically. 'We risk misreading, mishearing emphasis, even entirely missing the point. Negotiation of meaning and authority in Scripture are rendered almost infinitely complicated by the presence of irony.'[107] My reading and interpretation of Rebequita is therefore most vulnerable, but I think it is necessary to snatch her from Satan's claws. Rebequita had been mercilessly 'satanized' for acting as the accuser of Peter in a way similar to the high priest who accuses Jesus. 'She is persistent in her questioning and she refuses to be silenced by his denials of any knowledge of Jesus. Her charges mirror the accusations of the high priest. She takes the role of the accuser, which is traditionally associated with Satan.'[108] Moreover, other feminist scholars have concluded that Rebequita brought about Peter's total destruction in relation to Jesus. 'Yet this female character also brings about a reversal in Peter's fate, the complete destruction of Peter's relationship with Jesus, indicated by Peter's abject weeping.'[109] Through my hermeneutics of *descaramiento* I demonstrated

---

106. Miller, *Women in Mark's Gospel*, p. 144.
107. Sharp, *Irony and Meaning in the Hebrew Bible*, p. 8.
108. Miller, *Women in Mark's Gospel*, p. 152.
109. Connolly, *Disorderly Women and the Order of God*, p. 319.

the contrary. It was Rebequita's hailing of Peter who brought him back to Jesus. But scholars have forgotten that Peter was also with Jesus' enemies, and even worse that he denied Jesus three times, and was called 'Satan' by Jesus (Mk 8.33). Despite all this, Peter has been elevated to be the only protagonist worthy of our consideration. 'In the denial episode (Mark 14.54, 66-72), Peter plays the principal role and is, in fact, the only protagonist who merits our careful observation and analysis. The other minor role players (the attendants, the servant girl) are subordinated to Peter and are there merely to help in the presentation and development of Peter's part.'[110] I hope that I was able to demonstrate the contrary. If Gundry is correct in her observation that Mark plays up an attractive aspect of Jesus in his relationship with children while arguing that 'The Jesus who disregards seniority and teaches instead that the Kingdom of God belongs to ignorant, immature, morally deficient, and socially inferior little children is at the same time the one who brings the kingdom of God near with power and mediates it blessings',[111] then Rebequita has entered into the Kingdom of God by her own right.

My interpretation of both texts is open to mistakes and might be vulnerable on several fronts. However, by approaching the texts from *otros lados*, I find hope and freedom for all the wo/men who have been accused of being *marimachas, hociconas/es, malcriados/as* and *descarados/as*. Now that you have gazed upon these extraordinary wo/men, I would like to introduce you to other bodies who are also transgressing their gender. They are refusing to be 'men' and are behaving like 'women'. In Jesus' movement, everything seems to be done *al revés*, 'contrary to the norm'. I invite you to gaze on Simon *el del otro lado* (Mk 14.1-11), Nachito *el machito* (Mk 14.12-16), to see how they are undoing their gender.

110. Borrell, *The Good News of Peter's Denial*, p. 83.
111. Gundry, 'Children in the Gospel of Mark', p. 175.

3

NO SOMOS MACHOS PERO SOMOS MUCHOS /
WE ARE NOT MACHO BUT WE ARE MANY

Simón el del otro lado

The previous chapter reminded us that Mark opened his passion narrative by placing Jesus in Bethany, in the house of Simon the Leper (Mk 14.3). For Kristeva, the abject body is not concerned too much for his/her 'being' but rather for his/her place: '*Where am I* instead of *Who am I?*'[1] Etymologically, that Jesus is in Bethany could mean that he is in the house of the poor or the house of the afflicted.[2] Whatever the case, by eating with Simon the Leper, Jesus is clearly transgressing some boundaries. In Mark's Gospel, Jesus has been extremely busy announcing the Good News to a 'kingdom of nobodies',[3] that is, to those who are deemed as less than human, excluded from the law and forgotten by the community. Jesus has just predicted the total destruction of the Temple (Mk 13.2), and now he crosses to *el otro lado,* where Simon the Leper lives. He left Jerusalem (the 'place of peace') because in a few hours the city would become violent and murderous. And he entered Bethany (the house of affliction) to bring justice to *Simón, el del otro lado*. Jesus, by crossing to *el otro lado* from the place of 'peace and security' to a place of 'affliction', intends to announce to Simon the Leper that 'God has indeed heard' (which is the meaning of the name) Simon's stigma of being *del otro lado*. 'The departure from the doomed temple to the mount "opposite the temple" (13.3a) and subsequently to the house of a leper (14.3a) shows a shift in the strategy of the Jesus community. The specific reference to Simon as a leper seems to suggest a social-religious

---

1. Kristeva, *Powers of Horror,* p. 8.
2. K.W. Clark, 'Bethany', *IDB,* I, p. 387
3. The 'kingdom of nobodies' is a phrase that belongs to John Dominic Crossan, *The Historical Jesus: The Life of a Mediterranean Jewish Peasant* (New York: Harper-SanFrancisco, 1991), pp. 266-69.

border-crossing and the inclusive dynamic of the new community.'[4] But what happened was not just a social-religious border crossing. It was also a gender crossing.

Jesus is visiting and accepting hospitality from another excluded body called Simon the Leper. Most societies hide or in some other way get rid of sick, deviant and anomalous people; Israel was no exception. According to anthropologist Mary Douglas, the Jews understood holiness as total completeness. Holiness requires that individuals conform to the class to which they belong, where there are no blemishes, deformities or disabilities. And holiness requires that different classes of things should not be confused.[5] Simon the Leper became an outcast because his skin disease situated him in *el otro lado*. Simon as one of *del otro lado* is separated from the temple. By entering into a leper's household and by eating with Simon *el del otro lado* and Pola *la descarada,* Jesus is subverting the normative structure of the patriarchal household. Halvor Moxnes remarks that Jesus' household transgressed its boundaries; it had a different composition, and it lacked its hierarchy, 'Therefore we may say that the household of the kingdom has been "queered"'.[6] Simon *el del otro lado*, through his leprosy, speaks a subverted language.

It is striking that Mark did not give voice to Simon; we only know that his disease made him an outcast from the community. What is Jesus doing in the house of a polluted body? Eugene Boring notices that there are nine different persons named Simon in the New Testament (five in Mark).[7] For this reason, it was necessary to attach some sort of distinguishing label to each of them.[8] It is striking that all the Simons that appear in the New Testament have *muchos lados* of exclusion because of their ethnicity (Simon of Cyrene [Mk 15.21; Mt. 27.32; and Lk. 23.26]), profession (Simon the Tanner of Joppa [Acts 9.43; 10.6]), being a *practitioner* of witchcraft (Simon the Magician of Samaria [Acts 8.9]), politics (Simon the Zealot [Mk 3.18; Lk. 6.15; Acts 1.13]), having a shameful reputation (Simon the father of Judas Iscariot [Jn 6.71; 12.4; 13.2, 26]), being illegitimate (Simon the half-brother of Jesus [Mk 6.3; Mt. 13.55]), religious identity (Simon the Pharisee [Lk. 7.40]), and being ill (Simon the Leper [Mk 14.3; Mt. 26.6]).[9] In Butler's interpretation

4. Simon Samuel, *A Postcolonial Reading of Mark's Story of Jesus* (New York: T. & T. Clark, 2007), p. 144.

5. Mary Douglas, *Purity and Danger: An Analysis of Concept of Pollution and Taboo* (London: Routledge, 2004), p. 67.

6. Halvor Moxnes, *Putting Jesus in His Place: A Radical Vision of Household and Kingdom* (Louisville, KY: Westminster John Knox Press, 2003), p. 105.

7. Boring, *Mark*, p. 382.

8. Boring, *Mark*, p. 382.

9. In the previous chapter we studied Simon Peter's ironic character. I demonstrated how he fit the category of someone called *del otro lado*.

of Nella Larsen's novella *Passing*, she argues that Clare 'became' black because of her association with blacks. 'If she associates with blacks, she becomes black, where the sign of blackness is contracted, as it were, through proximity, where "race" itself is figured as a contagion transmissible through proximity.'[10] By the same token, Mark, by placing Jesus in the house of a leper, is crossing the boundaries of what is proper and acceptable. The strict and rigid boundaries of purity that separated clean bodies from unclean bodies have been 'contaminated'. Through his association with Simon *el del otro lado* Jesus has unmasked and disrupted the social boundaries demanded by the purity system and enforced by law.

In the history of interpretation some scholars have healed Simon's leprosy, affirming that Simon 'apparently has been cured of his disease, perhaps by Jesus himself'.[11] Other scholars, more audacious, would naively speculate that Simon *el del otro lado* 'was the husband of Martha or the father of Mary, Martha, and Lazarus'.[12] Moreover, scholars who like big families would suggest that not only was Simon *el del otro lado* the father of Lazarus, Mary and Martha, but also of Judas Iscariot (on the basis of Jn 6.71; 13.2, 26).[13] Speculation about Simon the Leper's marital status have not changed in the history of biblical interpretation between 1954 and 2009! Recently, biblical archaeologists are still speculating that Simon was married: 'In addition to the siblings Lazarus, Mary, and Martha, we also hear of another resident of Bethany: Simon the Leper, who may have been a Pharisee, and who was perhaps related (as a husband or father?) to Martha or to Mary.'[14] In this picture we are only missing the dog in order to have the happy American family! My culture is not exempt from this uneasiness toward men who are not married or have no family. They are accused of being *del otro lado* also. Some people like Celedonio Martinez are killed for refusing to get married. In the words of my friend Elkin: *Si no hubo casorio*

10. Butler, *Bodies That Matter*, p. 171.

11. Herman C. Waetjen, *A Reordering of Power: A Socio-Political Reading of Mark's Gospel* (Minneapolis: Fortress Press, 1989), p. 203. This author even suggests that Simon the Leper could be the anonymous leper of Mk 1.40-45.

12. E.P. Blair, 'Simon', *IDB*, IV, p. 357. Moreover, Charles F. Nesbitt, ('The Bethany Tradition in the Gospel Narrative', *Journal of the American Academy of Religion* 19.2 [1961], p, 119), referring to Bethany and Simon, claims: 'Through the centuries this has been traditionally regarded as the home of Lazarus and his sisters, Martha and Mary, but it is not quite so generally known as the residence of one Simon, a Pharisee and former leper, who was perhaps the husband of one of these sisters, or else the father of this well-known New Testament family.'

13. J.N. Sanders, 'Those Whom Jesus Loved (John IX.5)', *NTS* 1 (1955), pp. 29-41.

14. Shimon Gibson, *The Final Days of Jesus: The Archeological Evidence* (New York: Harper One, 2009), p. 21.

habrá velorio, 'If there is no wedding, there would be a funeral.'[15] A heter-onormative interpretation needs a hetero/sexual and healed Simon in order to provide the settings of Jesus' dinner. 'His hosting the gathering indicates that he was a *former* [emphasis in original] leper since active leprosy would exclude one from all social occasions.'[16] But Mark is mute on this 'heal-ing'; he wants to leave Simon *del otro lado* inflicted with the stigma of leprosy and singleness. Simon is using his afflicted body unabashedly with-out any stipulation of procreation. Scholars have noticed that Simon 'is not called the *"former* leper"', [emphasis in the original][17] but simply Simon the Leper; and by doing this Mark is inviting the community to cross to *otros lados* of exclusion and embrace the indecent women (Pola and Rebequita), the 'soft' man (Simon Peter) and the disabled person (Simon the Leper) as a sign that Jesus' 'queer' household indeed has arrived for people who have suffered violence for not doing their 'gender right'.

Jesus previously encountered a leper who 'came to him and begged him on his knees, "If you are willing, you can make me clean"' (Mk 1.40). Even there, it was not Jesus' initiative to cure him; it was the leper who demanded and challenged Jesus' power. But in the story of Simon *el del otro lado*, it is quite different. Jesus is unperturbed by Simon's leprosy and singleness. Jesus, by entering in his house and seeking fellowship through the ritual of the meal, somehow is denying 'the order that segregates those who cannot fulfill the conditions demanded by purity law and challenges the prevailing religious and social barriers'.[18] The encounter that Jesus had with Simon the Leper corroborates once again his solidarity with peo-ple who have suffered what Butler called 'the violence of gender norms',[19] or those who are confined to the 'unlivable life'. Samuel Chambers, inter-preting Butler regarding the one who has a 'livable life' and the ones who had the 'unlivable life' concludes, 'We would submit that a "livable life" is one which does not require radical deviations from the norms of sex and gender. An unlivable life is therefore one that proves incompatible with those norms.'[20] Simon *el del otro lado* 'joins' the status of the 'unlivable life' because his body deviates from the norms of sex and gender. Accord-ing to Josephus, a leper was as good as dead: 'Four are considered the

15. I want to express my gratitude to Elkin Nasrallah for sharing with me his unpub-lished poem that he wrote in lovely memory of Celedonio Martinez.

16. James R. Edwards, *The Gospel according to Mark* (Grand Rapids: Eerdmans, 2002), p. 413.

17. Boring, *Mark*, p. 382.

18. Hisako Kinukawa, *Women and Jesus in Mark: A Japanese Feminist Perspec-tive* (Maryknoll, NY: Orbis Books, 1994), p. 83.

19. Butler, *Gender Trouble*, p. xx.

20. Samuel A. Chambers and Terrell Carver, *Judith Butler and Political Theory: Troubling Politics* (New York: Routledge, 2008), p. 70.

equal of the dead person: the poor, the leprous, the blind and the childless' (*Ant.* 3.2.3).[21] Simon's humanity is at stake; his leprosy and his lack of children have situated him at the border of death. Biblical scholars have argued that disabled persons are typically seen first as disabled and only secondarily as a 'man' or a 'woman'.[22] However, Simon the Leper has been marked as a disabled person whose lack of voice makes him incapable of qualifying as a 'man'. Simon, as an inflicted and disabled body, remains 'without gender', the *other* to social norms.[23] It is striking that the disabled Simon does not express any desire to be healed from being *del otro lado*. As a matter of fact, Simon does not speak a single word. It has been argued that in antiquity to have a logos and be capable of reasoning was the sine qua non for being counted as human. Moreover, we have stated that in Greco-Roman culture, one of the ways in which real men gained and achieved masculinity was through the use of public discourse. For instance, in Rome, rhetoric and oratory were wholly male endeavors. These were taught, studied and practiced in public spaces—which is to say, in male space—by men, for men, to men, according to men's interests. It formed the core of Roman education and was the primary instrument of the law court, forum and senate.[24] I wonder why Mark does not depict Simon *el del otro lado* talking as a way to demonstrate that he was a 'real man'.

Simon speaks an abject language through his leprosy, and it is a language that Jesus seems to understand perfectly. Instead of Jesus sending him for therapy to the temple/priest to be cured of being *del otro lado*, Jesus himself *comes out* as one *del otro lado* by accepting hospitality and sharing a meal. 'Those who eat together share the material that becomes the human body; their bodies thereby become made of the same material.'[25] We saw in the previous chapter how Jesus entered into an ethic of *descaramiento* with Pola. Here Jesus through the meal forms an alternative family, where *descarados/as* and people *del otro lado* are welcome at the table. 'Those who share a meal are constituted by the meal as a family's bodies are connected

21. See also Eliseo Pérez-Álvarez, *Marcos* (Minneapolis: Augsburg Fortress, 2007), p. 123.

22. Thomas Hentrich, 'Masculinity and Disability in the Bible', in Hector Avalos *et al.* (eds.), *This Abled Body: Rethinking Disabilities in Biblical Studies* (Atlanta: Society of Biblical Literature, 2007), pp. 73-87 (73).

23. Helen Meekosha, 'The Meaning of Gender', in Gary L. Albrecht (ed), *Encyclopedia of Disability, II* (Thousand Oaks, CA: Sage, 2006), pp. 764-69 (765).

24. Joy Connolly, 'Virile Tongues: Rhetoric and Masculinity', in William Dominik and Jon Hall (eds.), *A Companion to Roman Rhetoric* (Oxford: Blackwell, 2007), pp. 83-97 (83-84).

25. Nicole Wilkinson-Duran, *The Power of Disorder: Ritual Elements in Mark's Passion Narrative* (London: T. & T. Clark, 2008), p. 64.

by genetics.'[26] Jesus' 'dysfunctional' family challenges all those people who had excluded lepers and women from the meal.

Matthew described Simon the Leper in the same way that Mark does: 'While Jesus was in Bethany in the home of a man known as Simon the Leper (Mt. 26.6-13)'. John substitutes Simon the Leper's body with Lazarus's body, which is passively reclining at the table (Jn 12.1-8). Lazarus does not say a single word. Contrary to Matthew, Mark and John, Luke portrays the 'Bethany narratives' by describing Simon as a Pharisee who is exercising his privilege of being male, judging both Jesus and the 'sinner' woman: 'When the Pharisee who had invited him saw this, he said to himself, "If this man were a prophet, he would know who is touching him and what kind of woman she is—that she is a sinner"' (Lk. 7.39). Notice that in Luke, Simon is not a leper but rather a Pharisee, a perfect body who observes the law and maintains his masculinity intact. Scholars argue that disabled men who are not able to behave in stereotypically competitive and masculine ways may adopt a variety of strategies to cope with the stigma they experience from others, such as redefining masculinity or creating alternative masculine identities that stress personhood rather than gender roles.[27] This is notably not the case with Simon *el del otro lado*. He could easily beg Jesus to be healed as his fellow leper did (Mk 1.40), but Mark intentionally leaves him in silence. I had previously referred to Hornsby's suggestion that silence does not necessarily signify 'passivity' or 'powerlessness';[28] indeed Simon *el del otro lado* is communicating that he is not obsessed with maintaining and redefining his masculinity. Simon *el del otro lado* could easily demonstrate his masculinity by becoming a talkative body like the one who appears in Lk. 7.36-50. But here he is mute, unwilling to prove his masculinity—or not needing to. One can even argue that Simon does not exist in the entire narrative! He does not exist as a 'hetero/sexual with children', but he does exist *as del otro lado* who knows his place in Jesus' queer household, where even unmanly bodies are welcomed. Simon's generous hospitality has provided the setting for Jesus' inauguration of the new household. The house of Bethany/affliction has become a model of hospitality for the house of Jerusalem where an effeminate man can proudly welcome Jesus' community.

Nachito el machito

Growing up in a place without electricity and running water, I understood that the well was an essential part of our lives. At the well wo/men fell in love, shared their struggles and socialized among themselves. The well was one of the few venues where women experienced a kind of freedom outside

---

26. Wilkinson-Duran, *The Power of Disorder,* p. 64.
27. Meekosha, 'The Meaning of Gender', p. 767.
28. Hornsby, 'The Annoying Woman', in *Bodily Citation,* p. 81.

of home. Of the three wells in my village only one produced potable water. Women went there either early in the morning or in the late afternoon to draw water, avoiding the midday sun at any cost. They would carry their *cántaros*, 'water jars', on their heads without holding them with their hands, making a kind of ring with their rebozo[29] on which they then placed the *cántaro*. Carrying a *cántaro* gave them a sense of pride in and mastery over their bodies. Walking with the *cántaro* full of water while engaging in a deep conversation without losing a single drop of water demanded a lot of discipline. Indeed, whereas for boys *la lumbrada* was a rite of passage to manhood, for girls carrying their *cántaros* on their heads was the rite of passage to womanhood. I can still remember my younger sister's happiness when she announced to us, *Ya puedo caminar con el cántaro de agua sin usar las manos,* 'I can walk with the *cántaro* on my head without using my hands.' My mother that day made special food to celebrate my sister's ability to carry her *cántaro*. I did not understand why women attributed such importance to that action, but my mother would remind me that it was not just a matter of holding the *cántaro* on one's head, but rather of walking with grace and harmony.

Men also went to the well to fetch water, but not at the same times as the women; and they carried their water in two containers suspended by rope from a yoke-like stick. This yoke was deemed more manly and appropriate for their macho bodies. Instead of walking with grace and harmony, they grasped the ropes on either side tightly as a way of showing their strength and control. The act of carrying these heavier containers of water without showing any pain or emotion was the perfect way to demonstrate one's manliness. Male children had to carry water like a man, albeit using a small container, but certainly never a *cántaro*. What happened if a male child transgressed these gender boundaries at the well? He would be publicly stigmatized, submitted to all kinds of vexations and punished for performing his gender incorrectly—as happened to a child called Ignacio from the neighboring village of San José de Peralta.

Though his name was officially Ignacio,[30] people called him 'Nachito'.[31] He was a smart, vivacious and friendly boy, who lived with his two sisters

---

29. Rebozo is a woman's garment that can vary in size and shape.

30. Thanks to Nachito for allowing me to use his story, and for opening up his heart to me. I hope one day he will understand that God will not send him to hell for being 'different'.

31. In Mexico the use of the diminutive is not restricted to children, but it is used for people who are sick or handicapped, although they are not children. Very often we hear expressions such as the following: 'Pobrecito/a está mailto/a/poor little fellow he/ she is sick.' Moreover, people used the diminutive also for persons who are 'different'; such is the case with 'Nachito' or 'Manuelito'. The common thread seems to be simple: that children, disabled bodies, and people del *otro lado* in the name of 'compassion' are considered incapable of reaching adulthood or humanity.

and his mother. Nachito's dad had passed away when he was two years old. He grew up among *puras viejas,* 'only women', as people from his town would comment. Perhaps for this reason men would classify him as being a little delicate and refined. Rumors began to circulate in Nachito's town that he did not like to play with others boys but preferred to play with girls. Nachito would go to the well with his mom and sisters, afraid to be by himself at home. One particular morning at the well Nachito, moved more by curiosity than by any desire of 'being a woman' (as he was accused of later on) decided to carry water in a small *cántaro*, because for him it was easier that way. Other men noticed what they perceived to be his exaggerated and effeminate way of walking, carrying the water jug like a girl. Immediately they reported Nachito's *descaramiento* to José Vazquez, Nachito's uncle. His uncle beat Nachito and broke the *cántaro* saying that he would not allow the memory of his brother to be shamed with such unmanly behavior.

In order to make a 'man' out of him, his uncle took Nachito to the 'city' to visit the whorehouse. Nachito was only eleven years old. This first journey to the city would be the beginning of many trips that he had to take in order to demonstrate that he was a *macho*. Some men were willing to make a donation to support the trip and the fees involved in such business. Men would 'comfort' Nachito's mom saying, *No se preocupe nosotros vamos a hacer un machito de su Nachito,* 'Do not worry, we are going to make a *machito* out of your Nachito.'[32] *El machito* Nachito did not know what was more humiliating: going to the whorehouse or answering the village men's question on his return *¿Ya se te paró? ¿Pudiste penetrar a las viejas? ¿Te veniste adentro de ellas?,* 'Did your penis become erect? Could you penetrate the women? Did you ejaculate inside them?' Week after week he had to confess that he was still a virgin, that he did not feel anything that 'males were supposed to feel when they are with women'. Men could not understand how they could not make a real macho out of Nachito. One day, Nachito *el machito* could not bear the pressure of his village any longer, especially when he discovered graffiti that proclaimed, *Aquí, en tierra de machos vive un joto,* 'Here in a land of machos lives a joto.'[33] That day he attempted to hang himself with the rope that was used to draw water from the well. When Nachito's mom found him almost dead, she promised him that he would never go back to the whorehouse. Men would say, *Hubiese*

---

32. *Machito* is the diminutive of *macho.*

33. In the next chapter I will demonstrate how words had the power not just to injure but even to kill. It seems that writing on public derogatory terms against people *del otro lado* had proved efficient. According to Human Rights Watch (*They Want Us Exterminated: Murder, Torture, Sexual Orientation and Gender in Iraq* [New York: Human Rights Watch, 2009]), in Iraq one often finds graffiti that reads, 'Death to the people of Lot.' 'People of Lot' is a derogatory expression in Arabic for men who engage in homosexual conduct, derived from the story of Sodom and Gomorrah.

sido mejor que se muriera, para evitar esa vergüenza, 'It would be better if he had died, to avoid such shame.' As soon as Nachito recovered, his mom sent him to Guadalajara to live with her older sister. The village men were relieved because their honor and masculinity were safe. *No queremos que la gente piense que en Peralta los hombres llevan agua en cántaros como las viejas,* 'We do not want people to think that in Peralta men carry water in *cántaros* like women,' Nachito's uncle would say. God forbid that anyone would dare to cross established gender boundaries of behavior!

Nachito el machito *of Mark 14.12-16*

We have witnessed how Jesus' queer behavior allowed for the crossing of all kinds of boundaries. Having moved from the Temple to the house of Simon *el del otro lado*, Jesus now leaves this house of affliction to enter into another dubious house in Jerusalem. We do not know too much from the Gospels about Jesus' movements in Jerusalem, but we can read between the lines that there were some sympathizers of Jesus' movement willing to provide a home in which Jesus ate his final meal. Scholars have been so intent on finding out if Jesus' meal was a Passover meal or not, it seems to me, that they have either overlooked or intentionally forgotten the only inhabitant of the house where Jesus had his last meal. We do not know anything about the host, and we are just left with Jesus' 'bizarre' instructions: 'Go into the city, and a man carrying a jar of water will meet you. Follow him' (Mk 14.13). In this section, I will attempt to 'go into the city' and find such a man, and for obvious reasons I will name him Nachito *el machito*, and I will follow him. Who is he? Is he a disciple of Jesus? Is he really un/doing his gender by carrying a jar? Why did Jesus introduce such an effeminate man as a sign of his last meal? What are the implications for Jesus' community in following him? Why does the water-carrying man not appear in Matthew's Gospel? Is Mark exhorting the community to move from a house of affliction to enter into a house of 'effeminacy'? Is this the way to be a disciple of Jesus? These are some of the questions that I will attempt to address in this retold story of Nachito *el machito*.

Scholars have pointed out that the characters in the Gospel of Mark are inextricably linked to the development of plot. Perhaps for this reason the characters in Mark's Gospel have received considerable attention. Articles, monographs, and dissertations have explored various character groups including the disciples, religious leaders, women, the crowd, Jews, minor characters and Gentiles. Other studies have examined individual characters in Mark's narrative, including God and Jesus.[34] Unfortunately, Nachito *el machito's* unmanly behavior has been found unattractive for their inves-

---

34. Kelly R. Iverson, *Gentiles in the Gospel of Mark: 'Even the Dogs under the Table Eat the Children's Crumbs'* (New York: T. & T. Clark, 2007), p. 2.

tigation. Recently some scholars have suggested that the story of Nachito *el machito* was probably not in Mark's passion source, but that this story circulated independently.[35] Nonetheless, for those of us who have been punished, excluded, tormented in useless therapies, obligated to go to our prostitute sisters, and forced to learn how to do our gender correctly, the story of Nachito *el machito* is a sign of hope and redemption. For our own study and analysis it is not important to trace the authenticity of such a story; indeed, I am not sure if anyone can claim to do so with any story that retells an event that purportedly happened so long ago. My hermeneutic *del otro lado* informs me that in Nachito *el machito's* life there is something sacred, profound and appealing that might sustain us in our daily battles as we struggle to be recognized as Jesus' disciples with all our *joterías*.

We notice the intimate relation that existed between Mk 14.13-16 and Mk 11.1-6. For Vincent Taylor these agreements show that the two stories were composed by the same author, but they do not suggest that they are doublets.[36] Mark 11.1-6 deals with the acquisition of an ass with which to ride to the walls of Jerusalem. In both instances, two anonymous disciples are sent to perform a mysterious errand. Jesus gives them certain signs to watch for and words to say which sound like instructions. In both cases, we are told that the disciples did as instructed and that things worked out exactly as Jesus had said. Vernon K. Robbins offers us the following parallel columns:[37]

Mark 11.1-6	Mark 14.13-16
1: he sent two of his disciples	13: he sent two of his disciples
2: and said to them,	And said to them,
'Go into the village …	'Go into the city …
and … you will find …	and … will meet you …
3: Say, "The Lord …"	14: Say…, "The Teacher …"
4: And they went away,	16: And they went out …
And they found …	And found
6: as Jesus had said,	as he had told them;
and…	and …

Despite these obvious similarities, there are also some sharp contrasts between these two texts. The object that they are supposed to find is quite different. In Mk 11.1-6 the two disciples find a tethered colt that needs to be untied in order to fulfill Jesus' messianic role. However, in Mk 14.13-16,

35. Adela Yarbro Collins, *Mark: A Commentary* (Minneapolis: Fortress Press, 2007), p. 646.

36. Vincent Taylor, *The Gospel according to St. Mark: The Greek Text with Introduction, Notes, and Indexes* (London: Macmillan, 1953), p. 536.

37. Vernon K. Robbins, *New Boundaries in Old Territory. Form and Social Rhetoric in Mark* (New York: Peter Lang, 1994), pp. 74-75.

the two disciples are met by an 'unleashed' Nachito, who is not restricted to any social boundaries whatsoever, but rather freely welcomes them and indicates to them the room for Jesus' final meal.

In Mk 11.1-12, Jesus wishes to enter into Jerusalem as a humble and meek Messiah riding upon an ass: 'Rejoice greatly, O Daughter of Zion! Shout, Daughter of Jerusalem! See, your king comes to you, righteous and having salvation, gentle and riding on a donkey, on a colt, the foal of a donkey' (Zech. 9.9). Did the disciples understand this humble gesture? Or did they see in Jesus' entry into Jerusalem the powerful figure of King David? The decorating of the colt with the disciple's garments, the laying of further garments to form a royal pathway for Jesus riding the decorated colt, and the spreading of leafy branches cut from the field are gestures that welcome Jesus as a powerful figure. They recall earlier solemn entries to take possession of Jerusalem.[38] The crowd and Jesus' disciples receive and welcome Jesus like a triumphant, nationalist hero who will scatter Israel's enemies from their land. 'The acclamation of Jesus in 11.9 makes explicit the failure of both the disciples and the crowds who prepare Jesus' way.'[39] The disciples still had a lot to learn about Jesus' kingdom of 'nobodies'.

Making a machito out of Nachito in the Matthean Tradition

The story of Nachito *el machito* has caused gender problems not only among contemporary scholars but also for the authors of the Synoptic Gospels. Luke repeats this story almost word for word, and discloses the identity of the disciples. For Luke it is Peter and John who are sent directly by Jesus to enter the city where Nachito *el machito* and his *cántaro* of water will meet them (Lk. 22.7-13). Matthew has removed, redacted and omitted Nachito's story from his Gospel. Let us observe the nuances of this particular story as it is described in the Synoptic Gospels. The common features emerge when Nachito's life is placed in parallel columns (see p. 77):

Elsewhere, Matthew typically adds to the details found in Mark's Gospel. That does not happen here. Whereas Mark and Luke describe the guide as 'a man carrying a jar of water', Matthew refers to him as 'a certain man'. Mark and Luke are uniform in their reference to Nachito *el machito* as a servant; they use a specific, noteworthy feature. That Matthew eliminates the detail about Nachito and his *cántaro* of water is particularly odd. Modern interpreters like the Matthean version of this pericope because it does not seem as legendary as the Markan and Lukan parallels, and 'it seems to approximate the actual events'.[40] Moreover, scholars have observed that

38. Moloney, *Gospel of Mark*, p. 219.
39. Moloney, *Gospel of Mark*, p. 219.
40. Luz, *Matthew 21-28*, p. 352.

Mark 14.13-15	Luke 22.10-12	Matthew 26.18
So he sent two of his disciples, telling them, 'Go into the city, and a man carrying a jar of water will meet you. Follow him. Say to the owner of the house he enters, "The Teacher asks: Where is my guest room, where I may eat the Passover with my disciples?" He will show you a large upper room, furnished and ready. Make preparations for us there.'	He replied, 'As you enter the city, a man carrying a jar of water will meet you. Follow him to the house that he enters, and say to the owner of the house, "The Teacher asks: Where is the guest room, where I may eat the Passover with my disciples?" He will show you a large upper room, all furnished. Make preparations there.'	He replied, 'Go into the city to a certain man and tell him, "The Teacher says: My appointed time is near. I am going to celebrate the Passover with my disciples at your house."'

Matthew shortened the Markan text by more than a third. 'The abbreviations are skillfully done. Everything that detracts from Jesus' order and its performance is omitted.'[41] This could be a way to understand why nothing remains of 'Mark's colorful prediction of meeting the man carrying water'.[42] Despite the fact that it is difficult to accept that the Matthean version seems to 'approximate the actual events' because of the layers and layers of interpretation and redaction, I would like to speculate that Matthew might have his own prejudices against men who are not doing their gender correctly. Even Ulrich Luz, who seems to advocate for the 'historicity' of Mt. 26.18, in the end concluded that 'the narrative was a completely theological creation by the evangelist on the basis of the Markan text and that it was not at all concerned with historical plausibility.'[43] If such is the case, we might ask why Matthew removed Nachito's *cántaro* from his narrative. My hermeneutic of *el otro lado* alerts me that there is some kind of *joterías* involved in this story. Matthew saw in Nachito's conduct a transgression of his gender, and perhaps for this reason he banished him to oblivion.

Matthew's community seems to be concerned with keeping the assigned gender roles in their proper places. In a society where 'men' were ideally 'physically strong, warlike, dominant, realistic, and intelligent; thrifty but

41. Luz, *Matthew 21-28*, p. 352.
42. Luz, *Matthew 21-28*, p. 352.
43. Luz, *Matthew 21-28*, p. 353.

generous with friends; capable of resisting strong emotions (sexual desire, fear, grief, pity, impulse); able to endure pain, fatigue, misfortune, hunger, and thirst; and reliable, straightforward, honest, brave, and informed in the ways of the world',[44] Nachito *el machito* would not even remotely have been manly in any way because of his effeminate *cántaro* and his association with meal preparation. Jerome Neyrey observes that objects and tools are likewise gender specific. Plows and draft animals, sheep, weapons and harvesting tools belong to the male world; looms, pots and pans and food-preparation instruments belong to the female.[45] Perhaps for this reason, Matthew has removed the sign of the *cántaro* in order to avoid any suspicion of a Jewish man doing a woman's job. The Matthean community knows by heart the significance of the woman-at-the-well scene, and this 'certain man' might cause some gender trouble. Actually it is not the first time that Matthew reverses details that point to some sort of transgression of gender roles. For instance, in the discourse of Luke 17, Jesus said that there would be two men sleeping on one bed, one would be taken and the other would be left (Lk. 17.13). Matthew removes these two men from their bed and locates them in a manlier place such as the field: 'Then there will be two men in the field; one will be taken and one will be left' (Mt. 24.40). Though Matthew throughout his Gospel has depicted Jesus fulfilling the Scriptures, in matters of gender he does not recall that the Scriptures allow two men to sleep together for the sake of keeping warm during cold nights: 'Also, if two lie down together, they will keep warm. But how can one keep warm alone?'(Eccl. 4.11). Moreover, the Mishnah would allow two men to sleep together under the same blanket (*m. Qidd.* 4.4) only because 'Jews are not suspected of homosexuality' (*b. Qidd.* 82a).[46] However, Matthew could apparently not take the risk, and so he erased any suspicion that might lead his community to transgress or subvert the gender roles.

If we use our hermeneutics *del otro lado*, we notice that Matthew does not bother with having just two disciples undertake the preparation, and he drops the elaborate process in Mark by which the chosen two would know where to make the preparations.[47] In Matthew, Jesus sent the disciples

44. Jeffrey Henderson, 'Greek Attitudes toward Sex', in Michael Grant and Rachael Kitzinger (eds.), *Civilization of the Ancient Mediterranean: Greece and Rome, II* (New York: Charles Scribner's Sons, 1988), pp. 1249-63 (1253).

45. Jerome H. Neyrey, 'Jesus, Gender, and the Gospel of Matthew', in Stephen D. Moore and Janice Capel Anderson (eds.), *New Testaments Masculinities* (Atlanta: Society of Biblical Literature, 2003), pp. 43-66 (44).

46. See Robert Kirschner, 'Halakhah and Homosexuality: A Reappraisal', *Judaism* 37 (1988), pp. 450-58.

47. John Nolland, *The Gospel of Matthew: A Commentary on the Greek Text* (Grand Rapids: Eerdmans, 205), p. 1062. Moreover, Matthew has also dropped the role of "two' at 10.1.

(plural) to find a 'certain man' on the street. Is Matthew suspicious that two male disciples would get into some sort of sexual misconduct on the way to Jerusalem? Above, I quoted the Mishnah that proclaims, 'An unmarried man may not herd cattle, and two men may not sleep together under the same cloak.' Scholars want us to believe that 'This shows that homosexuality was NOT prevalent in the Jewish community in Talmudic times. (This is not a cover up by the Rabbis, for if these acts indeed were found in the community, the Rabbis would not hesitate to forbid men from being alone.)'[48] It is difficult to know for sure whether or not 'homosexuality' was prevalent in the Matthean community, but describing two male disciples carrying out the task as Mark and Luke do might provoke some suspicion among Matthew's audience. Maimonides, who lived in the twelfth century, in interpreting the Talmud added, 'Those Jews who do refrain from being alone with a man or an animal are to be praised.'[49]

In Matthew's Gospel, when Jesus sends his disciples to go to a 'certain man', the author uses the term ὁ δεῖνα, which means a person or thing one cannot or does not wish to name.[50] Scholars since the patristic era have speculated why Matthew did not disclose the identity of the man. Did Jesus want to keep secret the name and the dwelling of the owner of the house? For Luz the word ὁ δεῖνα is used when a person's identity is not important. He concluded, 'Thus one cannot conclude from this text that the readers of the Gospel of Matthew must know the Markan story in order to understand Matthew's "abbreviated" text, only that Matthew has no interest in this man whom Mark emphasizes.'[51] It is obvious that for Matthew this man is not important, but we need to wrestle with the why question. Contrary to Luz's arguments, some interpreters of Mt. 26.14 in the patristic era associated this man with Nachito *el machito*. For instance, Cyril of Alexandria argues that this man is the same one that appears in Mk 14.13-14: 'So this "certain man" is the one with the "earthen pot washed with water" as described by Mark and Luke.'[52] Moreover, Origen in his allegoric interpretation of Mt. 26.16-17 also associated the 'certain one' with Nachito *el machito*: 'I think that the man "carrying a jar of water" whom the disciples met when they entered the city and whom Jesus wanted them to follow into his house was bringing it into the house not only that the house might be clean but also more richly

48. Nachum Amsel, 'Homosexuality in Orthodox Judaism' (accessed on 13 May 2009); online at http://www.lookstein.org/resources/homosexuality_amsel.pdf.
49. Amsel, 'Homosexuality in Orthodox Judaism'.
50. Frederick William Danker, *A Greek-English Lexicon of the New Testament and Other Early Christian Literature* (Chicago: University of Chicago, 2000), p. 215.
51. Luz, *Matthew 21-28*, pp. 353-54.
52. Quoted in Manlio Simonetti (ed.), *Ancient Christian Commentary on Scripture, Matthew 14-28* (Downers Grove, IL: InterVarsity, 2002), p. 245.

endowed.'[53] Moreover, in Matthew ὁ δεῖνα is the owner of the house, not a servant. 'I am going to celebrate the Passover with my disciples at your house' (Mt. 26.18). We know that in antiquity the public spaces belonged to men. The streets, plazas and marketplaces were the battlefields where men had to prove their masculinity among other males. Moreover, a man had to engage in constant battle to preserve the good reputation and honor of his household—which also meant protecting them from any unmanly behavior. 'In this public world, male citizens were exclusively in charge. A male citizen was a warrior and head of an *oikos*.'[54] Matthew, by placing 'such a man' in a public space and making him the owner of the house, has succeeded in maintaining and preserving traditional gender roles. Furthermore, he has artistically accomplished what Nachito's town folks were unable to do. Matthew has made a real macho out of 'such a man'.

In the same way as Nachito's uncle broke Nachito's *cántaro* in an effort to erase what he perceived as shameful behavior, so also Matthew would not allow Nachito's *cántaro* to shame the memory of this manly Jew. Matthew cannot allow his audience to suspect that a masculine and virile man would debase himself by doing a detestable, womanish and slavish job. Matthew's male community could easily affirm, like the people of Nachito's village, that 'We do not want other people to think that in our community men carry water in *cántaros* like women.' By breaking and erasing any reference to Nachito's *cántaro*, Matthew is reemphasizing and securing the masculinity of his male audience. He is keeping the gender roles in their proper place. Once Nachito's *cántaro* has been eliminated, and Nachito becomes not only *machito* but also a manly *macho,* the Matthean community can be sure that genders have not been subverted or crossed. The males in the community can again boast about their masculinity. But this is not the case with either Mark or Luke, who depict Nachito *el machito* as being as *joto* as can be.

Nachito el machito *Walking with Pride and Grace at the Well*

Scholars unanimously recognize that the instructions that Jesus gave to his disciples were 'unusual ... since this was usually the work of a woman'.[55] Morton Smith goes further in his assessment. He says, 'Carrying water was women's work, so this was like saying, "Look for a man wearing lipstick."'[56] However, Jesus knows what he is doing; he is reliable even when his

53. Quoted in Simonetti, *Ancient Christian Commentary*, p. 245.
54. Henderson, "Greek Attitudes toward Sex,' p. 1251.
55. Senior, *The Passion of Jesus*, p. 51.
56. Morton Smith, *The Secret Gospel: The Discovery and Interpretation of the Secret Gospel according to Mark* (New York: Harper & Row, 1973), p. 80.

instructions seem bizarre or outlandish.[57] I have been arguing that in antiquity being a man was linked very closely to the role of being an active agent rather than a passive one. Be it in politics, in sports, in war, in rhetoric or in the vast field of sexuality, what qualified an individual as a *man* was his active control of the situation. In ancient times, men were constantly threatened to death with the potential obsession of becoming 'weak' or 'effeminate' through a variety of activities: whether by bathing too much, or by eating the wrong foods, or engaging in too much sex, by wearing the wrong clothing, or even by taking too much enjoyment in supposedly unmanly tasks. Men were concerned about their loss of manliness, and the medical treatises of the time give testimony to the way in which physicians sought to ensure their patron's manliness.[58] In order to be manly, people under no circumstance would transgress the assigned gender roles for fear of being infected by the 'effeminate disease'.

We saw above that in Greco-Roman culture it was not enough to be born a 'man'; one had also to act the part of a man. Acting like a man required one to assume the active role in private sexual practice as well as in one's public life. We do not know exactly whether Nachito *el machito* walked with grace and harmony while carrying his *cántaro* or whether he exaggerated his 'effeminate' ways. The only thing that we can be sure of is that Nachito's gender performance was against the notion of masculinity and manhood. For this reason, Boring's interpretation that 'the meeting of a man carrying a jar of water is only moderately unusual'[59] is not convincing at all. Although Boring recognizes that carrying water was mostly women's work, and that when men carried water they usually used skin bottles rather than jars, he fails to take into consideration the strict observations of gender roles in the first century. Boring concludes that 'men, especially slaves, could be seen in the streets of Jerusalem carrying water jars without raising eyebrows'.[60] I suppose he had not been exposed to other cultures, such as my own, where Nachito, in response to walking just a few meters carrying his *cántaro* of water, was subjected to all kinds of humiliating acts because he was perceived to be 'threatening' the masculinity of other males. Joel Marcus notices that this insight about men carrying water in skin goes back to Marie-Joseph Lagrange, who lived at the turn of the twentieth century; and it is based on nothing more than his observation of Palestinian habits in

57. Theodore W. Jennings, *The Man Jesus Loved: Homoerotic Narratives from the New Testament* (Cleveland: Pilgrim Press, 2003), p. 160.
58. Hester, 'Eunuchs and the Postgender Jesus', p. 20. See also Aline Rousselle, *Porneia: On Desire and the Body in Antiquity* (New York: Basil Blackwell, 1988), pp. 5-23.
59. Boring, *Mark*, p. 388.
60. Boring, *Mark*, p. 388.

his own day ('if one can judge from modern custom').[61] I myself have seen in some Mexican villages men carrying water, or *pulque*,[62] in skin. However, gender roles are never crossed or subverted.

Like many stories of people *del otro lado* whose lives are considered dubious, unreal and unintelligible, scholars insist and persist in saying that Nachito's life 'is a legend or it has legendary features'.[63] Although Nachito's life is not real, nonetheless they see the necessity of making Nachito macho by associating Mk 14.12-16 with 1 Sam. 10.1-10,[64] where we find Saul, the masculine man, who had been just anointed king by Samuel. Note that in this particular story, there is no crossing of genders. In the Hebrew Bible there is a text where Israelites punish some men by making them carry water. The book of Joshua informs us that the Gibeonites tricked Israel by entering into a treaty with Joshua, arguing that they were not Israel's neighbors. However, three days later the Israelites learned that the Gibeonites were indeed their neighbors who lived near their lands. Because of the oath that Joshua took before God, he could not kill them. Instead, he punished them by forcing them to be woodcutters and water carriers (Josh. 9.21)—essentially emasculating them. He did not kill them physically, but he knew that living with the stigma of being treated as a woman was worse than death. Gorgias, the itinerant rhetorician, expressed this idea well: 'To good men death is more desirable than a shameful reputation. For one is the end of life, and the other a disease in life.'[65] The shameful story of the Gibeonites ended with the following remarks: 'And that is what they are to this day' (Josh. 9.27), referring to the shameful activity of being woodcutters and water carriers.

I often wondered what would have happened if instead of having a man carrying a jar of water in this biblical text, we had had a woman with her *cántaro*? Possibly our interpretation would have made sense immediately, and we would have interpreted it in terms of the long biblical tradition of women at wells with its concomitant wedding motifs. A decade ago, Dennis R. Macdonald argued that Mark transformed the famous woman-at-the well type of scene, in which typically, a male stranger arrives in a hostile or unknown area and meets a damsel drawing water, one of the few activi-

---

61. Joel Marcus, *Mark 8–16* (New Haven, CT: Yale University Press, 2009), p. 945.

62. The *pulque* was considerate a sacred drink to the Aztecs; they called it 'drink of the gods'. The *pulque* comes from the massive maguey cactus, and it is extracted by scraping the base, which stimulates the flow of this milky substance.

63. Yarbro Collins, *Mark*, p. 646.

64. Rudolf Bultmann, *The History of the Synoptic Tradition* (trans. John Marsh; New York: Harper & Row, 1963), p. 263.

65. Quoted in Willi Braun, *Feasting and Social Rhetoric in Luke 14* (New York: Cambridge University Press, 1995), p. 114.

ties that found ancient women alone and away from home. One function of such a scene was to provide the stranger with accommodations in a foreign environment, perhaps on the assumption that meeting another male might produce not hospitality but hostility.[66] Unfortunately, neither he nor all the other scholars who unanimously argued that Nachito's performance was unusual and dubious give him any credit for his service. Nachito seems to fulfill the requirements that Mark demands from all the people who wish to follow Jesus. Mark has been instructing the disciples to receive both Jesus and his message humbly, serving one another, accepting people who are *del otro lado*. Jesus' alternative household had welcomed people like Pola *la descarada*, Rebequita *la malcriada*, the unmanly Simon Peter, and Simon *el del otro lado*. To this list we can now add Nachito *el machito* for his *descaramiento* of carrying his *cántaro* of water on the holiest day in the holiest city.

Nachito el machito *as a Disciple of Jesus*

Earlier, we noted that characters in the Gospel of Mark are very important to his narrative. However, most studies of those characters focus on the role of the disciples. Elizabeth Malbon correctly argues that in the past, scholarly investigations have been inadequate because 'what Mark has to say about discipleship is understood in reference not only to disciples but also to other Markan characters who meet the demands of following Jesus'.[67] I find many inadequacies in the way people have interpreted Nachito's story. Scholars have transformed Nachito's life into a 'fairy tale'.[68] Nachito as a 'fairy' does not count. Nachito's service apparently 'has no value apart from the celebration of the Passover meal, and no Passover meal is mentioned in our gospels other than the present one, which took place "on the night in which Jesus was betrayed"' (1 Cor. 11.23).[69] He is 'merely a guide and may have been unconscious of his task'.[70] Nachito apparently does not deserve a single mention in books that have otherwise exhaustively analyzed the paradox of authority and servanthood in the Gospel of Mark.[71] And this when some have even associated Nachito with Mark himself: 'He [Mark] may even

66. Dennis R. Macdonald, *The Homeric Epics and the Gospel of Mark* (New Haven, CT: Yale University Press, 2000), pp. 120-21.
67. Elizabeth Struthers Malbon, *In the Company of Jesus: Characters in Mark's Gospel* (Louisville, KY: Westminster John Knox Press, 2000), p. 43.
68. D.E. Nineham, *The Gospel of Saint Mark*, (Baltimore: Penguin Books, 1963), p. 375.
69. Robert H. Stein, *Mark* (Grand Rapids: Baker Academic, 2008), p. 645.
70. Taylor, *The Gospel according to Saint Mark*, p. 537.
71. Narry F. Santos, *Slave of All: The Paradox of Authority and Servanthood in the Gospel of Mark* (Sheffield: Sheffield Academic Press, 2003).

have been the man carrying the pitcher.'[72] Once the scholar's imagination is allowed to come forth, the identity of Nachito is endless. Nachito can be the husband of Mary, or the young man who ran away naked during Jesus' arrest, as Vernon Bartlet speculates: 'If he [Nachito] was Mark, and had come from the house where the Last Supper was held, he may have been the son of the head of the house—himself, then, the husband of Mary, Mark's mother, whose house was later a *rendezvous* of the Christians at Jerusalem where Peter was a familiar figure' (Acts 12.12ff.).[73]

Although Bartlet does not inform us why he speculates this way about Nachito's identity and 'hetero/sexual' life, it is very likely that he is using the reconstruction that Severus of Al'Ashmunein (955-987 c.e.) made about Mark the evangelist. In the Coptic tradition Mark is linked with several anonymous characters that appear in the Gospels.[74] Of course, in the Coptic tradition, Nachito is neither married nor has siblings.

> And Mark was one of the Seventy Disciples. And he was one of the servants who poured out the water which Our Lord turned into wine, at the marriage of Cana in Galilee. And it was he who carried the jar of water into the house of Simon the Cyrenian, at the time of the sacramental Supper. And he also it was who entertained the disciples in his house, at the time of the Passion of the Lord Christ, and after his resurrection from the dead, where he entered while the doors were shut.[75]

One of the things that we learn about Mark/Nachito from the Coptic tradition is his constant service toward the community. I believe the inadequacies and misfortunes of Nachito can be resolved if we admit that he is a disciple of Jesus with all his *joterías*. Our interpretation might yield more fruit if we just accept that in Jesus' new household, true disciples are the ones who are not constrained by gender roles but rather are moved by hospitality to one another.

It is striking that Mark depicts Jesus' last days sharing meals in two households where all kinds of transgressions occur. These households are ones in which wo/men do not do their gender right. In Mk 14.13-16 Jesus again sends two of his disciples, 'presumably from Bethany, where Jesus and his disciples remain' (Mk 14.3),[76] to a house of 'effeminacy'. Archae-

---

72. J. Vernon Bartlet, *St. Mark* (New Century Bible; Edinburgh: T. & T. Clark, 1925), p. 380.

73. Bartlet, *St. Mark*, p. 401.

74. In order to see the influence of the Gospel of Mark in the Coptic tradition, see Thomas C. Oden, *The African Memory of Mark: Reassessing Early Church Tradition* (Downers Grove, IL: InterVarsity, 2011).

75. Severus of Al'Ashmunein, *History of the Patriarchs of the Coptic Church of Alexandria* (ed. and trans. B. Evett; Paris: Firmin-Didot, 1948), p. 141.

76. Senior, *The Passion of Jesus*, p. 51.

ologists inform us that Nachito *el machito's* house was at a location close to the Gihon Spring, or to the Siloam Pool. This is where people filled their jars with water and carried them back home.[77] For our purposes, it is not important to locate Nachito's presumed house. For us it is more important that other men might consider this particular house suspicious. If males from Nachito's town were able to comment about the house where a *joto* lives, males from Jesus' time could easily point out, *Aquí, en tierra de machos vive un joto,* 'Here in the land of machos lives a *joto.*' By sending two of his disciples to a house with a dubious reputation, Jesus is confirming that discipleship is open for all *descarados/as* who do not fit into the so-called normal, natural and hierarchical order of the household that the Greco Roman world promoted.

In the Gospel of Mark, being a disciple is not an easy task (Mk 8.34; 10.21, 25). There is no doubt that Mark somehow intended to present to the audience the Twelve as a model of discipleship throughout the Gospel (Mk 3.14). And yet in the end, these Twelve fail totally. Even Jesus as 'disciple of the kingdom'[78] struggles in being faithful to God's plan, especially at Gethsemane (Mk 14.33-36). In the end, one can ask if there is any faithful disciple in the entire Gospel. We saw in the previous chapter that following Jesus required breaking away from certain values, and embracing Jesus' dislocation and marginality:

> *Como los niños, los discípulos ejemplares en el Evangelio son todos personas 'liminales', las cuales por una razón u otra se encontraban socialmente 'desubicadas' o al margen de la 'normalidad' en aquella sociedad,*
> Like children, the exemplary disciples in Mark's Gospel are all 'liminal', people who for one reason or another were socially "dislocated" or living on the margins of 'normalcy'.[79]

If being liminal, abnormal, dislocated or living on the margins of society are the prerequisites for entering Jesus' new household, then Nachito *el machito* fits the bill. Nachito has willingly left behind his manliness, masculinity, honor and the privilege of having a phallus. As a *descarado,* he is serving in another's house, one where liminal, marginalized and dysfunctional disciples like him can dwell.

Scholars notice that in Mk 14.12-16, the evangelist emphasizes the servanthood of the two disciples in two ways. First, he includes a servant's question (14.12b). Mark records how the disciples take the initiative to prepare for the Passover by asking a question (14.12a): 'Where do you want us to go and make the preparations for you to eat the Passover?[80] It is true that they

77. Gibson, *The Final Days of Jesus,* p. 50.
78. This insight belongs to Dr Vena.
79. Vaage, 'En otra casa', pp. 27-28.
80. Santos, *Slave of All, p. 238.*

are the ones who initiated the preparation of the meal, but it is Nachito who does the shameful job of carrying the water for the Passover meal. He is the one who meets them and shows them the house that is already prepared. Mark closes this pericope by saying, 'They prepared the Passover meal.' We might assume with most scholars that they helped in the preparation of the food, but it was Nachito who endured the difficulty of the work. Mark uses the verb βαστάζω, which denotes the sense of being able 'to bear up under especially trying or oppressive circumstances'.[81] Nachito's *descaramiento* in 'carrying' his *cántaro* of water probably provoked all kinds of violence, insult and aggression against him. Nonetheless, this kind of dubious behavior is what Jesus required of a person to become part of his alternative household. Besides, the word βαστάζω is strongly linked with the idea of carrying one's cross. 'The metaphor τὸν σταυρὸν βαστάσαι originally denotes the outward carrying of the cross by Jesus (Jn 19.17), then the personal attitude of the disciples (Lk. 14.27).'[82] In the same way that Jesus made Pola *la descarada* a symbol of discipleship, he is instructing us to follow this effeminate man wherever he goes.

We have been arguing that *descarados/as* disciples are often silent, that they speak only through their excluded bodies. Nonetheless, Nachito *el machito* comes into existence through Jesus' words that legitimate and recognize his life. Jesus' words become Nachito's words, and the disciples must follow Nachito wherever he goes. To follow Nachito *el machito* is to follow Jesus, because both are also bound by the ethic of *descaramiento*. Nachito, by carrying his jar of water, is prefiguring the shameful behavior that Jesus is going to endure in a few hours when he carries his own cross. The verb ἀκολουθέω in the Gospel of Mark has strong sense of discipleship (Mk 1.18; 2.14, 15; 3.7; 5.24; 6.1; 8.34; 9.38; 10.21, 28, 32, 52; 11.9; 14.13, 54; 15.41; 16.17). Jesus is giving his male disciples another opportunity to enter into an ethic of *descaramiento* with Nachito *el joto*. We must remember that in the previous house of affliction, the male disciples were indignant toward Pola *la descarada*. Here perhaps these same male disciples have a chance of redeeming themselves by following, working and eating with a *joto*.

Jesus had previously sent out the Twelve two by two, warning them that they might find resistance to his message: 'If any place will not welcome you or listen to you, shake the dust off your feet when you leave, as a testimony against them' (Mk 6.11). Here Jesus is confident that his disciples will be received with hospitality rather than hostility because he is the διδάσκαλος (teacher). Jesus as a teacher has followers in Jerusalem who are willing to prepare the Passover meal for the community and to welcome them into a new household. However, this household has the mark of effeminacy, and

81. Danker, *A Greek-English Lexicon*, p. 171.
82. F. Büchsel, 'βαστάζω', *TDNT*, I, p. 596.

only bodies that are not afraid of being made contagious by this 'disease' can celebrate the meal. Jesus the teacher has changed the rules of commensality and membership. His household is open to all the unwanted, unwelcomed, undesirable and disposable bodies. This time the male disciples cannot misunderstand the instruction that Jesus is giving them, can they?

The disciples ask Jesus, 'Where do you want to us to go and make the preparations *for you to eat the Passover*?' (Mk 14.12) [my emphasis]. Assuming that two disciples prepared the Passover meal, why then is Mark not using the plural, 'so that we may eat'? Are they already distancing themselves from Jesus' meal? What is wrong with them? Eating implies fellowship, and in this particular context, discipleship. Jesus' order was to follow Nachito and to say to the owner of the house, 'The teacher asks, "Where is my guest room, where I may eat the Passover *with my disciples*?"' Jesus' intention is to celebrate the Passover together as a new family. Mark informs us that 'the disciples left, went into the city and found things just as Jesus had told them. So they prepared the Passover' (Mk 14.16). This could be an indication that these disciples indeed followed Jesus' order, but the fact that they themselves are excluded from the meal gives me pause. Joel Marcus resolves this dilemma by affirming that the use of the second person singular ('so that *you* may eat'), when the first personal plural might be expected ('so that *we* may eat'), emphasizes Jesus' centrality and the disciples' reverence for him; it is crucial that *he* should consume the festal meal. Presumably they will eat as well, but they modestly refrain from mentioning this [italic in the original].[83] This could be a way of redeeming the disciples, but I am not so sure if the male disciples in the Gospel of Mark had any reverence for Jesus at all. Moreover, modesty is hardly the adjective that I would use to describe the male disciples' ambition for power that is evident in Mark's Gospel!

Mark presents Jesus in Bethany relaxing and accepting table fellowship with some unwanted people. He apparently has the intention to participate neither in the Jewish Passover nor in the Feast of the Unleavened Bread— or at least we are not informed about them. For those two feasts are symbols of oppression and exclusion for people like Pola, Simon, and Nachito. 'Where do you want to us to go and make the preparations for you to eat the Passover?' (Mk 14.12). This question is abrupt and out of context; Jesus is already celebrating among friends the true feast of liberation with people who were excluded from it. The male disciples, witnessing that the time of the national feast was at hand and perceiving that they might lose the opportunity to disclose Jesus' identity as the new liberator of all Israel, take the initiative and seem confident that Jesus legitimates their motifs. The disciples' question shows that they are still trapped in their nationalistic ideology of a warrior messiah. However, Jesus would take this opportunity to teach them the true meaning of his Passover celebration.

Mateos and Camacho correctly observe that the initiative to celebrate the Passover feast comes not from Jesus but rather from the male disciples, followers of the Judaist tradition: *Por eso sólo le preguntan dónde quieres celebrar la cena, insistiendo en que van a prepararla para él (prepararte)*, 'For this reason they not only asked him, where do you want to celebrate the Passover, they also insist on preparing it for him.'[84] These male disciples have not yet learned about Jesus' alternative feast, which is open for all and not just for the Jews. They have not made any progress in their understanding of Jesus' alternative household, meals and celebration, and for this reason they associate him with the old Passover and Israel's total revindication in front of the other nations: *Asocian a Jesús a los ideales judíos de liberación representados por la antigua Pascua, que incluyen la reivindicación de Israel frente a las naciones paganas*, '[They] associate Jesus with the Jewish ideas of liberation represented by the old Passover, which included Israel's revindication in front of pagan nations.'[85] However, Jesus has other ideas and motivations in mind, and he would give precise instructions on how to celebrate the Passover feast.

As we have already noted, Mark does not disclose the identity of the two disciples; however, the number two reveals Jesus' intention of forming his alternative society. The number two represents the alternative community, as in Mk 6.7: 'Then Jesus went around teaching from village to village. Calling the Twelve to him, he sent them out two by two and gave them authority over evil spirits.' Mark uses the verb ἀποστέλλω, which defines the essential characteristics of any disciple. They must be called by Jesus to be with him and to be sent out to preach (Mk 3.14). Once Jesus sends out his alternative community and introduces the figure of Nachito *el machito*, the male disciples must change their understanding of the Passover. For the Spaniard Markan scholar Salvador Santos Pacheco, Nachito's presence is the only guarantee that both disciples have of finding the house and preparing the meal; without Nachito, both disciples would be disorientated, without destiny and incapable of fulfilling Jesus' order. In this context, Nachito is not just another disciple, but a model disciple: *El hombre invertido aparece en el texto como modelo de discípulo*, 'The inverted man appears in the text as a model disciple.'[86] Santos Pacheco adds that Jesus' alternative

84. Mateos and Camacho, *El Evangelio de Marcos*, p. 456.
85. Mateos and Camacho, *El Evangelio de Marcos*, p. 456.
86. I have been in communication via email with Salvador Santos Pacheco, and he has shared many insights about this anonymous man. He confessed to me that this is the first time he has seen this character as a disciple, thanks to my hermeneutic *del otro*

society would be distinguished not by privileges but rather by service to one another. Nachito *el machito* marks the route to the last setting where Jesus' community celebrates the definitive freedom and meaning of the Passover. The οἰκοδεσπότης as a master of the house and Nachito *el machito* have done their part. They are willing to receive Jesus' Twelve disciples. But these two disciples, by separating themselves from Jesus' meal, do not want to be associated with a *descarado*. Besides, it is in the context of the meal that Jesus categorically affirms that one of the Twelve will betray him, one that is eating with him (Mk 14.17). In both households there are some anonymous *descarados/as* disciples who enter into a relationship with Jesus, but there are also some male disciples who keep their distance from Jesus' company. It is as if Jesus has been betrayed prior to his own prediction. He has been with the disciples, but the male disciples throughout the Gospel have not been with him. In the previous chapter I demonstrated how the male disciples were nervous about being emasculated by associating themselves with Pola *la descarada*. If in sharing a meal one becomes connected as a family, these male disciples certainly do not want to be part of this alternative household where a man behaves like a wo/man. Once again we observe how when the proper gender roles are transgressed, subverted and blurred tremendous panic and anxiety occur among the male community.

We do not know what the reaction was of the male disciples when Nachito found them in the crowded city of Jerusalem. Did they exclaim like in Mexico, ¡*Mira un joto!* 'Look A faggot!'? Did they draw attention to his effeminate way of walking, his unmanly *cántaro*? Did they notice his sissy voice? According to Seneca, one could easily recognize an effeminate man by his walk. 'An effeminate man (*impudicus*) is revealed by his walk, from [the way] he brings his finger up to his head, and from his eye movement' (*Epistulae* 52.12).[87] Human beings, argues Cicero in *On Duties*, are disposed by nature to disapprove morally of ways of sitting and standing that displease the eyes and ears. He includes among the postures to be avoided those of the effeminate and the rustic (*De officiis* 1.128-29).[88] Scholars have speculated that the 'two were to follow in silence, and enter the house into which they saw him pass'.[89] This implies that the two disciples were not

---

lado. He graciously provided many insights that are reflected in my interpretation of Mk 14.12-16. I would like to express my gratitude for his solidarity and encouragement in continuing to embrace my *otro lado*.

87. Quoted in Anthony Corbeill, 'Political Movement: Walking and Ideology in Republican Rome', in David Fredrick (ed.), *The Roman Gaze: Vision, Power, and the Body* (Baltimore: Johns Hopkins University Press, 2002), pp. 182-215 (189).

88. Quoted in Corbeill, 'Political Movement', p. 188.

89. Henry Swete Barclay, *Commentary on Mark* (Grand Rapids: Kregel, 1977), p. 329. Also R. Alan Culpepper (Mark [Macon: Smyth & Helwys, 2007], p. 489): 'Perhaps without even a word being spoken, they would follow him to a house.'

walking together with Nachito. It is not easy to walk with a *joto* in a macho
land without losing one's masculinity. They might be accused of also being
a *joto*. There is a saying in Latin America that goes, *Dime con quién andas y
te diré quién eres,* 'Tell me with whom you walk and I will tell you who you
are.' A person is known by the company that she or he keeps, and Nachito
does not have a good reputation. Therefore, his company must be avoided at
all costs. How many times did my friend Nachito hear his friends' mothers
warning them, *No quiero que te juntes con ese joto,* 'I do not want you to
keep company with that *joto.*' Being a *joto* is a contagion, a disease that one
must avoid at all costs.[90] The disciples had probably found out that in such
a house of effeminacy, the proper genders were not observed. In the same
way that they had found it difficult to accept Pola *la descarada* as a disciple,
they are now finding it difficult to eat with a *joto* and enter into fellowship
with him through the symbolism of the meal. Eating or living with people
del otro lado requires boldness. In Mexico, for instance, in May 2009, the
National Commission for Human Rights (CNDH) found that 66 percent
of the population would not live under the same roof as a homosexual. A
total of 39.4 percent expressed that homosexuals should not participate in
politics, and 40 percent responded that they would not accept a homosexual
living in their home. Sadly, the male disciples insisted on maintaining their
privileges, although Jesus had announced a new exodus and liberation for
all through the symbolism of the meal.

We stated above that the conflict between Mark's narrative and the actual
historical practice of the Passover meal has provoked long and hot debate.
I understand that Jesus wants to celebrate his meal after the manner of the
original Passover, eating 'as those in flight' (Exod. 12.11).[91] Jesus is calling
his community to 'come out' in a new exodus. The process of *coming out* is
not easy for some disciples. Thus, from Jesus' perspective it is only though
the *coming out* that they can celebrate his Passover meal. This *coming out*
from slavery into freedom must be done in the inverse direction: 'It is an
exodus in the inverse direction [italics in the original] that is to take place,
since Israel has in its turn become a land of slavery because of money, the
state-temple, the god of the dead.'[92] Israel is not just the land of slavery
because of an orchestration of economic power, but also because it keeps

90. To understand the disease of effeminacy in antiquity, see Diana M. Swancutt, 'The Disease of Effemination': The Charge of Effeminacy and the Verdict of God
(Romans 1:18–2:16)', in Stephen D. Moore and Janice Capel Anderson (eds.), *Masculinities on the New Testament* (Atlanta: Society of Biblical Literature, 2003), pp. 193-
234.
91. Myers, *Binding the Strong Man*, p. 361.
92. Fernando Belo, *A Materialist Reading of the Gospel of Mark* (trans. Matthew J.
O'Connell; Maryknoll, NY: Orbis Books, 1981), p. 208.

all those unwanted, unwelcome and unmanly people out of the community. Jesus' exodus and covenant are not anything new; they are just bringing into historical memory what God has done in the past with Israel. The exodus of liberation includes everyone, citizens, illegals, slaves and effeminate servants. 'Carefully follow the terms of this covenant, so that you may prosper in everything you do. All of you are standing today in the presence of the LORD your God—your leaders and chief men, your elders and officials, and all the other men of Israel, together with your children and your wives, and the aliens living in your camps *who chop your wood and carry your water*' [my emphasis] (Deut. 29.9-11). In Jesus' new covenant, or exodus, people who were ashamed, those who were reduced to nothing, and those who transgressed their gender boundaries are now encouraged to *come out* to experience the new exodus that Jesus just announced. Jesus is not just embracing Nachito *el machito* as a disciple, he is also giving him a new way of being human before God.

Fernando Belo observes that Jerusalem becomes the 'city', and the temple is replaced by 'one house' among all the houses of the city. 'This means that we are no longer in the Jewish symbolic field and its center, but in a space that is marginal to this field and that is therefore anonymous in the Jewish text.'[93] If this is true, we can argue that an effeminate household where a marginal Nachito dwells is the paradigm for being a disciple. Jesus has displaced the household from the center to the margins and is allowing his disciples to redefine the notion of masculinity, a meaning other than the manhood that the Greco Roman culture promoted. Because it is a place on the margin, Jesus' household is in some way unfamiliar, and all his disciples are exhorted to move to the periphery: 'Discipleship in Mark is demanding and antifamiliar or a project of the socially marginal.'[94] For disciples such as Pola *la descarada*, Rebequita *la malcriada*, Simon *el del otro lado,* and Nachito *el machito,* who have been constantly displaced to the bottom of society, Jesus' invitation is indeed Good News. These liminal and peripheral people at least have a place to go now. As *descarados/as* disciples they have been called by Jesus not to be homeless, as Leif E. Vaage correctly states, but rather to create an alternative household as the requirement for entering into the Kingdom of God. 'At the same time, it is not a call to homelessness but, rather, to inhabit "another home" whereby one enters into the Kingdom of God.'[95] However, this idea of 'anonymous houses in a field that no longer has a center'[96] might be a cause of anxiety and fear for some male disciples who are concerned with their masculinity and manhood.

93. Belo, *A Materialist Reading,* p. 209.
94. Vaage, 'En otra casa', p. 42.
95. Vaage, 'En otra casa', p. 42.
96. Belo, *A Materialist Reading,* p. 209.

We have been exploring the possibility of seeing in Nachito *el machito* the prototype of the discipleship that Jesus requires. His openness, marginality, service and *descaramiento* in leaving behind his manliness for something called the Kingdom of God puts him in a favorable place. In the same way that Jesus praised Pola *la descarada* for her good work in a previous household, here Jesus gives us Nachito and his *cántaro* as the mark of discipleship. After all, Jesus' kingdom is for people who like Nachito have left behind a 'normal life' in order to be a true disciple of Jesus. As Vaage suggests, *Dejar la vida normal y pasar a una vida más marginal es el primer paso hacia el reino de Dios,* 'To leave a normal life and enter into a marginal life is the first step toward God's kingdom.'[97] Can someone be more marginal or liminal than the unmanly Nachito, who dared to transgress assigned gender roles? Here we have an extraordinary disciple who has left behind the manly task in order to enter into Jesus' alternative household where genders have been subverted and all kinds of disciples dwell. In the house of effeminacy each disciple has the opportunity to show his or her fidelity or betrayal to Jesus, to defend their honor or to become *descarados/as*. Now that we have seen how Nachito has exposed his *joterías* and become Jesus' disciple, let us turn our attention to Jesus' broken, powerless and abject body.

97. Vaage, 'En otra casa', p. 42.

4

Jesus' Abject, Precarious and Vulnerable Body

Jesus as an Abject Body

In every era, the human body has been an essential focus of reflection, discussion and meditation on the antagonistic relationship between the body that is sacred and the body that is profane, the body that is merely flesh and the spiritualized body, the body that is beautiful and the body that is grotesque, the body that is normalized and the body that is abject. However, the human body is not just a physical being; the body has become both one of the more heavily burdened bearers of meaning of culture and religion and one of the richest sources of meaning. As anthropologists observe, the body is indeed a complex structure. The function of its different parts and their relation to one another afford a source of symbols for other complex structures in society.[1] How then should we read Jesus' body? Can we really read Jesus' body as an abject being in Mark's account of the Last Supper?

We have learned from anthropologists that how a particular society understands the human body is often emblematic of how that society functions and ascribes meaning. Jesus' body therefore likewise 'represents the social body of which he is a member'.[2] We saw in the previous chapter how Jesus symbolically speaking had displaced his alternative household to the periphery where there is no longer any center, where all kinds of abject bodies dwell. According to the anthropologist Mary Douglas, 'The body is a model which can stand for any bounded system. Its boundaries can represent any boundaries which are threatened or precarious.'[3] Relying on Douglas's insight, Butler would argue that 'all social systems are vulnerable at their margins, and that all margins are accordingly considered

---

1. Douglas, *Purity and Danger,* p. 142.
2. Wilkinson-Duran, *The Power of Disorder,* p. 116.
3. Douglas, *Purity and Danger*, p. 115.

dangerous'.[4] Living at the liminal border is not an easy task to accomplish. Borders and margins are always dangerous places to cross or in which to live. However, by freely moving in those dangerous places, Jesus calls into question the systems that promote and enforce order and demarcation. Jesus as an abject body demonstrates that borders are malleable and permeable, and by doing so he makes room for those abject bodies that were pushed beyond the margins to push back, to challenge the stability of readable and enforceable norms that condemn them to 'live the unlivable life'. If abjection is what 'disturbs identity, system, order ... [and] does not respect borders, positions, rules',[5] then Jesus in Mark's Gospel is the promoter of a kingdom of abject bodies. Perhaps for this reason, bodies like those of Pola *la descarada*, Rebequita *la malcriada*, Simón *el del otro lado* and Nachito *el machito* have found a place in Jesus' alternative household. Liew correctly observes that those 'others' or these abjects in Mark turn out to be the Romans, the disciples and the women, all of whom have ambiguous and ambivalent relationships with Jesus.[6] Although Liew does not describe Jesus as an abject being, Jesus' ministry, miracles and deeds could easily be classified as abject because they question recognized borders. So in the Gospel of Mark, Jesus voluntarily touches a leper (Mk 1.40-45) and takes a corpse by the hand (Mk 5.41). He is touched by a menstruating woman (Mk 5.24-28) and invites a sinner to follow him (Mk 2.13-14). Jesus continually crosses boundaries that he is expected to avoid (Mk 4.35-42; 7.31), for example, by entering into public debate with a Syro-Phoenician woman (Mk 7.24-30). Jesus very often is in contact with the possessed and all kinds of mutilated bodies such as the blind, the lame and the deaf.[7] Jesus defies established codes by declaring all foods to be clean (Mk 7.19). He shares and seeks fellowship with sinners (Mk 2.15). He applies his own spittle to the eyes of a blind 'body' (8.23) and to the tongue of a dumb body (7.33). Jesus heals on a Sabbath (Mk 3.1-6) and interrupts and cleanses the temple (Mk 11.15).[8] From these texts we can see that Jesus' behavior sums up Kris-

---

4. Butler, *Gender Trouble*, p. 180.

5. Kristeva, *Powers of Horror*, p. 4.

6. Tat-siong Benny Liew, 'Re-Mark-able Masculinities: Jesus, the Son of Man, and the (Sad) Sum of Manhood?' in Stephen D. Moore and Janice Capel Anderson (eds.), *Masculinities on the New Testament* (Atlanta: Society of Biblical Literature, 2003), pp. 93-135 (113).

7. Jesus' crossing of boundaries is observed in the miracles that he performed. Geographically speaking, Jesus performed his miracles in both Jewish territory as well as in Gentile territory. For more on Jesus' crossing of boundaries in performing his miracles, see the excellent article by Jesús Peláez, 'La praxis curativa de Jesús en el Evangelio de Marcos. Una salvación que se brinda a todos', *Éxodo* 56 (2000), pp. 37-42.

8. For further information how Jesus transgresses all kind of boundaries see Jerome Neyrey, 'The Idea of Purity in Mark's Gospel', *Semeia* 35 (1986), pp. 91-128.

teva's notion of the abject as that one who 'transgresses the boundaries of the clean, the pure and the proper'.[9] Furthermore, we can argue that all bodies—not just Jesus' body—that we have examined so far in Mark's passion narrative are not just *descarados/as* or *del otro lado*, but also abject beings because they transgress all kinds of boundaries and cause confusion to the recognized unity and order that the Jews of the first century promoted. In Mark's Gospel, Jesus is defining a new order and new borders by his zeal in announcing Good News for all the abject bodies.

So why does Mark transgress so many boundaries in his passion narrative? The easy answer would be because Mark's Gospel is told at the margins of Judaism. 'This story, told at the margin of Jewish life amid the instability of the 70s, exhibits a strong interest in the overcoming of boundaries—social, physical, religious, geographical—and this too reflects the situation of the community.'[10] Perhaps it is for this reason that Mark has 'marked' and presented us with some characters who 'house abjection' in their bodies. To most people, these bodies did not matter, and they were therefore already considered socially, religiously, and psychologically dying or indeed dead. Some characters that we have already examined were not even really considered to be human. Abjection is, after all, what distinguishes what is not fully human from what is. The process of becoming human or inhuman is a rigid and well-orchestrated mechanism of exclusion. Mark has depicted some characters in the passion narrative as being excluded from society, the temple, and the household due to their gender, illness and effeminacy. Butler, using Kristeva's concept of abjection, would say that some bodies become 'the Other' or a set of 'Others' through exclusion and domination. In keeping and reinforcing the borders of the 'inner' and the 'outer' in their 'proper place', a few bodies would become subjects, but many more bodies become 'shit'.[11] So it is through the breaking, transgressing and challenging of boundaries that Jesus accepted the neglected, abused and broken bodies of Pola *la descarada*, Rebequita *la malcriada*, both Simons (Simon Peter and Simon the Leper) with their many *lados* of exclusion, and Nachito *el machito* as the promoters of a new ontology. Bodies that were once understood and treated as 'shit', Jesus calls to become part of his abject kingdom.

The crossing of borders with all their precarious margins comes to a climax during Jesus' passion narrative. By associating with Pola *la descarada*, Simon *el del otro lado,* and Nachito *el machito,* Jesus interrogates the construction of borders, identities, gender, masculinity and wo/men. By

Also, David Rhodes, *Reading Mark: Engaging the Gospel* (Minneapolis: Fortress Press, 2004), pp. 140-75.

9. Kristeva, *Powers of Horror,* p. 85.
10. Broadhead, *Mark,* p. 17.
11. Butler, *Gender Trouble,* p. 182.

entering into an ethic of *descaramiento* with those nobodies, Jesus debunks the idea that borders are 'secure'. Jesus' dubious and abject behavior demonstrates that boundaries can be crossed, confused, consolidated and collapsed. The crossing, confusion and collapsing of borders come to a head when Jesus identifies his own body with the broken bread. For Xavier Pikaza, once the disciples decide to follow and imitate Jesus' way of eating, the borders are erased that once divided and separated, '*hombres y mujeres, puros e impuros, enfermos y sanos, judíos y gentiles. Todos participan de su signo, se hacen cuerpo en Jesús*, 'Men from women, pure from impure, sick people from healthy people, Jews from Gentile. All of them participate in Jesus' sign-act, and thus become bodies in Jesus.'[12] We will see how Jesus' identification with the broken bread somehow proclaims that the boundaries that were set up to define and separate all kind of people are after all merely human constructions, and that these 'boundaries can also be revised, reconceived, redesigned or replaced',[13] by something that Jesus would call the Kingdom of God.

My Body Is Mine and Not Mine, or Take It 'This Is my Body"

I have pointed out that Jesus' way of eating was scandalous in that he shared a meal with people that he was expected to avoid and that he sought solidarity with people of dubious reputation. Jesus as an abject being is redefining the norms of who belongs where and who eats with whom. Scholars who have traced the meal motif in Mark's passion narrative conclude that Mark portrays Jesus as the consummate boundary transgressor.[14] Transgressing, crossing and redefining boundaries in Mark's Gospel seem to be Jesus' modus vivendi; he pursues this revolutionary way of being in order to include in the larger community once again the abject bodies of those who were already socially dead, without any chance of being considered human. In his last two meals, at Bethany and Jerusalem, Jesus presents us with two abject bodies—Pola *la descarada* and Nachito *el machito*—as signs of discipleship. Jesus' fellowship with these abject and degraded bodies provoked some negative feelings toward Jesus by his own male disciples. Yet at his last meal, in a house where a *joto* lives, Jesus would do something even

---

12. Xavier Pikaza, *Pan, casa palabra: La iglesia en Marcos* (Salamanca: Ediciones Sígueme, 1988), p. 385.

13. Robert McRuer, *The Queer Renaissance: Contemporary American Literature and the Reinvention of Lesbian and Gay Identities* (New York: New York University Press, 1997), p. 124.

14. Dietmar Neufeld, 'Jesus' Eating Transgressions and Social Impropriety in the Gospel of Mark: A Social Scientific Approach', *BTB* 30.1 (2000), pp. 15-26 (22).

more bizarre and provocative. He would identify his body with the broken bread.

Jesus arrived at the house where Nachito *el machito* dwells, but for some unknown reason, Mark, or perhaps an editor, removed from the meal not just Nachito and his *cántaro* but also other disciples. Mark abruptly replaced the disciples with the Twelve ('And when evening had come, he came with the Twelve' [Mk 14.17]). This wording might lead us to deprive other wo/men, slaves and children from sharing Jesus' final meal. However, 'the room is μέγα, "large", because Jesus, the Twelve, other disciples (such as the two unnamed disciples who had been sent ahead to make preparations), and women (as we might rightly infer from passages such as Lk. 10.38-42) will be present'.[15] Moreover, scholars have recognized that even though Mark distinguishes to a limited extent between the disciples and the Twelve, narratively the two groups are used similarly.[16] It would be ironic if once Nachito *el machito* had endured the hard work of drawing and carrying water like a woman, and probably helped in the preparation of the room, he would be excluded from the very meal he had prepared. Perhaps Mark is using the figure of the Twelve because they as men are the ones who are struggling to show solidarity and fidelity to both Jesus and Jesus' abject disciples, as I demonstrated in the previous chapters. Myers observes that Mark divides this narrative into two sections, each beginning with 'they were eating' (14.18, 22). 'These two contrasting vignettes portray the lack of, and reassertion of, solidarity between Jesus and his followers.'[17] Pola *la descarada*, Simon *el del otro lado* and Nachito *el machito* have already demonstrated their alliances with Jesus, and Jesus in return has entered into solidarity with those *descarados/as*. Now it is the turn of the Twelve to show if they are really with Jesus or not.

And while they were at the table and eating, Jesus said, 'Truly I say to you, one of you will hand me over, who is eating with me' (Mk 14.18). Betrayal, lack of solidarity and desire for power and privilege had accompanied the Twelve throughout their relationship with Jesus. In Mk 3.13-19 we had been informed that Judas Iscariot was the one who betrayed him. In Chapter 2 we saw how, for Althusser, the subject is formed when it is acknowledged by an authority figure. We briefly mentioned how for Butler someone turns to the voice of the law because the person is guilty of some infraction. Here the Twelve turn to the voice of the teacher, who is dis-

15. Craig A. Evans, *Mark 8:27–16:20* (Nashville, TN: Thomas Nelson, 2001), p. 374.

16. Ernest Best, 'Role of the Disciples in Mark', *NTS* 23 (1977), pp. 377-401. See also Paul L. Danove, *The Rhetoric of Characterization of God, Jesus, and Jesus' Disciple in the Gospel of Mark* (New York: T. & T. Clark, 2005), pp. 90-126.

17. Myers, *Binding the Strong Man*, p. 361.

tressed and anxious because they are guilty. As soon as Jesus, the authority figure, announces to his Twelve that one of them is going to betray him and identifies that one as 'one who is eating with me', the Twelve have in effect been acknowledged or identified by Jesus' announcement and been found guilty! They begin to become distressed and to say to him, one by one, It is not I, is it? (Mk 14.19). In a certain way all of them are guilty! Otherwise why would Jesus be calling out when we were already informed in Mk 3.19 of the identity of the betrayer? Or as Origen would ask, 'Perhaps someone will ask: If the twelve apostles all had clean consciences (that is, if they were all innocent of any act of betrayal against the teacher), why were they "sorrowful" at the news that he would be betrayed, as though it could have been one of them to whom he was referring?'[18] They responded out of guilt or because their consciences told them to do so. The question reflects Mark's picture of the flaws of the Twelve throughout the Gospel; they are never really sure of their own commitment.[19] Jesus' announcement 'evokes grief and protests'.[20] Mark previously had used the word λυπέω ('grief, distress') to describe the failing of the young man who was unable to follow Jesus because he had great wealth (Mk 10.22). Now Mark is using this word for the last time to describe another kind of failure to respond to Jesus' radical call of discipleship. Edwards seems to be right when concluding that in both cases this word describes 'those who fail Jesus'.[21]

But there is more to it than this. For it is not just anyone who is going to betray Jesus; it is one of the 'magnificent' Twelve: 'It is one of the Twelve, who is dipping with me in the bowl' (Mk 14.20). The betrayer is not one of the broader groups of disciples who might be eating with Jesus, but one of the Twelve, one of Jesus' intimate friends. Instead of asking Jesus, 'It is not I, is it?' They should simply admit their guilt, Butler suggests: '"Here I am"—through the appropriation of guilt.'[22] However, for all the time they have spent with Jesus, the Twelve still have a long way to go in learning how to be with Jesus and his abject friends. In the previous chapter we showed how some male disciples were already keeping their distance after they learned that Jesus chose to stay in a house marked by the disease of effeminacy, and that his meals were for all. Here Judas, one of the Twelve, would change his alliances and disrupt the unity of the meal. Instead of becoming one of the community, one of those who ate together and shared their struggles together, Judas would take a different path. After all, meals,

18. Quoted in Simonetti (ed.), *Ancient Christian Commentary*, p. 245.
19. Donahue and Harrington, *The Gospel of Mark*, p. 394.
20. Edwards, *The Gospel according to Mark*, p. 423.
21. Edwards, *The Gospel according to Mark*, p. 423.
22. Butler, *Psychic Life of Power*, p. 107.

in Douglas's words, are 'the line between intimacy and distance'.[23] Soon not just the Twelve but all the disciples would keep their distance from the teacher's scandalous meal by imitating and then following Judas instead of Jesus.

And while they were eating, he took bread, gave praise, broke it and gave it to them and said, 'Take this is my body' (Mk 14.22). Anthropologists have helped us to understand how food is everything! Food marks social differences, boundaries, bonds and contradictions. Eating is an endlessly evolving enactment of gender, family, and community relationship.[24] In the Christian tradition we have become so accustomed to repeating and hearing these Eucharistic words that they have lost their provocative and revolutionary tone. In order to recover their meaning it is necessary to hear them once again in their abject context. Mark repeats these words almost in the same way on three occasions (Mk 6.41; 8.6; 14.22). In these feeding stories, Jesus is moved by compassion and solidarity with the crowd that is in a borderless desert, struggling between life and death. In both instances Jesus demanded of his disciples that they feed the crowd, be in solidarity with it; but the disciples fail to do so. Nonetheless, Jesus gives to the disciples the bread that he had taken, broken and blessed (Mk 6.41; 8.6) in order that they might be fully implicated in the lives of the community. Food sharing creates solidarity, and food scarcity damages the human community and the human spirit.[25] In both feeding stories the disciples have the opportunity to nourish their brothers and sisters, or to diminish their lives by sending them away with an empty stomach.

Jesus, out of compassion for these abject bodies, identifies himself with the bread that can nourish them. It is not clear who the ones are who are supposed to take Jesus' body/bread. καὶ ἔδωκεν αὐτοῖς ('and gave to them'). The personal pronoun αὐτοῖς, which functions as the indirect object of ἔδωκεν, is not specified.[26] Is it the Twelve? It is more likely that the entire community is encouraged to take Jesus' broken and abject body. 'Take it, this is my body.' This saying is terse, lacking the word φάγετε ('eat'), which is found in Mt. 26.26, and the phrase τὸ ὑπὲρ ὑμῶν ('which is for you'), which is found in 1 Cor. 11.24.[27] Butler makes some suggestions why this

23. Mary Douglas, 'Deciphering a Meal', in Carole Counihan and Penny Van Esterik (eds.), *Food and Culture: A Reader* (London: Routledge, 1997), pp. 36-54 (41).

24. Carole Counihand and Penny Van Esterik, "Introduction' in *Food and Culture*, pp. 1-7 (1).

25. Carole Counihand and Penny Van Esterik, "Introduction' in *Food and Culture*, p. 1.

26. Joachim Jeremias, *The Eucharistic Words of Jesus* (trans. Norman Perrin; New York: Charles Scribner's Sons, 1966), p. 177.

27. Yarbro Collins, *Mark*, p. 655.

is so. In the first instance, she says, we cannot claim any autonomy over our bodies without being fully implicated in the lives of others. For her, to be a body is to be given over to others even as a body is emphatically 'one's own body'.[28] The first step to claiming one's autonomy over one's body is through the connectedness to the other. For Butler, 'our' bodies are never an isolated event, they must be intrinsically implicated in the struggles, despairs, anxieties, sufferings, miseries and hopes of *others*. Here Jesus can legitimately claim his body because, as we have seen, he fully implicated himself in the lives of those who were confined to the 'shadowy regions of ontology'.[29]

We stated above how for Butler our bodies can never be fully ours: 'My body is mine and not mine,' she writes.[30] In a certain way, Jesus' body is his and 'it' is not. His broken body belongs to the community that has been with him and has demanded from him solidarity. 'Take it, this is my body' is the most revolutionary statement not just in Mark's Gospel but in the entire Christian Scriptures! It is here that Mark gives us a glimpse of Jesus' identity. We as readers know that Jesus' 'messianic secret' will be fully revealed officially when Jesus confesses that he is the son of the Blessed One (Mk 14.62). However, here Jesus' identity has been unmasked, revealed, taken, blessed, broken and given as a sign of solidarity with those whose precarious lives were threatened by death. Jesus is neither the Messiah nor king whom some male disciples were expecting. He is just a piece of perishable bread whose intention is to give life. The Mexican biblical scholar Carlos Bravo imagined Jesus saying the following words regarding the bread

> *Esto que pasa con el pan es lo que pasa conmigo: seré partido y repartido para dar vida ... Como este pan, jamás he buscado nada para mí; sólo he buscado dar vida. No soy el Rey que esperan, no soy blasfemo, no estoy loco, no soy el mesías guerrero; soy esto: pan que se parte y se reparte. Este pan soy yo,* What is happening to the bread is going to happen to me. I will be both broken and given in order to give life ... Like this bread, I have never sought anything for myself. I have only sought to give life. I am not the King that you expect, I am not a blasphemer, I am not crazy, I am not the warlike Messiah. I am this: bread that is broken and shared. I am this bread.[31]

Mark, by identifying Jesus' body with the broken bread, is announcing all kinds of violence that he will endure, as we are going to see.

28. Butler, *Undoing Gender*, p. 20.
29. Butler used this phrase in an interview to refer to the abject body. See Meijer and Prins, 'How Bodies Come to Matter', pp. 275-86.
30. Butler, *Undoing Gender*, p. 21.
31. Bravo, *Galilea año 30*, p. 146.

By associating his body with the bread, Jesus has started the painful process of abjection. According to Kristeva, we first experience abjection at the point of separation from the mother/father and food. 'I expel myself, I spit myself out, I abject myself.'[32] She notes that abjection represents a revolt against that which gives us our own existence or state of being. This happens because there is no longer a clear demarcation between subject and object or between self and other. Some scholars have pointed out that the exact meaning of 'this is my body' is not clear; 'this is …' language may imply complete identification of the signifier with the thing signified, but does not necessarily do so (see, e.g., Jn 15.1-6).[33] Others strongly affirm that 'Jesus does not mean to say that the bread is literally his body. The sense in Aramaic may have been "this (bread) represents me".'[34] Though we are in no position to resolve this problem, we do well to remember that we are dealing with the symbolic universe of abjectness, where the abject body is, above all, ambiguity![35] By identifying himself with the bread, Jesus threatens the meaning of subject/object. As Kristeva notes, 'It is thus that they see that "I" am in the process of becoming an other at the expense of my own death.'[36] Jesus is giving birth through his giving body/bread to a community of abject disciples. From death emerges life, as Belo notes: every meal confirms for the participants that 'to live means to feed upon death'.[37]

We stated above that Mark deliberately has omitted the word 'to eat'. Thus, the emphasis is not primarily on eating but rather on the disciples' 'taking of the bread'. Francisco Pérez Herrero observes that Mark does not depict Jesus eating from the bread that he just broke and shared.[38] Mark seems to put the emphasis not on the eating but rather on the taking of the bread, through which the disciples are to learn to be in solidarity with other bodies. The meal in Mk 14.22-25 is the third in a series of messianic meals in the Gospel, and all of them are uniform in this detail. For instance, in both stories about feedings, after Jesus had taken the loaves, after he had given thanks to God and had broken the loaves, Jesus 'gave them to his disciples to set before the people' (Mk 6.41; 8.7). For some unknown reason, Mark does not depict Jesus commanding the disciples in the first place 'to eat' in the three meals. Can the disciples eat when there is a hungry crowd expecting some solidarity? The disciples cannot eat the bread if they are not impli-

---

32. Kristeva, *Power of Horror*, p. 3.

33. Marcus, *Mark 8–16*, p. 965.

34. Evans, *Mark 8:27–16:20*, p. 390.

35. Kristeva, *Powers of Horror*, p. 9.

36. Kristeva, *Power of Horror*, p. 3.

37. Belo, *A Materialist Reading*, p. 40.

38. Francisco Pérez Herrero, *Pasión y pascua de Jesús según san Marcos: Del texto a la vida* (Burgos: Imprenta Santos, 2001), p. 93.

cated in the struggles of the community as Jesus had been. For this reason, Jesus offers his straightforward words: 'You give them something to eat' (Mk 6.37). However, the disciples show little concern for the needs of the crowds. The similarities between the feeding stories are remarkable, and yet the settings are quite different. On the one hand, the feeding story in Mark 6 takes place in Jewish territory. On the other hand, the second feeding story happens in Gentile territory. The feeding stories therefore take place on the both sides of the lake, one Jewish and the other Gentile, in Mark's configuration. Jesus feeds both Jews and Gentiles, which indicates the universal scope of his mission.[39] By placing each of the stories in different territories Mark is inviting his community to cross, to transgress, to embrace and to feed both: Jew and Gentile, clean and unclean, men and women; the manly man as well as the effeminate one. Jesus' bread/body, as Belo suggests, is destined to *'lose its center'* (italic in original).[40] Without reference to the phrase 'do this in memory of me' (Lk. 22.19; 1 Cor. 11.24), the community must learn to take Jesus' body/bread that has now become a source of power for bodies subject to a curse.[41] These seem to be some of the obligations and implications that 'the taking' of Jesus' bread/body entails for the Markan community.

In Mark's last meal, Jesus 'took a cup, gave thanks, and gave it to them, and they all drank from it' (Mk 14.23). If we examine carefully Mark's description of Jesus' words and deeds, we notice that Jesus does not order the disciples to drink from it. At the least, we are not informed of this. 'Jesus gave the cup to them.' Once again the emphasis seems to be on taking the cup. I find Wilkinson-Duran's insight helpful: 'Jesus talks about the blood as though it were not drunk, but only spilled.'[42] Once the disciples had the cup in their hands, all of them freely and willingly took the initiative to drink from it. Now they seem to be in a position to accept the cup. The crux now is to understand what kind of symbolism the cup that Jesus gave to them holds. What does the cup mean from Jesus' point of view? What does Jesus require of all those who take freely of the cup? Did the disciples understand the symbolism of the cup? Are they willing to accept the responsibilities that come along with drinking from the cup? The symbolism of the cup had previously appeared in the Gospel (Mk 10.38-39) and referred to Jesus' death. On that occasion Jesus examined the ambition of Zebedee's sons, who were looking for power in the community. Jesus asked them, 'Are you able to drink the cup that I am to drink, or to be baptized with the baptism with which I am baptized?' (Mk 10.45). They

---

39. Senior, *The Passion of Jesus*, p. 75.
40. Belo, *A Materialist Reading*, p. 211.
41. Belo, *A Materialist Reading*, p. 211.
42. Wilkinson-Duran, *The Power of Disorder*, p. 66.

were talking like 'macho men', who endure pain, suffering and privation, but when push comes to shove they behave more like effeminate persons; they fail. They did not know how to take their words 'like a man'. The cup in Mark is always connected with the death of Jesus, and this is confirmed in Gethsemane when Jesus prays to his Father to remove the cup from him (Mk 14.36). Donald Senior notices that in both instances (Mk 10.35-45; 14.22-25) the disciples are invited to share in Jesus' sacrificial death for the world.[43] However, in both instances the disciples fail to be engaged in such a mission. It is striking that, in Mark, Jesus' blood is identified with the wine only after all the disciples had drunk from the cup. By taking and drinking from the cup without 'knowing' exactly what the cup entails, they are like Judas. 'Mark's comment that all of the twelve drank from the cup is undoubtedly connected with Mark's notion that by eating this meal all of the twelve are party to the betrayal of Jesus.'[44]

As soon as the disciples drank from the cup, Jesus identifies his blood of the covenant with the wine. We saw above how, in Mark, Jesus does not command his disciples to eat his body/bread or to drink his blood/wine, as Matthew does: 'Take and eat; this is my body' (Mt. 26.26); 'Drink from it, all of you' (Mt. 26.27). We could say that Mark's Gospel is less cannibalistic than the other Gospels.[45] However, Jesus, identifying the wine with his blood that would be poured out for many, has accomplished his process of total abjection. For Kristeva, most of what is abject centers around the body—blood, excrement, urine, vomit, saliva, filth, waste, pus, body fluids and open wounds, those substances that are disturbing and disgusting because they turn our insides out, dissolving the acceptable boundaries between inner and outer, living and dead, clean and defiled, order and disorder. Jesus' blood soon would be out of order, drawing us 'toward a place where meaning collapses'.[46] Ironically it is Jesus' borderless and 'out-of-place' blood that announces a new order, a new beginning, a new creation for bodies who are suffering violence, exclusion and segregation. Jesus' blood re-appropriates the scene in which Moses sprinkled the Israelites with the sacrificial blood at Mount Sinai, saying, 'This is the blood of the covenant that the LORD has made with you in accordance with all these words' (Exod. 24.8). Jesus' blood has sacrificial connotations. It could be interpreted as an elaboration of the idea of the covenant: the blood is poured out for the benefit of many, with the result that they become members of a

43. Senior, *The Passion of Jesus*, p. 60.

44. Lee E. Klosinski, *Meals in Mark* (PhD diss., Claremont Graduate School, 1988), p. 200.

45. See Albert J. Harrill, 'Cannibalistic Language in the Fourth Gospel and Greco-Roman Polemics of Factionalism (John 6:52-66)', *JBL* 127.1 (2008), pp. 133-58.

46. Kristeva, *Power of Horrors*, p. 2.

renewed covenant with God.[47] In the previous chapter we saw how Jesus was calling his community *to come out* to a new kind of exodus, in order to enter in a new covenant with Jesus and his God. We showed how people like Nachito *el machito* found liberation through his *coming out* in Jesus' new community. Here Jesus' blood is not just for Nachito, but for all of those abject bodies that he has ministered to during his life. Jesus' new covenant is for bodies that are living in a state of perpetual suspension between life and death.

Jesus' broken bread/body and poured-out blood/wine has drawn the community to another reality, to another symbolic universe, where life is expected. We have seen how Jesus' identification with the bread and wine had muddied boundaries, caused confusion and ambiguity, in order to extend some possibilities of recognition to other bodies. Butler succinctly argues, 'Possibility is not a luxury; it is as crucial as bread.'[48] Perhaps it was for this reason that Jesus adopted the symbolism of the bread that is broken but also gives life. When Jesus said, 'This is my body' and 'This is my blood', he is not just accomplishing his abjection at the expense of his own death, but rather he is 'exposing' his body, which implies, brokenness, vulnerability, violence and mortality, that the community might experience life. After all, 'abjection is a resurrection that has gone through death (of the ego). It is an alchemy that transforms death drives into a start of life, of new significance.'[49] Jesus' abject meal had the power to nourish and bind together all kinds of people through the symbolism of the bread and wine. For this reason Jesus is giving up his body, a body that has been fully implicated in the struggles of the community since the beginning of the Gospel.

We opened this section by noting Butler's idea that we cannot in the first instance reclaim any autonomy over our own bodies. For her, the body is 'given over from the start to the world of others, bearing their imprint, formed within the crucible of social life.'[50] This describes perfectly Jesus' new incarnation, a body given for others since the beginning of his ministry. In Jesus' last meal we observed how eating food and drinking wine formed a new table fellowship in which issues of superior/inferior, inclusive/exclusive, men/women, pure/impure, manly/effeminate, slave/free, inside/outside, and decent/indecent no longer seem to count. In Jesus' abject Last Supper, table fellowship symbolizes the establishment of relationships based not so much on conventions of social stratification as on a radically inclusive companionship in which boundaries between people are being broken down. Exclusion from the table implies a lack or loss of status,

47. Yarbro Collins, *Mark*, p. 656.
48. Butler, *Undoing Gender*, p. 29.
49. Kristeva, *Powers of Horror*, p. 15.
50. Butler, *Undoing Gender*, p. 21.

whereas invitation to the table implies reconciliation, that is, full restoration within the community.[51] Unfortunately, there are some male disciples who are not ready to cross boundaries in order to include everyone. Judas is one of those abject characters who instead of showing fidelity, loyalty and solidarity to Jesus shifts his alliances to Jesus' enemies. By betraying Jesus, Judas becomes what Octavio Paz describes as *el chingaquedito,* the one who is 'silent, deceptive, fashioning plots in the shadows, advancing cautiously and then striking with a club'.[52]

Judas el chingaquedito

For Butler the body is not just an abject being, but it is also vulnerable to violence. According to her, it is through the body that notions of gender, sexuality, race and ethnicity become exposed to others, implicated in the social process, inscribed by cultural norms and apprehended in their social meanings. Therefore, the body is both dependent on others and subject to violation by another, by others. 'The body implies mortality, vulnerability, agency: the skin and the flesh expose us to the gaze of others but also to touch and to violence.'[53] Jesus' body is not an exception to this catena of violence that he received during his passion. Jesus' body would be totally exposed to violence during his arrest, trials and finally death. Mark had depicted Jesus as a man in perpetual violence and conflict with himself and with the political, economical, social, and religious institutions that exploited the poor.[54] Those institutions in the end would use their power to kill him. Mark has informed us about Jesus' sentence to death early in the Gospel. In Mk 3.6 we are informed that the Pharisees and the Herodians plotted how to kill Jesus. Since then, Jesus has been fully aware that his actions and teaching have placed him at risk of violent persecution and death (8.31; 9.31; 10.33-34).[55]

In Mark's passion narrative Jesus' body has been surrounded by violence, deception and intrigue not just from the chief priests, Pharisees and scribes but also from his disciples, as we have seen. After Jesus' last meal, he announced that all his disciples would abandon him. This prediction is

---

51. Neufeld, 'Jesus' Eating Transgressions', p. 20.
52. Paz, *Labyrinth of Solitude*, p. 76.
53. Butler, *Undoing Gender*, p. 21.
54. To see how Jesus is a man in conflict with such institutions, see Carlos Bravo, *Jesús, hombre en conflicto*. Also, Jack Dean Kingsbury, *Conflict in Mark* (Minneapolis: Fortress Press, 1992).
55. Michael E. Vine, 'The "Trial Scene" Chronotope in Mark and Jewish Novel', in Geert Van Oyen and Tom Shepherd (eds.), *The Trial and Death of Jesus: Essay on the Passion Narrative in Mark* (Leuven: Peeters, 2006), p. 193.

fulfilled immediately when Jesus' disciples fall asleep instead of keeping watch with him. Mark depicts Jesus confessing, 'My soul is very sad, to the point of death. Stay here and keep awake' (Mk 14.34). In Chapter 1, we affirmed that the act of confessing entails some moral demands on the person who hears one's confession. Here Jesus is demanding solidarity of his best friends (Peter, James and John), but they do not utter a single word in response. As a matter of fact, they did not know what to answer him (Mk 14.40). Mark depicts Jesus praying three times. We know even his personal prayer; we know how he addressed God; we know Jesus' struggles in being faithful to God. Although Mark does not depict Jesus sweating blood as Luke does (Lk. 22.44), nonetheless, for Mark it is clear that Jesus' anguish is real to the point of death. It is striking that during Jesus' prayer, his words did not have any power to 'wake the disciples up' and move them to action. Those disciples who previously had heard Jesus' words, whose words had provoked in them the desire to follow him (Mk 1.18, 20; 10.28), here do not seem to have 'authority' over them at all. However, Jesus' words would hail their enemies, who emerge out of the night, breathing violence toward him.

We are informed that from the time of the arrest, the Markan Jesus speaks only four times: Mk 14.48-49; 14.62; 15.2; 15.34, yet the few times that he does speak become critically important.[56] Mark opens the account of the arrest while 'he was still speaking' (Mk 14.43). Immediately, Mark re-introduces to the audience the abject figure of Judas in the company of a crowd that had been sent by Jesus' enemies. I have been arguing that Judas had previously betrayed Jesus on a different occasion. However, now we are in the 'official betrayal', where the creativity and talent of Mark would bring on stage all the possible characters to witness the encounter between the teacher and his 'beloved' disciple. 'The only persons named are Judas and Jesus, and the arrest is narrated as a fateful and final meeting between them.[57] Surrounded by a night of terror and violence Mark would unmask the figure of Judas *el chingaquedito*.

I argued how, for Butler, we exist through the use of language, but this language can also inflict violence and deny our very existence. 'If language can also threaten its existence',[58] Butler affirms. We had seen how after Pola's *descaramiento*, Judas Iscariot,[59] one of the

---

56. Webb, *Mark at the Threshold*, p. 185. I will argue the contrary, that Jesus is speaking even when he is 'silent'.

57. Edwards, *The Gospel according to Mark*, p. 437.

58. Butler, *Excitable Speech*, p. 5

59. The character of Judas Iscariot is very ambiguous and complicated to understand in Mark's passion narrative. Judas somehow is there at the wrong time, with the wrong people, doing the wrong things. However, the other disciples are not less guilty in Jesus' death. For further information regarding the character of Judas through history,

Twelve, went to the chief priests to betray Jesus to them (Mk 14.10). In that particular moment, Mark did not reveal Judas's exact words; we only know that from that moment on they were looking for an opportunity to kill Jesus. Jesus was injured and wounded through Judas's words by being reduced to an object of conversation. Now, Mark informs us about the injurious language that Judas used against Jesus. 'Now the betrayer had given them a signal, saying: "The one whom I kiss—he is the one. Seize him and lead him away securely"' (Mk 14.44). We have focused so much on Judas's kiss that we have forgotten his previous actions and injurious language toward Jesus' body. We are informed that Judas had given (δίδωμι) a sign to iden-tify Jesus. It is ironic that prior to his arrest, Jesus had willingly given his bread/body to the community. Here Judas is giving, sealing, selling and affirming Jesus' sentence upon Jesus' body. *El beso pertenece a la mayor intimidad entre personas, que no sólo comparte el pan* (cf. 14,18-20) *sino el aliento y vida*, 'The kiss is a symbol of deep intimacy among persons, who not only share bread (cf. 14.18-20) but also breath and life.'[60] I argued above that Jesus, by giving his body/bread, formed an abject community. Judas as an abject member would corroborate Kristeva's notion that 'abjec-tion is immoral, sinister, scheming, and shady: a terror that dissembles, a hatred that smiles, a passion that uses the body for barter instead of inflam-ing it, a debtor who sells you up, a friend who stabs you'.[61] Jesus and Judas are both abject beings, but with different purposes and missions. While Jesus has given his body/bread for sustaining the precarious life of his com-munity, Judas, on the other hand, is giving Jesus' body for violence, which will culminate in Jesus' death.

'Seize him and lead him away securely' (Mk 14.44), Judas said. The verb 'to seize' (κρατέω) in the Synoptics is 'often used of the attempts of the opponents of Jesus to arrest Him, to lay hands on Him, e.g., Mk 12.12; 14.1'.[62] One of the characteristics of a body made abject is the confusion of roles: 'the killer who claims he is a savior'.[63] Judas probably did not claim to be the savior, but he is for sure a killer by his injurious language. Judas as a *chingaquedito* has commanded that Jesus be led away under guard, and the crowd without hesitation 'laid hands on him and seized him' (Mk 14.46). We are not informed why the crowd was so easily manipulated by Judas. It is true that the crowd had been sent by the chief priests, the scribes, and the elders (Mk 14.43), but it is Judas who announces Jesus'

see the exhaustive work of Susan Gubar, *Judas: A Biography* (New York: W.W. Norton, 2009).

60. Pikaza, *Pan, casa palabra*, p. 397.
61. Kristeva, *Power of Horror*, p. 4.
62. W. Michaelis, 'κρατέω', *TDNT*, III, p. 911.
63. Kristeva, *Power of Horror*, p. 4.

arrest. Judas's words are powerful, and he speaks with authority, just as Jesus had spoken in the past (Mk 1.27). Judas's words and actions confirm, as the flyleaf of *Words That Wound* indicates, 'Words, like sticks and stones, can assault; they can injure; and they can exclude.' Some words can, that is, be 'used as weapons to ambush, terrorize, wound, humiliate and degrade'.[64] Judas's words had the power to wound and inflict violence on Jesus. I find it intriguing that Mark depicted Judas first calling Jesus 'Rabbi' and then kissing him. According to M. Aberbach, 'a student was never to refer to his master by name or greet him in a familiar light-hearted manner without the appellation "Rabbi"'.[65] Judas is playing fast and loose with the expected formalities of the greetings. His actions show that he is a devoted pupil of Jesus, but the audience knows that he is a *chingaquedito*. He is 'passing' for something that he is not. The fact that Judas hailed or invoked Jesus as a Rabbi and then kissed him makes perfect sense from a Butlerian point of view. Recall that for Butler, 'language sustains the body not by bringing it into being or feeding it in a literal way; rather, it is by being interpelleted within terms of language that a certain social existence of the body first becomes possible'.[66] Thus, there cannot be a kiss without first the greeting, 'Rabbi!'

By calling out the name 'Rabbi', Judas is not only threatening Jesus' life, but he is also extending some 'possibilities' for his social existence. 'By being called a name, one is also, paradoxically, given a certain possibility for social existence.'[67] Jesus, using his 'linguistic survival' skills, as Butler would say, responded to the violent mob: 'you have come out to seize me with swords and clubs as you would [come out] against a robber' (Mk 14.48). Language has the power to enable social existence and to injure, and in this sense there is a kind of linguistic vulnerability at the heart of subjectivity, but this very vulnerability carries within it the possibility for resistance.[68]

Jesus is not surprised by his arrest. During his life many people had attempted to 'seize him' for different purposes. Even his family attempted to seize him because they considered him to be out of his mind (Mk 3.21). However, he resists and protests the way that his arrest is taking place and

64. Mari J. Matsuda *et al.* (eds.), *Words That Wound: Critical Race Theory, Assaultive Speech, and the First- Amendment* (Boulder, CO: Westview, 1993), p. 1.

65. M. Aberbach, 'The Relation between Master and Disciple in the Talmudic Age', in H.J. Zimmels, J. Rabinnowitz, and I. Finestein (eds.), *Essays Presented to Chief Rabbi Israel Brodie on the Occasion of his Seventieth Birthday* (London: Soncino, 1967), pp. 1-24 (13).

66. Butler, *Excitable Speech*, p. 5.

67. Butler, *Excitable Speech*, p. 2.

68. Gill Jagger, *Judith Butler: Sexual Politics, Social Change and the Power of the Performative* (New York: Routledge, 2008), p. 116.

his identification as a 'robber'. After all, robbers do not have good reputations! Scholars who have studied the character of bandits in ancient novels charge them with a catena of vices such as 'inclined to undisciplined and luxurious "soft" (and thus "feminine") living and unkempt appearance; prone to excessive drinking, insatiable lust, and despair from unrequited same-sex love; practitioners of human sacrifice and cannibalism; and likely to meet an ignoble death'.[69] Perhaps Mark was aware of such vices, and he would depict Jesus attempting to defend his honor and masculinity. 'Jesus is complaining about the manner of his arrest—as if he were really an armed and dangerous man.'[70]

The Greek word ληστής, which Marks uses, can be translated as 'robber', 'brigand', 'rebel' or 'insurrectionist'.[71] Jesus' trial has begun here during his arrest. It is not knowing the charges against him that makes him vulnerable, disoriented and powerless in front of the ones who represent the law. In Butler's words, 'To be addressed injuriously is not only to be open to an unknown future, but not to know the time and place of the injury, and to suffer the disorientation of one's situation as the effect of such speech.'[72] With this injury that Jesus has suffered, Judas had inaugurated Jesus' night of terror. He has been 'framed' as a criminal, as Butler says; and Judas, the mob and the religious leader have found him guilty even before the trial. Butler argues that when an innocent person is framed by a nefarious police force, the innocent person is found guilty. 'If one is "framed", then a "frame" is constructed around one's deed such that one's guilty status becomes the viewer's inevitable conclusion.'[73] Jesus from now on would be treated as a criminal, rebel, effeminate, and insurrectionist; and his crucifixion between two known criminals (Mk 15.27) would publicly confirm his guilt.

Jesus' arrest and trial are a cruel parody because there is no crime to punish, only envy on the part of his enemies (Mk 15.10). Nonetheless, he has been framed as a robber, and the entire judicial and religious system must find him guilty. It does not matter if the ruling priest and the entire council did not find any testimony against him (Mk 14.55), or if the testimonies against Jesus were not in agreement (Mk 14.57), or even worse that Pilate

69. Thurman, 'Looking for a Few Good Men: Mark and Masculinity', in Stephen D. Moore and Janice Capel Anderson (Atlanta: Society of Biblical Literature, 2003), pp. 137-61 (141). In order to understand the role of the unmanliness *bandidos y ladrones* (*lēstai; latrones*), see the remarkable commentaries that Thurman develops in his dissertation entitled *Writing the Nation/Reading the Men: Postcolonial Masculinities in Mark's Gospel and the Ancient Novel* (PhD diss., Drew University, 2010), pp. 100-106.
70. Donahue and Harrington, *The Gospel of Mark*, p. 416.
71. Evans, *Mark 8:27–16:20*, p. 425.
72. Butler, *Excitable Speech*, p. 4.
73. Judith Butler, *Frames of War: When Is Life Grievable?* (New York: Verso, 2009), p. 8.

pointedly asks them, 'What evil has he done?' (Mk 15.14). We, the audience, know that Jesus is innocent; however, he has been framed, and there is no power to unframe him of his supposed guilt. After all, to be framed means 'to be subject to a con, to a tactic by which evidence is orchestrated so to make a false accusation appear true'.[74] During his trial, Jesus is 'invisible'; his body is an object of discussion, and his words and actions have been twisted against him. The high priest asks Jesus a second time if he is indeed the Son of the Blessed One (Mk 14.62), and Jesus authoritatively gives an account of himself. In this connection, Butler notes that we tend to give an account of ourselves only because we are interpellated as beings that are rendered accountable by a system of justice and punishment.[75] Jesus could have remained silent as a way of resisting or calling into question the false charges against him. From Mark's point of view the high priest does not represent God but rather Satan. Joel Marcus notices that the priest's question is reminiscent of earlier Markan pericopes in which the demons shout out Jesus' identity (1.24; 3.11; 5.7), and he concludes, 'The high priest is therefore unmasked by his own question; it is not Jesus who is on the side of Satan, but the high priest and his collaborators.'[76] For some unknown reason Jesus breaks his silence, and decides to expose his identity. He is giving his account only in the face of the priest who directly demanded to know if Jesus is the Messiah. We have seen how, for Butler, prior to judging another we must be in some relation to him or her. 'This relation will ground and inform the ethical judgment we finally do make.'[77] The high priests throughout Mark's Gospel have been described in opposition to Jesus' words and deeds. They have not been in relation to Jesus and his God, but rather they have entered into an alliance with Satan and Pilate. They have not been engaged in an ethic of *descaramiento*, and so the high priest, the Sanhedrin and Pilate used condemnation as the way to inflict violence on the condemned in the name of the law, and do not recognize in the face of the *other* God's voice that utters 'You shall not kill' (Exod. 30.13).

Jesus el descarado *Utters 'You Shall Not Kill'*

We stated above that the body implies mortality, vulnerability and openness to violence. The body is the medium of our relations with other bodies. It is a 'porous boundary, given over to others'.[78] As a consequence, Butler

---

74. Butler, *Frames of War*, p. 11.
75. Butler, *Giving an Account*, p. 10.
76. Marcus, *Mark 8–16*, p. 1017.
77. Butler, *Giving an Account*, p. 45.
78. Butler, *Undoing Gender*, p. 25.

notes, the corpus is not just open to violation by those other bodies, but, as Levinas says, it too can violate: that is, the vulnerability of the other might elicit a violent response from us—we might desire to kill, maim or beat them.[79] After Jesus' confession the high priest tore his garments, and some began to spit on Jesus and to cover his face and to hit him and to say to him, 'Prophesy!' And the attendants received him with slaps (Mk 14.65). Through his confession Jesus had been exposed to others, but instead of finding recognition of his messiahship, he is received by violence. When the high priest affirms, 'You heard the blasphemy. How does it seem to you?' (Mk 14.64), he is instigating everyone to violate and abuse Jesus' body. He is hailing violence, and demands solidarity of all those who heard Jesus' blasphemy. Even the slaves (presumably of the high priest) (cf. v. 54) join in and 'get him with slaps'.[80] Jesus' face is the target of the slaps and spitting, and he is blindfolded. Some members of the Sanhedrin are anticipating Jesus' flogging by the soldiers. It is striking that Matthew omits the blindfold motif from his account. Matthew mentions Jesus' face but not the covering of the face. According to Gundry, Matthew omits the covering not because it was absent from the original text of Mk 14.65 but because Matthew wants to make a clear allusion to Isa. 50.6.[81] We have been showing that Matthew does not appreciate Mark's confusion of gender. Perhaps, the Matthean community knows that victims who were blindfolded were also stripped of their clothing, as I will argue below. Matthew, of course, would not submit Jesus to this kind of sexual humiliation. In Matthew, Jesus can prophesy who hit him because he is not blindfolded. Luke 22.63-64 mentions the blindfolding of Jesus but does not mention his face. For Gundry, the fact that 'Matthew 26.67-68 mentions Jesus' face but not the covering, and Luke 22.63-64 the covering but not his face, favors that the original text of Mark 14.65 mentioned both'.[82] As some scholars remark, the behavior of some members of the council is surprisingly very similar to the behavior of a lynch mob; they abuse the prisoner. 'They spit on his face, punch him, and demand that he prophesy.'[83] Moreover, they are behaving like Gentiles, who, according to Jesus, were supposed to spit on him (Mk 10.34). Mark exposes Jesus' face as the most vulnerable part of his body that is mercilessly exposed to the gaze of others.

In the interpretation that Butler makes of Levinas, the face of the other demands responsibility, and protection. For Levinas, violence is one temp-

79. Lloyd, *Judith Butler*, p. 139.

80. Yarbro Collins, *Mark*, p. 707.

81. Robert H. Gundry, *Mark: A Commentary on his Apology for the Cross* (Grand Rapids: Eerdmans, 1993), p. 918.

82. Gundry, *Mark*, p. 918.

83. Yarbro Collins, *Mark*, p. 702.

tation that a subject may feel in the encounter with the precarious life of the other that is communicated through the face. 'The face, for its part, is inviolable; those eyes, which are absolutely without protection, the most naked part of the human body, nonetheless offer an absolute resistance to possession, an absolute resistance in which the temptation to murder is inscribed.'[84] For Butler there are situations in which responding to the face of the other feels horrible, impossible and where the desire for murderous revenge feels overwhelming.[85] Perhaps these feelings motivated the entire mob to do violence to Jesus' face. They did not recognize in Jesus' face the voice of God that had uttered from the beginning of creation, 'You shall not kill.' In Levinas's words, 'To see a face is already to hear "You shall not kill," and to hear "You shall not kill" is to hear "social justice".'[86] The mob could not resist their murderous intention, and they decided to kill the beloved son (Mk 1.11; 9.7; 12.6). It is ironic that the one who sought justice for all does not find justice for his agonizing body. The religious system had given '"sentence first—verdict afterward", and everyone seems to go along with this mockery of justice, chiming in with a unanimous death sentence'.[87]

Jesus' vulnerable, precarious and naked face receives the worst aggressive violence when he is spat upon by the mob. For Belo, all kind of force and violence is unleashed against the body of Jesus, 'which is defiled by spittle and has blows rained on it'.[88] We need to keep in mind that saliva and all kinds of body fluids out of their proper place are causes of defilement. However, Jesus as an abject body had used his own saliva for healing purposes. This was the interpretation that the church father Cyprian gave us: 'He was even covered with the spittle of his revilers, when, but a short time before, with his own spittle he had cured the eye of the blind man.'[89] There are two healings stories in the Gospel of Mark in which Jesus uses his saliva to restore life. Usually Jesus heals by his words or merely by touching the afflicted body. Yet in the healing of the deaf mute (7.31-37) and of the blind man of Bethsaida (8.22-26) he uses the defiled saliva to bring light/life into these abject bodies. With the deaf mute Jesus puts his finger into the man's ear, spits and touches his tongue (7.33). With the blind man of Bethsaida, Jesus spits on the man's eyes before touching them, and has to make a sec-

84. Emanuel Levinas, *Difficult Freedom: Essays on Judaism* (trans. Seán Hand; Baltimore: Johns Hopkins University Press, 1990), p. 8.

85. Butler, *Giving an Account*, p. 92.

86. Levinas, *Difficult Freedom*, p. 8.

87. Marcus, *Mark 8–16*, p. 1017.

88. Belo, *A Materialist Reading*, p. 220.

89. Quoted in Thomas C. Oden and Christopher A. Hall (eds.), *Ancient Christian Commentary on Scripture: Mark* (Downers Grove, IL: InterVarsity, 1998), pp. 226-27.

ond attempt before the man's sight is fully restored (8.23-25).[90] The spit that had been used previously to cure, to heal and to make visible the face of the blind man is used here to humiliate, to shame and to dehumanize Jesus' face. Jesus' saliva and hands brings light/life to those bodies that he touched. Fatefully, the saliva and hands of Jesus' adversaries bring blindness/death to his abused body.

In the Hebrew Bible to spit upon someone's face is a great insult. In Num. 12.14 we are told how when Miriam was castigated by God with leprosy, Moses interceded before God for her; and God replied to him, 'If her father had spit in her face, would she not have been in disgrace for seven days? Confine her outside the camp for seven days; after that she can be brought back' (Num. 12.14). Moreover, in Deut. 25.9, in a section that deals with the levirate law, the author describes how the community should treat a man who fails in marrying his sister-in-law. 'Then the elders of his town shall summon him and talk to him. If he persists in saying, "I do not want to marry her", his brother's widow shall go up to him in the presence of the elders, take off one of his sandals, spit in his face and say, "This is what is done to the man who will not build up his brother's family line."' Observing that in these verses it is in the transgressor's face that one spits, scholars conclude, 'it is not surprising that some manuscripts of Mark 14.65 read, "And some began to spit in his face."'[91] Others scholars also appeal to the Hebrew Bible to corroborate the shameful aspect of being spat at on one's face. However, they erroneously conclude that 'the abuse is meant not to physically harm Jesus but to shame him (cf. Num. 12.14; Deut. 25.9; Job 30.9-10)'.[92] It is obvious that spit is meant to shame Jesus, but there is no way to separate the shame from the physical violence that Jesus is receiving. To give some idea about how shameful and detestable it was to be spat upon, we note that the Mishnah years later would prohibit spitting on the Temple Mount or in the Temple saying that it is equivalent to spitting into the Lord's eye (*m. Ber.* 62b). Here this angered mob is not just spitting in the most holy place, but they are spitting on the face of the Messiah, the Son of the Blessed One, who demands an ethical response. Sadly, the mob has not shown any respect to Jesus' face through the Gospel. They have not understood Butler's insight

---

90. The use of saliva or spitting in someone's eyes, which the abject Mark vividly describes, was not appealing to the other evangelists, with the exception of Jn 9.6-7. Eric Eve ('Spit on your Eye: The Blind Man of Bethsaida and the Blind Man of Alexandria', *NTS* 54 [2008], pp. 1-17 [2]) correctly observes that 'Luke omits this section of Mark altogether, and to the extent that Matthew can be said to have any parallels to these Markan stories (Matt 9.27-31; 15.30-31)'. Eve finds a parallel between Mk 8.22-26 and Vespasian's use of spittle while healing a blind man at Alexandria.

91. Evans, *Mark 8:27–16:20*, p. 458. Matthew faithfully follows Mark while affirming 'that they spit in his face' (Mt. 26.67; 27.30).

92. Stein, *Mark*, p. 687.

that 'Whatever the Other has done, the Other still makes an ethical demand upon me, has a "face" to which I am obligated to respond.'[93] Once the mob failed to respond to the demands of Jesus' face, they would no doubt cover 'it' as a way to disclaim any further responsibility.

After the 'sentence first—verdict afterward' is passed, some begin to spit on him, and to cover his face, and to strike him and to say to him, 'Prophesy!' (Mk 14.65). Mark does not reveal the identity of the 'someone' who has perpetrated all this violence. Perhaps the 'someone' represented the 'all' who had failed Jesus' face by announcing his deadly sentence. Jesus' blindfold functions as a sort of anti-mask, intended not to prevent others from recognizing him, but to prevent him from recognizing the other.[94] The 'someone' knows that there is power in gazing upon him without being seen. This voyeuristic ritual puts in control the one who gazes over the one who is gazed upon. Gazing upon another without being gazed at is a way in which the Roman emperors gained power and control over their citizens. The one 'who observes without being observed becomes, to an extent, godlike'.[95] For the Greeks, Zeus was figured as that all-seeing enforcer of mortals.[96] Moreover, the involuntary act of covering one's head in the Greco-Roman culture was a brutal humiliation. 'The community might deny personhood to those they shamed by covering or wrapping the head, the focus of one's social being.'[97] Jesus' enemies became 'invisible' and elevated to superior rank. They had power and authority to deny Jesus' identity, because they had gazed upon Jesus; and Jesus is 'unable' to return their gaze. By behaving like a god who sees everything without being seen, the religious authorities are somehow changing their alliance; they become followers of the Gentiles' deities instead of the God whom Jesus represents. Jesus for the first time had *come out* with power as the Son of the Blessed One, the Messiah and the Son of Man, coming out from behind the clouds, from where God sees everything. However, Jesus' personality has been robbed, and he has been deprived of the power to see who is slapping his face.

Butler argues that the encounter with the 'face' and the way in which we respond to violence is the core of what it really means to be human.

93. Butler, *Giving an Account*, p. 91.

94. Wilkinson-Duran, *Power of Disorder*, p. 95.

95. Olivier Hekster, 'Captured in the Gaze of Power, Visibility, Games and Roman Imperial Representation', in Olivier Hekster and Richard Fowler (eds.), *Imaginary Kings: Royal Images in the Ancient Near East, Greece and Rome* (Stuttgart: Steiner, 2005), pp. 156-76 (172).

96. Shadi Bartsch, *The Mirror of the Self: Sexuality, Self Knowledge, and the Gaze in the Early Roman Empire* (Chicago: University of Chicago Press, 2006), p. 134.

97. Carlin Barton, 'Being in the Eyes. Shame and Sight in Ancient Rome', in David Fredrick (ed.), *The Roman Gaze: Vision, Power, and the Body* (Baltimore: Johns Hopkins University Press, 2002), pp. 216-35 (230).

The process of being humanized or dehumanized depends on our response to the vulnerability and precariousness of the *other*. Perhaps Robert Gundry is correct in rejecting O. Böcher's interpretation, which argues that the mob covered the face of Jesus to protect themselves from Jesus' evil eye.[98] Jesus' face has more power than that of a simple evil-eye spell, for Jesus' face has the power to humanize the other. However, the mob passed up the opportunity to become humanized, and it is for this reason that they cover Jesus' face. Jesus' defiled eyes remind them of their murderous act. In the same way that they seized the beloved son, killed him and threw him outside the vineyard (Mk 12.9), in a few hours Jesus would be seized again, and he would be given over to Pilate (Mk 15.1) to be killed outside the city. The mob cannot tolerate Jesus' face, which had acquired new meaning and 'form', still uttering 'You shall not kill.'

In the Greco-Roman culture 'the face' and its expressions, naturally enough, carried great meaning. This symbolic meaning of reciprocity and solidarity was supposed to emerge through the mutual observation of the other's face that goes on during elite gift-exchange in order to assess the value of the gift and the gratitude owed in return.[99] For Butler, 'the face' does not speak in the same sense that the mouth does; 'the face is neither reducible to the mouth nor, indeed, to anything that mouth has to utter'.[100] For this reason, Jesus' 'face' cannot be covered, blindfolded or deprived of the mob's sight. There is no way to cover, deprive or hide Jesus' identity. We have shown how Jesus, by entering into an ethic of *descaramiento* with Pola, Simon, and Nachito, had himself become a *descarado/sin cara*, 'without face'. How can they cover a *descarado's* face when it is no longer reduced or connected to Jesus' body? How can they cover or blindfold a face when Jesus himself had decided to live *sin cara*, 'without a face'? How can they cover a *descarado's* face when Jesus' *descaramientos* are still celebrated by some *descarados/as* disciples that are not there to be controlled, restricted and tortured? What kind of face do they intend to cover? Jesus' physical face? Or Jesus' *descarados* behaviors? Once we displace Jesus' face to another symbolic order, the face of the *other* becomes sacred and demands an ethical response. Jesus' martyred body has become the face that still speaks despite intention of his enemies to maim him, silence him, deface him and kill him.

> The face describes the human back, the craning of the neck, the raising of the shoulder blades like a 'spring'. And these bodily parts, in turn, are said to cry and to sob and to scream, as if they were a face or, rather, a face with

---

98. Gundry, *Mark*, p. 919.
99. Bartsch, *The Mirror of the Self*, p. 123.
100. Judith Butler, *Precarious Life: The Power of Mourning and Violence* (New York: Verso, 2004), p. 133.

a mouth, a throat, or indeed, just a mouth and throat from which vocaliza-
tions emerge that do not settle into words. The face is to be found in the
back and the neck, but it is not quite a face.[101]

It is interesting that as late the seventh century C.E., Isidore of Seville would
derive *vultus,* 'face or expression', from *voluntas,* 'will', because the one
could throw light on the other (*Etymologiae* 11.34.).[102] Unfortunately, the
religious authorities are not willing to read Jesus' face/body that is now
speaking more loudly than ever. It is not through sounds or words, but rather
through his wounded, inflicted and vulnerable body that Jesus continues to
proclaim, 'You shall not kill.'

   Through his new acquisition of the face, Jesus is still seen and heard, but
the mob is both blind and deaf because they have failed to respond both to
Jesus and to God. They do not know how to read, hear and interpret Jesus'
broken body that is still speaking on behalf of God. They have attempted to
hide from Jesus' gaze in order to claim divine inspiration, because in their
minds, they are seeing without being seen. Sadly, they do not realize that
Jesus somehow became God's eyes with the power to see and speak though
his precarious body. By observing that Jesus during his passion is surrounded
by silence (Mk 15.17-19, 22, 23, 29-30, 31-32), some scholars conclude that
'the reader has the impression that Jesus endures every humiliation and pain
inflicted on him in silence'.[103] For others, Jesus during his passion narrative
somehow 'lost his speech', and Jesus, who was the sower, sowing the word
of God, the image of the conquering male master of disciples, in the end had
become like a submissive and silenced woman.[104] Others see in Jesus' silence
the *macho* man who endures pain, suffering and dies with honor.[105] One of
the few scholars who interprets Jesus' silence as a way to resist, engage,
disengage and obstruct the judicial system of both the Sanhedrin and Pilate
correctly argues that 'silence was an uncommon but legitimate defense tactic
in antiquity'.[106] Therefore, it is necessary to read and to interpret Jesus' body
from *otros lados* of communication. Indeed Jesus' face still speaks, prophesying through his broken, abused and naked face/body.

---

   101. Butler, *Precarious Life,* p. 133.
   102. Bartsch, *The Mirror of the Self,* p. 124.
   103. Bas M.F. van Iersel, *Mark. A Reader-Response Commentary* (trans. W.H. Biss-
cheroux; Sheffield: Sheffield Academic Press, 1998), p. 453.
   104. Connolly, *Disorderly Women,* p. 314.
   105. John J. Pilch, 'Death with Honor: The Mediterranean Style Death of Jesus in
Mark', *BTB* 25 (1995), pp. 65-70.
   106. William Sanger Campbell, 'Engagement, Disengagement and Obstruction:
Jesus' Defense Strategies in Mark's Trial and Executions Scenes (14.53-64; 15.1-39)',
JSNT 26.3 (2004), pp. 283-300 (286).

Those who have studied the effect of pain during interrogation and torture have found that pain destroys not just a person's self and world but also
language: 'World, self, and voice are lost, or nearly lost through the intense
pain of torture.'[107] The only language that remains after torture is the fragile
body, which is still speaking though its lacerated and incurable wounds.[108]
Butler, referring to Elaine Scarry's work, argues that one of the injurious
consequences of torture is that the one tortured loses the ability to document
in language the event of torture; thus, torture eradicates its own witness.[109]
Perhaps for this reason, Mark emphatically brings into his political drama
all the witnesses that he can summon to make sure that Jesus' language is
not lost in torture. Jesus has had a long night; he has been disconnected
from his friends and 'blinded' from his enemies; his body has been used as
boxing bag, but his body is still present 'shouting in silence'. David Tombs
in his remarkable study about *desaparecidos/as* ('disappearances') as a tool
of state terror points out how official silence and denials greeted relatives
who tried to find out what had happened to their beloved ones. 'As anxious
enquires were made with the different authorities, the official answer was
invariably the same, *No está aquí, No está aquí* "He/She is not here, He/
She is not here."'[110] Contrary to *los/as desaparecidos/as* of Latin America,
Jesús está aquí, 'Jesus is here', and his face has become 'the vocalization
of agony that is not yet language or no longer language.'[111] Jesus' agony is
a subversive language with power to *come out* as the Messiah and as the
Son of God.

Jesus responds to the high priest with the powerful Ἐγώ εἰμι— although
in this case it is not a claim to his divinity but an affirmation that 'I am
the messiah, the son of the Blessed'.[112] Mark portrays Jesus as replying
'boldly, clearly, and fully to the high priest'.[113] As torture advanced and danger approached, Jesus' ability to speak 'boldly and clearly' becomes more

107. Elaine Scarry, *The Body in Pain. The Making and Unmaking of the World* (New York: Oxford University Press, 1985), p. 35.

108. Human Rights Watch (*They Want Us Exterminated*, p. 1) had reported how many gay men in Iraq who had been exposed to torture had lost the ability to speak. Such is the case of Hamid, 35, who developed a speech impediment from strain and grief after the murder, in April 2009 in Baghdad, of his partner of ten years. In Hamid's words: 'Since then, I've been unable to speak properly. . . . I can't believe I'm here talking to you because it's all just been repressed, repressed, repressed.'

109. Butler, *Excitable Speech*, p. 6.

110. David Tombs, '"He Is Not Here." Disappearance, Death and Denial', in Michael A. Hayes and David Tombs, (eds.), *Truth and Memory: The Church and Human Rights in El Salvador and Guatemala* (Leominster: Gracewing, 2001), pp. 194-210 (199).

111. Butler, *Precarious Life*, p. 139.

112. Yarbro Collins, *Mark*, p. 704.

113. Yarbro Collins, *Mark*, p. 713.

ambiguous. When the tyrant Pilate asked him if he was the king of the Jews, Jesus plainly responded, 'You say so' (Mk 14.2), which is neither a denial nor an affirmation.[114] We showed above how Jesus became the abject messiah through his identification with the bread. Since then, Jesus' identity has become more ambiguous, because he is both the messiah and the king but with different purposes and a different mission to accomplish. For this reason I find appealing Willoughby Charles Allen's argument that Jesus replied ambiguously because 'He claimed to be the Messiah, but in a sense different from any current meaning attached to the title'.[115] Jesus is both Messiah and king but his messiahship and kingship reside not in power or rhetoric but rather in the abjectness of his body that is still speaking on behalf of God who says, 'You shall not kill.'

For Butler, God's voice is represented by the human voice, because it is God who says, through Moses, 'Thou shalt not kill.' 'The face that at once makes me murderous and prohibits me from murder is the one that speaks in a voice that is not its own, speaks in a voice that is not a human voice.'[116] Even though Jesus speaks in a human voice, his voice is not his own: his voice is the voice of the God who protects life. God's voice is heard through the Gospel legitimizing Jesus as the beloved son: 'You are my Son, whom I love; with you I am well pleased' (Mk 1.11). Moreover, God emerges from the cloud to testify that Jesus indeed is the beloved son, and God exhorts the entire community to listen to him: 'This is my Son, whom I love. Listen to him!' (Mk 9.7). Therefore, to hear and read Jesus' face is to hear and obey God's commands. Through the use of irony, Mark depicts Jesus' opponents trying to cover God's face and silence God's voice. Nonetheless, Jesus' face/body makes various utterances at once: 'it bespeaks an agony, an injurability, at the same time that it bespeaks a divine prohibition against killing.'[117]

It is from this vulnerability, abjectness, helplessness and brokenness that Jesus' face must be read and interpreted, and not from the perspective of the powerful and eschatological Messiah. Marcus's great insights into this issue deserve to be quoted in full:

> In the mockers' eyes, Jesus' claim to be the eschatological redeemer and rebuilder of the Temple is vitiated by his present state of helplessness and subjection to their will. For the evangelist and biblically literate reader, however, the echoes of the Suffering Servant passages in Isaiah 50-53 (silence before judge, spitting, slapping) may suggest that this absorption

114. Yarbro Collins, *Mark*, p. 713.

115. W.C. Allen, *The Gospel according to Saint Mark: With Introduction, Notes, and Map* (London: Rivingtons, 1915), p. 182.

116. Butler, *Precarious Life*, p. 135.

117. Butler, *Precarious Life*, p. 135.

of abuse is actually effecting the defeat of the rulers of this world. Jesus, then, is not being vanquished but triumphing in his very humiliation.[118]

Sadly, the angered mob, the blinded religious authorities, the violent Roman soldiers and some unfaithful disciples neither see nor hear Jesus' agonizing voice asking to preserve his life. In this sense, some of Jesus' intimate friends, the religious authorities, as well as the Roman government's soldiers are responsible for Jesus' death, for letting him die alone, for being bound in a murderous act and for asking him to prophesy.

Jesus' face/body resists dying; his face/mouth has still something to communicate; his language has not halted completely; and he is still in a position to 'prophesy' as his adversaries demand. Scholars have noticed that Jesus' being blindfolded and the demand to prophesy are reminiscent of a children's game. The challenge 'to play the prophet' is the relatively simple one of asking Jesus to tell who hit him, as is done in children's games.[119] Unfortunately, in Jesus' game there are no warnings about his enemies who are striking his head. His abusers are not offering any signs by which to be recognized; they act anonymously as a way of avoiding any responsibility for their deeds. 'They hit Jesus without fear of reprisal, in part because he is at their mercy, in part because he cannot see which of them is doing

118. Marcus, *Mark 8–16*, p. 1018.

119. Gerard S. Sloyan, *Jesus on Trial. A Study on the Gospels* (Minneapolis: Fortress Press, 2006), p. 48. Also, Raymond Brown (*The Death of the Messiah: From Gethsemane to the Grave, I* [New York: Doubleday, 1994], p. 574) believes that the 'Marcan phrase about covering the face is quite intelligible in light of a game that would have been known to the readers'. According to the *Encyclopedia Britannica* ('blindman's buff', n.p [accessed 3 November 2009]; online at http://www.britannica.com/EBchecked/topic/69380/blindmans-buff), this kind of game had been played as early as two thousand years ago in Greece. 'The game is variously known in Europe: Italy, *mosca cieca* ('blind fly'); Germany, *Blindekuh* ('blind cow'); Sweden, *blindbock* ('blind buck'); Spain, *gallina ciega* ('blind hen'); and France, *colin-maillard* (named for a medieval fight between a French lord of Louvain [Leuven] and a man named Colin who fought with a mallet and was blinded in the battle). The game blindman's bluff is played in many areas other than Europe, however. For instance, in Papua New Guinea the game is known as *kamu namu*. As a child I remember playing a version of *la gallina ciega*, 'blind hen'. In our games the body of the blind person was in constant movement. We began by spinning around several times and disorienting the blindfolded player. After that, we commanded him/her to *híncate que ya viene el padre, párate que ya pasó*, 'Kneel the priest is coming; get up because the priest has gone.' Then we asked him/her if s/he wanted to hear *ruido o silencio*, 'noise or silence', in order 'to orient' him/her. As soon as s/he chose either one, we gently knocked on his/her head, avoiding being caught by his/her hands. When finally s/he caught one of us, everyone would asked him/her if s/he was able to recognize the person who had knocked on his/her head just by touching and exploring the body. If s/he guesses correctly, the child who hit him/her must take his/her place as the next to be 'blinded'.

the striking. Because he does not know them they feel free to strike, and because they do not know him, they have the impulse to do so.'[120] Moreover, Jesus is not part of the game, but is the game itself. Jesus' face is there mercilessly disoriented, receiving blow after blow.

We have seen how language can injure, disorient and put the person out of context. However, language also provides an opportunity to recognize the person as a human being. When Jesus' abusers ask him to prophesy, they are extending to him some recognition of his humanity; and Jesus, using his 'linguistic survival', would indeed prophesy. They do not want him dead yet, for there is more torture to come. Jesus must demonstrate that in fact he is the true Messiah, able to identify his assailant by smell without seeing him.[121] Through his body and his voice, Jesus is indeed prophesying and fulfilling his previous prophesies (Mk 8.31; 9.31; 10.33-34). 'This is the first instance of mockery that ironically utters the truth, for Jesus' words are being fulfilled even as his opponents speak.'[122] Moreover, Mark, using irony, has depicted Jesus' prophesying practically throughout his passion narrative. In the house of Simon *el del otro lado* Jesus has predicted his burial (14.8), as he has also in the retelling of Pola's anointing of Jesus wherever the gospel is preached (14.9), and in the disciples' meeting with Nachito *el machito* and his *cántaro* (14.13), in Judas's betrayal (14.18), in his own death (14.21), and in the coming of the eschatological banquet (14.25), in the scattering of the disciples (14.27), in his resurrection and meeting with them in Galilee (14.28) and in Peter's denial (14.30). 'Therefore, when Jesus is mocked and challenged to prophesy (14.65), the reader knows full well that Jesus has already prophesied and that his prophecies are all coming to pass.'[123] Yet the blind mob is not willing to accept those kinds of prophecies, which testify against their evil deeds. There is no doubt that Jesus has been accepted as a prophet by the people (Mk 6.15; 8.28; cf. 6.4),[124] but Jesus' prophecy has been moved either by acceptance or rejection through the Gospel. Jesus even speaks of the future coming of false prophets who will perform extraordinary signs and wonders to deceive the chosen ones (Mk 13.22). Ironically, he is the one whose prophecies are found to be illegitimate; he is the one from the chief priest's point of view who is causing division among the community, and thus he is the one who

120. Wilkinson-Duran, *The Power of Disorder*, p. 95.

121. J. Duncan M. Derrett, *Law in the New Testament* (London: Darton, Longman & Todd, 1970), p. 338.

122. Myers, *Binding the Strong Man*, p. 377. See also Mary Ann Tolbert, *Sowing the Gospel: Mark's World in Literary-Historical Perspective* (Minneapolis: Fortress Press, 1989), p. 278.

123. Culpepper, *Mark*, p. 496.

124. Stein, *Mark*, p. 687.

must die. The Temple authorities have found Jesus to be a false prophet, who acts without a mandate from God and keeps people from observing the Torah, the way of life revealed by God to God's people. According to Deut. 13.1-6 and 18.9-22 such a false prophet must be executed.[125] But before he dies, he will be subjected to all kinds of sexual vexations by the Roman authorities.

Conclusion

We have seen in this chapter how Jesus became abject through the continuous transgression and redefinition of boundaries. His scandalous last meal confused the boundaries of what was thought to be proper and acceptable in order that some bodies that were thought 'impossible', 'unintelligible' and unlivable were included in his commensality. Unfortunately, the implication of Jesus' eating with all kinds of *descarados/as* provoked anxiety in Judas, who decided to give him over to the religious authorities. We showed how Judas's injurious language damaged Jesus' precarious body. Instead of receiving Jesus' abject body and becoming bound with him throughout the ethic of *descaramiento,* Judas gave him to the religious authorities, becoming bound to them by a murderous act. The high priests, the scribes and the Pharisees, instead of recognizing in Jesus' face God's voice who uttered, 'You shall not kill', decide to give him over to the Romans authorities, becoming bound to them by a murderous act. Yet it is not my intention to engage in the endless discussion of whom to blame for Jesus' death. My hermeneutics of *el otro lado* allow me to bring to trial all characters that did not recognize God's presence in Jesus' fragile, vulnerable and precarious body. From this perspective, even some of Jesus' male disciples were responsible for Jesus' death for not engaging in an ethic of *descaramiento* and for allowing him to die alone. The religious authorities were responsible for Jesus' death by not recognizing in Jesus' face their own humanity. Now let us turn our attention to the Roman authorities and see how Jesus is reduced to an object, stripped of his humanity and 'penetrated' by the gaze of others. Once Judas and the religious authorities have inflicted violence on Jesus' precarious body, the Romans finish the dirty job of crucifying *al hijo de la Chingada.*

125. Van Iersel, *Mark*, p. 453.

5

LA MUERTE DE UN HIJO DE LA CHINGADA /
THE DEATH OF A SON OF A BITCH

In the previous chapter we saw that in antiquity men established their dominion, power and masculinity through the dynamic of the gaze. The male spectator was located in a position of power, and bodies on display were situated in a position of powerlessness or at least had less power than the spectator. Effeminate men and slaves who were gazed upon became vulnerable, objects and capable of being penetrated by the 'razor sharp eyes'[1] of other manlier men. In this chapter, we will see how Jesus was 'penetrated' and 'fucked' by other men during his trial, crucifixion and death.

Biblical scholar Wilkinson-Duran has argued that 'Mark writes out his message on Jesus' body'.[2] How then do we read Mark's message? Markan scholars such as Tat-siong Benny Liew have shown how Jesus' masculinity in the Gospel of Mark juxtaposes contradictions and is itself eventually self-contradictory.[3] On the one hand, Jesus embodied the idea of being a virile and manly man according to the masculine stereotype of the Greco-Roman world. On the other hand, Mark depicts a contradiction by showing Jesus in total submission to the control of his God-Father. According to Eric Thurman, Mark depicts Jesus in 'unstable masculinity'.[4] Both Liew and Thurman have 'unearthed contradictions, ambiguity, and ambivalence',[5] regarding Jesus' masculinity as it is depicted in Mark's Gospel. Colleen M. Conway more recently states, 'The Markan Jesus is a divinely appointed strong man, critic of Roman 'great ones', noble martyr, but also a passive, emasculated victim who suffers a humiliating death'.[6] My reading *del otro lado* would support the understanding of Jesus as a broken, precarious and

---

1. I am borrowing this phrase from Barton, 'Being in the Eyes', p. 225.
2. Wilkinson-Duran, *The Power Of Disorder,* p. 116.
3. Liew, 'Re-Mark-able Masculinities', p. 129.
4. Eric Thurman, 'Looking for a Few Good Men', p. 160.
5. Colleen M. Conway, *Behold the Man: Jesus and Greco-Roman Masculinity* (Oxford: Oxford University Press, 2008), p. 89.
6. Conway, *Behold the Man,* p. 89.

vulnerable body that suffered all kinds of violence and vexation at the hands of more manly men. After all, it is during the passion narrative that 'Jesus' body is powerless, itself pierced and penetrated, its boundaries transgressed, assailed by thirst and pain, abandoned by God and human being both'.[7] In this chapter, I will demonstrate how Jesus becomes and dies as a *hijo de la Chingada*.

Tie Me Up, Tie Me Down, but Please Do Not Leave Me: Jesus among chingones

We showed in the previous chapter how Jesus was beaten all over his body, how he had been reduced to the status of an object by the will of the religious authorities who had bound him, taken him away and handed him over to Pilate (Mk 15.1). We saw how Judas's words inflicted violence upon Jesus' body while saying, 'Seize him and lead him away securely' (Mk 14.44). Judas's words nonetheless had the power to move Jesus' opponents, including the chief priest, the scribes and the whole Sanhedrin (Mk 8.31; 11.27; 14.43, 53), to inflict violence upon Jesus' exposed body. Judas's words are both illocutionary and perlocutionary[8] at the same time. His words do what they said, and such words produce effects after being uttered. 'Yet this is the first mention of Jesus being bound, though the forcible arrest in 14.46 might have included binding (so Jn 18.12)'.[9] We might speculate that the binding, the blindfold and the torture form part of the repertoire of a crucified body. Marcus finds some similarities between the crucifixion of a Roman soldier in which people 'bind his hands, veil his head, [and] hang him on the tree of shame!' (Cicero *Rubirius* 13), and Jesus' own trial. 'The Markan Jesus' head is veiled (14.65), his hands are bound (15.1), and he is crucified (15.24-25).[10] Moreover, Jesus' opponents not only bound him, they also brought him and handed him over to Pilate. Judas started the process of giving Jesus over (Mk 14.10, 11, 18, 21, 41, 42, 44) as if Jesus were a piece of meat, an expendable torso for purchase—to be sold, given or thrown away. Judas marked and wrote upon Jesus' body Jesus' own destiny and fate. Once Judas opened this floodgate of violence, the high priest, the elders, the scribes and

---

7. Wilkinson-Duran, *The Power Of Disorder*, p. 117.

8. Illocutionary and perlocutionary are two concepts that Butler borrowed from J.L Austin, *How to Do Things with Words* (Cambridge: Harvard University Press, 1975). According to Butler (*Excitable Speech*, p. 3) Austin distinguishes 'illocutionary' from 'perlocutionary' speech acts: the former are speech acts that, in saying do what they say, and do it in the moment of the saying; the latter are speech acts that produce a certain effect as their consequence; by saying something, a certain effect follows.

9. R.T. France, *The Gospel of Mark: A Commentary on the Greek Text* (Grand Rapids: Eerdmans, 2002), p. 627.

10. Marcus, *Mark*, p. 1026.

the whole council would follow Judas's script and would leave their mark of violence on Jesus' malleable body. 'It is as though Jesus is suddenly completely at the disposal of the men of violence, entirely plastic and malleable, as though he is an unresisting register on which any and every mark can be made.'[11] But the religious authorities are not the only ones who will write violence upon Jesus' body, for Pilate will also give Jesus' body over to the soldiers to be flogged and finally to be crucified (Mk 15.15).

Once the soldiers were given Jesus' body by Pilate, they led Jesus into the courtyard, that is, the praetorium, and called together the whole cohort (Mk 15.17). Jesus had already been led several times, and on each of these night tours of the city[12] the violence increased considerably. In Jesus' first guided tour from Gethsemane to Jerusalem (the house of the chief priest) the mob laid hands on him and arrested him (Mk 14.46). On his way from the house of the high priest to outside the praetorium, where Pilate presumably addressed the crowd,[13] Jesus had already been mocked, beaten over all his body, blindfolded and had his face spat upon. From outside the praetorium to inside the courtyard, Jesus would be 'dressed up', crowned with thorns, greeted as a king of the Jews, hit on the head with a reed, spat on (his face?), knelt before in reverence, mocked again, disrobed of the purple cloak, dressed up in his own clothes, and finally guided to his last tour outside of the city where he would be killed (Mk 15.16-20). I have been arguing that Mark gathers together in his passion narrative all kinds of characters to witness the abject Messiah being killed at the hands of the powerful Romans. For T.E. Schmidt the gathering of the whole cohort is meant to evoke the presence of the entire praetorian guard as an imperial triumph.[14]

A few scholars have observed that the soldiers' dressing of Jesus in a purple garment (πορφύρα) (Mk 15.17) implies that Jesus' own clothing was removed.[15] Robert Gundry thinks Jesus was already undressed for the flogging, even though Mark does not mention it. Gundry asks, 'Is he playing down the shame?'[16] David Tombs, comparing Mark, Matthew and John

---

11. Connolly, *Disorderly Women,* p. 323.

12. I learned while working in Ciudad Juarez (border town with the United States) that when someone 'disappeared' in the middle of the night, people often would say that such person was taken on a tour at night 'to see' the city.

13. Culpepper, *Mark,* p. 545. The crux lies in deciding where the Praetorium was located. There are two candidates for the location of the Praetorium of the passion. The first one is the Fortress Antonia, and the second one is the palace of the king. My focus of interest is to show how Jesus' abuses increase from place to place. For the full arguments about these two sites, see Raymond Brown, *Death of the Messiah,* pp. 705-10.

14. See T.E. Schmidt, 'Mark 15.16-32: The Crucifixion Narrative and the Roman Triumphal Procession', *NTS* 41 (1995), pp. 1-18.

15. Yarbro Collins, *Mark,* p. 726.

16. Gundry, *Mark,* p. 942.

with regard to the flogging of Jesus, observes that 'all three present the first act of mockery as the soldiers dressing Jesus in a crown of thorns and a purple cloak (Mark 15.17), purple robe (John 19.2) or scarlet robe (Matthew 27.28). There is no mention of needing to strip him before doing so.'[17] Tombs has exposed Jesus' naked body to the biblical scholars' gaze in order to consider Jesus' sexual humiliation during his trial and crucifixion.

> Based on what the Gospel texts themselves indicate, the sexual element in the abuse is unavoidable. An adult man was stripped naked for flogging, then dressed in an insulting way to be mocked, struck and spat at by a multitude of soldiers before being stripped again (at least in Mark 15.20 and Matthew 27.31) and reclothed for his journey through the city—already too weak to carry his own cross—only to be stripped again (a third time) and displayed to die whilst naked to a mocking crowd. When the textual presentation is stated like this, the sexual element of the abuse becomes clear; the assertion is controversial only in so far as it seems startling in view of usual presentation.[18]

Wilkinson-Duran has accepted Tombs's suggestion, and she notices that 'Luke notably softens this aspect of the crucifixion, but Matthew follows Mark in presenting Jesus' humiliation as sexual, among its others properties.'[19] Have Tombs and Wilkinson-Duran somehow 'clothed' Jesus' body too quickly? Have they too quickly spared us of the dis/pleasure of gazing upon Jesus' naked body?[20] Whatever the case, both scholars have awakened my curiosity to gaze once again upon Jesus' naked body to see if

---

17. David Tombs, 'Crucifixion, State Terror, and Sexual Abuse', *USQR* 53 (1999), p. 102. Actually, Matthew informs us that the soldiers 'stripped' Jesus in order to dresses him with the scarlet robe. W.F. Albright and C.S. Mann (*Matthew: Introduction, Translation and Notes* [New York: Doubleday, 1971], p. 346) inform us that 'some manuscript have the word *endusantes* (clothed him)'. They concluded that 'Jesus would have been stripped already for the flogging'. Why then did Matthew give us this extra information that the soldiers stripped Jesus of his clothes? We have been arguing how Matthew seems to be more 'sensitive' to some issues of 'gender trouble'. For Matthew's community it would have been more shameful to present Jesus already naked walking at night in the company of a battalion of soldiers. Matthew protected Jesus' naked body as much as he could. He allows us to glimpse at Jesus' naked body only when it is needed.

18. Tombs, 'Crucifixion, State Terror', pp. 89-109 (104).

19. Wilkinson-Duran, *The Power of Disorder*, p. 94.

20. Despite their great insight and radical interpretation both prudently seem to conclude that Jesus, after all, was not 'sexually assaulted' or 'raped'. Tombs ('Crucifixion, State Terror', p. 107) concluded: 'Whereas the texts offer clear indications of sexual humiliation, the possibility of sexual assault can only be based on silence and circumstance.' By the same token, Wilkinson-Duran, 'Jesus: A Western Perspective', in Daniel Patte *et al.* (eds.), *Global Bible Commentary* (Nashville, TN: Abingdon, 2004), pp. 246-349 (349), argues that 'there is no mention of rape in the text of the passion in the Gospels, and so no solid ground on which to build this case'.

there were 'other properties' involved in Jesus' sexual humiliation. Tombs seems to suggest that 'something' might happen to Jesus inside the praetorium, but he also concludes that 'The Gospels indicate a high level of public sexual humiliation in the treatment of Jesus, and the closed walls of the praetorium present a disturbing question about what else might have happened inside.'[21]

Gazing and Saying chingaderas
as Mortal Weapons of Sexual Penetration

I have been arguing that a gaze turns a subject into an object, but also that everything depends on the one who does the gazing or is gazed upon. In Mexican culture when a male stares at another male, often his gaze is met by a violent response: *¿Qué me ves güey?*, 'What are you looking at, asshole?'[22] In this dynamic, the one gazing seizes control, power, authority and superiority from the one being gazed upon. And the one who is gazed upon loses not only power or authority, but he is reduced to a sexual object capable of being penetrated. 'The other may experience the male gaze as a violation, a rape; the object of the gaze is no longer another person, but someone to be possessed or disposed of.'[23] A simple gaze between two *macho* men is enough reason to prompt maiming and killing in revenge in some Mexican villages. This is the case of Gabino Barreda,[24] who killed his friend while drinking beer in a remote village of Puebla. When I asked him about the reasons, he plainly confessed, *Lo maté porque me vio como si fuera vieja*, 'I killed him because he gazed upon me as if I were a woman.' He continued, *Primero me quiso emborrachar para después chingarme*, 'First he got me drunk with the purpose of *chingarme*.'[25] When Gabino noticed my incredulity about the motives for his murderous deeds, he added, *El maricón me desnudo con la vista, me empezó a decir chingaderas, hasta que le dije 'te va llevar la Chingada'*, 'The *maricón* undressed me by his gaze; he began to say, "*chingaderas*", until I said to him, "*te va llevar la Chingada*".'[26] Paz's insights are helpful here: 'The macho commits *chingaderas*, that is,

21. Tombs, 'Crucifixion, State Terror', p. 109.
22. Like any other injurious concept *güey* is quite difficult to translate; it depends on the context in which it is used.
23. Phillip Culbertson, 'Designing Men: Reading the Male Body as a Text', *Journal of the Society for Textual Reasoning* 7 (1998) [accessed 13 November 2009]; online at http://etext.virginia.edu/journals/tr/archive/volume7/Culbertson1.html.
24. I heard this story during a confession. I have changed the name and the state where this murder happened.
25. *Chingarme* in this context could either mean 'to fuck' or 'to kill'.
26. *Te va llevar la Chingada* could be translated as 'you are a dead man', or something like that.

unforeseen acts that produce confusion, horror and destruction.'[27] In this story, gazing upon other men and saying *chingaderas* were the reasons why Gabino felt his masculinity was threatened and why he felt as if he had been reduced to a penetrable object, like a woman.

Gazing and saying *chingaderas* are mortal weapons, able to inflict violence on others. In Chapter 1 we affirmed that for Paz the verb *chingar* denotes the desire to penetrate another by force, to inflict violence, to injure and destroy the body of an object by simple acts of saying *chingaderas*. Paz points out that the verb *chingar* has sexual connotations but that it is not a synonym for the sexual act, for 'One may *chingar* a woman without actually possessing her'.[28] Gabino Barreda similarly felt penetrated by his friend's gaze and *chingaderas;* even though his body was intact, he felt dispossessed of his masculinity, degraded and humiliated for being treated, as he perceived, like a woman. In Paz's words, 'The person who suffers this action is passive, inert and open.'[29] In Mexico for instance, in order to protect women from the sexual harassment that they suffer daily, La Asamblea Legislativa approved a decree on 29 January 2008, that punishes *miradas o palabras lascivas*, 'gazes or lascivious words'.[30] This decree has unleashed all kinds of responses because it does not define exactly what constitutes a 'lascivious gaze'. Nonetheless, gazing and saying *chingaderas* upon other bodies have the power to inflict violence and reduce the other to a sexual object. Despite the time and culture that divides the Mexican culture from the Greco-Roman culture, one can find some similarities between them having to do with gazing and having one's body gazed at, and saying *chingaderas*.

The Romans believed that there was force and power in the act of gazing. This idea is attested in Varro's *De lingua latina,* which states, *Video a visu, <id a vi>: qui<n>que enim sensuum maximus in oculis* ('I *see* from *sight*, that is, from *vis*, "force", since it is the strongest of the five senses').[31] Varro derives *video* from *vis*, and then goes on to quote a verse on the Actaeon

---

27. Paz, *Labyrinth of Solitude*, p. 81.
28. Paz, *Labyrinth of Solitude*, p. 77.
29. Paz, *Labyrinth of Solitude*, p. 77.
30. The decree states: 'Toda acción u omisión que amenaza, pone en riesgo o lesiona la libertad, seguridad, integridad y desarrollo psicosexual de la mujer, como miradas o palabras lascivas, hostigamiento, prácticas sexuales no voluntarias, acoso, violación, explotación sexual comercial, trata de personas para la explotación sexual o el uso denigrante de la imagen de la mujer.' See *Ley de acceso de las mujeres a una vida libre de violencia del distrito federal* [accessed 14 November 2009]; available online at http://www.asambleadf.gob.mx/al/pdf/010803000083.pdf.
31. Quoted in David Fredrick, 'Introduction', in David Fredrick (ed.), *The Roman Gaze: Vision, Power, and the Body* (Baltimore, MD: Johns Hopkins University Press, 2002), p. 1.

myth: *Cum illud o<c>uli<s> violavit <is>, qui invidit invidendum* ('When he violates with his eye, who looked upon what ought not to be seen'). Again, 'the link between seeing and force, or violence, is apparent.'[32] David Fredrick argues that Varro associates visual command of the natural world with the power of the male gaze to violate the female body—not surprisingly, since *vis* sometimes 'means violence', 'rape'.[33] Classics scholars have illuminated for us how for the Greco-Roman culture the mere act of gazing involved the entire body or what they called 'the tactile quality of seeing'. Here we find significant differences from our own understanding of vision; theoretically informed or not, most of us do not think of seeing as a tactile phenomenon, and certainly not as an action that physically acts upon the things seen.[34] However, we are dealing with the Greco-Roman world where physical penetration was possible by the 'manly' eyes. '[T]he notion of the erotic penetration of the body by corpuscular bodies entering in through the eyes proves a remarkably consistent ancient paradigm for the working of the gaze upon the soul'[35]—and body, I would add. Some ancient poets, such as Achilles Tatius in his work *Clitophon and Leucippe* in the second century C.E., would find more appealing and attractive the sexual penetration of the body by someone's gaze than by using the actual penis.

> Doing this is more pleasurable than actual consummation. For the eyes, mutually reflecting each other, receive *simulacra* of the body as in mirrors. This outward emanation of beauty, which flows through the eyes into the soul, is a kind of copulation between separated bodies, and it is not far from physical sex. (*Clitophon and Leucippe* 1.9.4-5).[36]

In Mk 15.15 once Pilate had satisfied the crowds by releasing Barabbas, he had Jesus whipped and handed over to be crucified. Scholars agree that the flogging was a preliminary act to crucifixion.[37] The flogging was accompanied by the removal of the clothes

> *Al suplicio de los golpes se añadía la vergüenza de la desnudez, ya que al que iba a ser flagelado se le despojaba previamente de sus vestidos,*

32. Hekster, 'Captured in the Gaze of Power', p. 162. For an overview of the various aspects and meanings of *vis,* see A. Ernout, 'Vis-vires-vis', *Revue de philologie* 28 (1954), pp. 165-97.

33. Fredrick, 'Introduction', in *The Roman Gaze*, p. 2.

34. Bartsch, *The Mirror of the Self: Sexuality*, p. 3.

35. Bartsch, *The Mirror of the Self: Sexuality*, p. 58.

36. Quoted in Bartsch, *The Mirror of the Self: Sexuality*, pp. 57-58. It is in this context that I will understand Jesus' sexual penetration. Although there is not any evidence that he was sexually penetrated, nonetheless, the stigma, dishonor and shame of being penetrated by the gaze in the Greco-Roman culture might be equated with physical sexual penetration.

37. See all the data that Gundry provides on this issue, *Mark*, p. 938.

*quedando tendido en el suelo o siendo atado a un poste o columna pre-
parada para el efecto*, To the torture of the flogging was added the shame
of being naked, because the person who would be flogged was previously
stripped of his clothes. Then he was laid on the ground or he was tied up
to a post or column, which was prepared for such action.[38]

In the Greco-Roman culture there was a strong connection between sexual
activity and literal assaults on the body, such as whipping or beating, for
example.[39] Perhaps for this reason, the evangelists are extremely prudent
about recollecting the scourging of Jesus. 'One word— in the first three
Gospels a simple participle—expresses it. Mark (15.15) and Matthew
(27.26) mention the fact itself. In Luke (23.14, 22) the scourging is only
announced as Pilate's intention, without any mention of its being inflicted.'[40]
Perhaps they want to avoid giving an explanation for Jesus' nakedness in
public. 'It is generally assumed that the scourging was carried out before
the eyes of the people on the public square in front of the praetorium'.[41] For
Simone Légasse, Mk 15.16 is a clear indication that 'Jesus was flogged in
public'.[42] However, in Mark's account, Jesus' body is immediately removed
from both Pilate's gaze and the public's gaze after the flogging and led into
the courtyard. Did Mark know that there was power in gazing and saying
chingaderas in public? Did Mark know that Jesus could be penetrated by
being exposed naked to other men?

But the soldiers were probably not the first ones to gaze on Jesus' penetrable body. They might not have the 'distinction or privilege' of being the first
sexual abusers of Jesus' body. Probably Jesus had already 'lost his virginity'
during his trial before the Sanhedrin and religious authorities. It is possible
that during Jesus' trial before the Sanhedrin, as a part of his humiliation and
abuse, he was deprived of his clothes. Throughout his Gospel, Mark uses
his rhetorical technique of grouping three events for theological purposes.[43]

---

38. Pérez Herrero, *Pasión y Pascua de Jesús*, p. 266.

39. Bartsch, *The Mirror of the Self: Sexuality*, p. 175.

40. Simone Légasse, *The Trial of Jesus* (trans. John Bowden; London: SCM Press, 1997), p. 76.

41. Josef Blinzler, *The Trial of Jesus* (trans. Isabel and Florence McHug; Westmin-ster: Newman Press, 1959), p. 225.

42. Légasse, *The Trial of Jesus*, p. 77.

43. Osvaldo Vena (*Evangelio de Marcos* [Miami: Sociedades Bíblicas Unidas, 2008], p. 5) lists the following triads for theological purposes. Jesus called three times to discipleship (1.16-20; 3.13-19; 6.7-13); Jesus called three intimate friends (5.37; 9.2; 14.33); three times Jesus predicted his passion (8.31; 9.30-32; 10.32-34); three times Jesus visited the Temple (11.11, 15, 27), three times Jesus woke up his disciples at Geth-semane (14.32-42); there are three titles that describe Jesus' relation with God: 'son of Man', 'Christ', and 'Son of God' (14.61-62). Peter denied Jesus three times (14.66-72). There are three women at the cross and then at the tomb (15.40; 16.1). On three

Over the course of his three predictions, Mark is increasing the violence that Jesus suffered. In Mk 8.31-32 Jesus as the Son of Man announces that he must be rejected by the elders, chief priest and the teachers of the law, and that he must be killed. There is not any announcement of any other kind of torture. In Mk 9.31-32, the prediction is almost the same, with the exception that Jesus is going to be betrayed not by the religious authorities but rather by 'men'. Finally in Mk 10.33-34, the author combines the two groups who hand him over, the religious authorities and the Gentiles. It seems that Mark is bonding together these two antagonistic powers through the brokenness and penetrable body of Jesus. Mark has informed us that the Gentiles (not the religious authorities) are the ones who supposedly will mock Jesus, spit on him, flog him and kill him (Mk 10.33-34). Surprisingly, the religious authorities behave more like the Gentiles. They all condemn Jesus as worthy of death (Mk 14.64); they will mock him during his crucifixion (Mk 15.31); and some members of the Sanhedrin will spit on him (Mk 14.65). The only thing that Mark does not report as happening during Jesus' trial with the Sanhedrin is the flogging of Jesus' body. Instead, Mark informs us about the blindfold and the slaps that Jesus suffered. However, scholars have shown that the blindfolding and the flogging typically accompanied the sentence of death. 'Flogging and torture, especially the blinding of eye and the shedding of blood, generally accompanied the sentence.'[44] If such is the case, then Jesus at one time must have been naked in order to be flogged by the religious authorities. At one moment Jesus' genitalia must have been exposed, and at that moment the spectators' glance must have penetrated him as if he were a woman. Jesus' penetration could be accomplished by the 'simple' act of gazing upon his genitalia. In a world where the genitals were the 'shameful' parts of the body, one could violate the body 'only when the veils of shame were torn away (which violation could be accomplished simply by staring at them or speaking of them)'.[45] Jesus was not exempted from degradation, penetration and submission if we understand the implications of the spectators' gaze this way.

Scholars have observed the similarities that exist between the mockery of Jesus by the Sanhedrin and the mockery of the soldiers. Sloyan observes that the theme of the mockery of Jesus occurs in Mark at 14.65 (as a prophet, by certain members of the Sanhedrin); at 15.16-20 (as a king, by Roman soldiers); and at 15.29-32 (as the rebuilder of the Temple, by

occasions three different groups mocked Jesus: the religious leaders (14.65), the soldiers (15.16-20), and three different groups on the cross (15.29-32). Three crosses were erected at Golgotha at the third hour (15.26-27).

44. Jerome Neyrey, 'Despising the Shame of the Cross: Honor and Shame in the Johannine Passion Narrative', *Semeia* 69 (1996), pp. 113-37 (113).

45. Barton, 'Being in the Eyes', p. 218.

passersby; also by chief priest and scribes and those crucified with him). Gerard S. Sloyan unites these mockery motifs by alluding to some Hebrew texts: 'undoubtedly certain biblical passages were influential in the creation of [these] motif[s], in particular Psalm 22.7-8; 69.10-13; Wisdom 2.16-20'.[46] However scholars have paid little attention to the notion that Jesus' penetrable body is actually the motif that connects these mockery stories. It is Jesus' abject body that bonds all kinds of people together. Anthropologist Gayle Rubin, in identifying the nature of structural domination by men over women through the mechanisms of the kinship system, has demonstrated how through the 'exchange of women', men become the 'givers' and women become the 'gifts' that they exchange. Women's bodies are the conduit through which men are linked among themselves in order to maintain their power over women. They become the subjects and women become objects through the trafficking of bodies. 'If it is women who are being transacted, then it is the men who give and take them who are linked, the women being a conduit of a relationship rather than a partner to it.'[47] Using Rubin's idea of the exchange of bodies, we can observe how Jesus' body is the one that creates the link between the religious authorities and the soldiers. Jesus' womanized body has become the perfect conduit to connect violent people.

Michele Connolly uses Jesus' body as the medium by which the soldiers, by abusing Jesus, become bonded together.

> Jesus is denigrated, beaten and spat on, made the sport of men using violence to bond with one another. A reverse male bonding occurs in this scene. These men bond not with Jesus as a leader, eschewing self-indulgent violence, but with one another, over against Jesus.[48]

Moreover, Jesus' penetrable and malleable body bonds together also the chief priest, the Sanhedrin and all those who abused him with slaps, such as the soldiers. It is striking that both groups—religious authorities and Pilate's soldiers—repeated exactly the same kind of behavior toward Jesus' body. On the one hand, Mk 14.65 depicts the mocking of the high priest, the members of the Sanhedrin and some servants spitting upon Jesus' face, blindfolding Jesus' eyes, slapping Jesus' face and concluding the mockery with the demand to prophesy. On the other hand, Mk 15.18 depicts the soldiers' mockery in the following way. They first mocked him by hailing him as 'King of the Jews!', then they struck him on the head and spat on him. Juan

46. Sloyan, *Jesus on Trial*, p. 48.
47. Gayle Rubin, 'The Traffic in Women: Notes on the "Political Economy" of Sex', in Ellen Lewin (ed.), *Feminist Anthropology: A Reader* (Malden, MA: Blackwell, 2006), pp. 87-106 (93).
48. Connolly, *Disorderly Women*, p. 323.

Mateos and Fernando Camacho point out that the mockery of the soldiers is 'inversely' related to Jesus' mockery by the religious authorities. *Aquí en el pretorio, las acciones se desarrollan en orden inverso: comienzan con la burla de la dignidad real y, solamente antes del último homenaje, se intercalan golpes y esputos,* 'Here in the praetorium, the actions are developed in an inverse order: the soldiers began to mock Jesus as if he were a royal dignitary, and only after the last homage, the soldiers began to beat him and spit on him.'[49] Jesus as a 'versatile' body could accommodate all kinds of insults and abuses. It does not matter if the abuse happened at the 'inverse', his malleable body could be used as a medium or conduit to bond two antagonistic forces such as the religious authorities and the Roman authorities. Jesus' inverted body is a gift to be taken by other manlier men.

We have been arguing how Jesus' body might be penetrated by being gazed upon. However, this was not the only way in which a penetration could be accomplished. Classics scholars argue that 'sexual penetration and beating, those two forms of corporeal assault, are in Roman terms structurally equivalent'.[50] J.N. Adams suggest that the verb *futuo,* 'to fuck', may be related to *futo,* which mean 'hit' or 'beat'. He concluded, 'Verbs of striking and the like are often applied metaphorically to the act of the male in intercourse.'[51] In Mk 15.16-20, the sexual humiliation that Jesus suffers is present throughout the pericope. We have already pointed out how Mark seems to indicate that Jesus was naked when the soldiers dressed him in a purple cloak. At that point the soldiers had the opportunity to gaze upon his naked body and penetrate him with their gaze. After crowning him with thorns, they began to say *chingaderas,* such as 'welcome, king of the Jews!' (Mk 15.18). These *chingaderas,* as we have seen, have the power to penetrate, wound or even kill when they are uttered by manlier men. To the humiliation of being treated like an object, now the soldiers add beating Jesus with a reed. In this scene of sexual degradation there are only two 'characters' to gaze upon: the Roman soldiers, who represent the 'impenetrable penetrators',[52] and Jesus, the 'penetrable penetrated' one.

49. Mateos and Camachos, *Evangelio de Marcos,* p. 664.

50. Jonathan Walter, 'Invading the Roman Body: Manliness and Impenetrability in Roman Thought', in Judith P. Hallett and Marilyn B. Skinner (eds.), *Roman Sexualities* (Princeton: Princeton University Press, 1997), pp. 29-43 (39).

51. J.N. Adams, *The Latin Sexual Vocabulary* (Baltimore, MD: Johns Hopkins University Press, 1982), p. 118. See especially pp. 145-49 for the use of expressions of striking or beating as a metaphor for sexual penetration.

52. For Fredrick ('Mapping Penetrability in Late Republican and Early Imperial Rome', in David Fredrick (ed.), *The Roman Gaze: Vision, Power and The Body* [Baltimore: Johns Hopkins University Press, 2002], pp. 236-64 [258]) the 'impenetrable penetrable' occupy the pinnacle of what it means to be a 'real' man. The impenetrable pen-

Paz's understanding of *el chingón* and *la Chingada* might help us to understand the relationship between the soldiers and Jesus. For Paz, the *chingón* is the *macho,* the male; he rips open the *Chingada,* the female, who is pure passivity, defenseless against the exterior world.[53] In our context, the soldiers are *los chingones,* and Jesus is *la Chingada* or *el chingao.* The relationship between them is violent, and it is determined by the cynical power of the first and the impotence of the second.[54] Biblical scholars more or less agree that the soldiers were Greek-speaking men from the eastern province, not Latin-speaking Romans or Italians.[55] Nonetheless, they represent the powerful Roman army, and their mission is to control, to submit and *chingar* anybody who might cause trouble to the empire's interests. The contrast between *los chingones* and *el chingao* is clear. On the one hand, we have the Roman soldiers, who were viewed as a symbol of all that is manly in Roman society and whose bodies were understood as sexually inviolable.[56] On the other hand, we have Jesus' open and wounded body, whose effeminate body is capable of being penetrated.

We have been arguing that in the inability to defend and protect one's body, especially one's 'borders', which are more vulnerable, one becomes like a woman, capable of being penetrated. 'Ocular penetration is, after all, a form of violation of the integrity of bodily boundaries.'[57] Jesus inside the palace is subjected to all kinds of sexual humiliation, for his body has been penetrated at different levels. 'Verbal propositions and pestering, touching, beating, sexual penetration—all are seen as degrading invasions of the personal space of the victim of these assaults.'[58] Jesus has been 'touched', beaten and verbally abused. The soldiers have uttered *chingadera* after *chingadera,* and Jesus is there as a mere object of the soldiers' power. Butler remarks that in the case of sexual torture, a noxious deployment of power, humiliation and sexual freedom is at work. The one who tortures has the freedom and power to inflict violence, and the one who is tortured becomes powerless through the continuous acknowledgement that s/he is a prisoner. 'We embody that freedom, you do not; therefore, we are free to coerce you, and so to exercise our freedom, and you, you will manifest your unfreedom to us, and that spectacle will serve as the visual justification for our

etrators were the emperor, the free men, the elite men, the soldiers. At the bottom of the pyramid we find the most penetrable body, the least important—slaves and foreigners.

53. Paz, *Labyrinth of Solitude,* p. 77.
54. Paz, *Labyrinth of Solitude,* p. 77.
55. Yarbro Collins, *Mark,* p. 724.
56. Walter, 'Invading the Roman Body', p. 40.
57. Bartsch, *The Mirror of the Self: Sexuality,* p. 73.
58. Walter, 'Invading the Roman Body', p. 41.

onslaught against you.'[59] It is obvious that the soldiers had the freedom to punish and inflict violence toward Jesus, and he is just there, disposed, vulnerable, shamed, without even a proper name. Mark does not mention Jesus' name during the soldier's mockery. Jesus only exists through the actions of his abusers.

> *Nótese que en la narración no aparece su nombre; doce veces está designado por un pronombre, siempre como término de una acción ejecutada por los soldados. Jesús se muestra en la escena enteramente pasivo; no opone resistencia a los ultrajes ni expresa protesta alguna,* Notice that during the narration, Jesus' name does not appear. Jesus is named twelve times with a pronoun. This pronoun is always connected with an action performed by the soldiers. Jesus is depicted in this scene as being totally passive. He neither shows any resistance to the mockery nor expresses any kind of protest.[60]

The soldiers embody the freedom to coerce, to do violence, and to deny even Jesus' own identity.

The soldiers as *chingones* have the power to transform the flagellation into a grotesque scene staged for their own amusement.[61] Pilate only orders Jesus to be flogged and to be crucified. However, *los chingones* take the initiative to make a 'drag queen show' out of *el chingao*. 'This is Jesus in drag, dressed in a royal purple cloak with a crown of thorns. He is the subject of laughter and derision, just [like] the transvestite.'[62] In Greco-Roman culture, actors were not considered to be glamorous or fabulous but rather were characterized as being sexual effeminates, as having bodies 'broken' or emasculated (*fracti*) by softness; their gestures in particular were effeminate and indecent.[63] Mark depicts the soldiers, the faithful and obedient servants of the empire, as having the power to present a drag queen show in which Jesus is the main actor. *Marcos presenta a los fieles servidores del imperio como espectadores complacidos del escarnio al impotente rey de los judíos,* 'Mark presents the faithful servants of the empire as satisfied spectators of the mockery of the powerless king of the Jews.'[64] Jesus as the effeminate actor is there, providing his drag show to the avid eyes of the soldiers. We must constantly remind ourselves that in antiquity showing oneself to a crowd of onlookers seems to have been *ipso facto* associated with deviancy and effeminacy. The Roman satirist Juvenal (*Sat.* 2.117-20)

---

59. Butler, *Frames of War*, p.131.
60. Mateos and Camacho, *Evangelio de Marcos*, p. 667.
61. François Bovon, *The Last Days of Jesus* (trans. Kristin Hennessy; Louisville, KY: Westminster John Knox Press, 2006), p. 51.
62. Althaus-Reid, 'Mark', p. 518.
63. Bartsch, *The Mirror of the Self: Sexuality*, p. 153.
64. Mateos and Camacho, *Evangelio de Marcos*, p. 664.

compares the disgrace of a male citizen who acts as a gladiator before a crowd to the disgrace of his being another man's wife: both of these activities represent the breaching of the citizen's body, whether by the eyes or by the phallus, as well as the submissive position of being the provider of pleasure.[65] Jesus had became another man's wife, reduced to nothing, obligated to renounce his own identity. He had been forced to impersonate other bodies, to act and behave as if he were a *chingón*. He is forced to pass for something that he is not. By clothing him with royal garments, greeting him like a king and kneeling before his body, the soldiers are attempting to make a *chingón* out of Jesus, a 'manly emperor'. Jesus had been invested with the 'manly clothes' of the emperor, and he must behave and act as if he were *el gran chingón*.[66] Jesus as impersonator of the emperor cannot behave in a way that endangers or confuses his manliness. 'An emperor who behaved in a way that threatened his manliness could not be tolerated.'[67] However, the audience knows, the reader knows and the soldiers know that everything is a cruel drag parody, because Jesus is not a *chingón* but a *chingao*.

'And when they had mocked him, they took the purple cloak off of him and put his clothes on him' (Mk 15.20). Here Mark reveals both Jesus' identity and his theatrical performance: he is not a *chingón* but a *chingao*, and he is not performing but he is performed upon. This is manifest in the striptease that he is forced to perform in public. Thanks to this change of clothing, Jesus is exposed once again in his penetrable body. For Wilkinson-Duran it seems clear that Jesus was wearing only the purple robe. 'The possibility that the makeshift robe around his shoulders left his genitals exposed adds a whole new note of shame to the spectacle.'[68] Jesus has been reduced to a mere object, 'a toy for crowds and Roman soldiers, so lacking in sovereignty that the very idea of Jesus as sovereign became a joke'.[69] Jesus' body became like that of a puppy,[70] so immature and inhuman that he needs to be dressed and undressed 'like an infant or a doll'.[71] Only the soldiers are not children but *chingones,* 'exerting unlimited power over another man'.[72]

---

65. Bartsch, *The Mirror of the Self: Sexuality*, p. 154.

66. The emperor was seen as the ideal man, full of virtues and manliness. See Conway, *Behold the Man*, pp. 35-66.

67. Matthew Kuefler, *The Manly Eunuch: Masculinity, Gender Ambiguity, and Christian Ideology in Late Antiquity* (Chicago: University of Chicago Press, 2001), p. 89.

68. Wilkinson-Duran, *The Power of Disorder*, p. 96

69. Wilkinson-Duran, *The Power of Disorder*, p. 117.

70. Human Rights Watch (*They Want Us Exterminated*, p. 3) defines 'puppies' as a vilifying slang term of apparently recent vintage; it implies that the men are immature as well as inhuman.

71. Wilkinson-Duran, *The Power of Disorder*, p. 96.

72. Wilkinson-Duran, 'Jesus: A Western Perspective', p. 348.

Mark emphasizes that the soldiers dressed Jesus with his own clothes. A naked body is a vulnerable body. This is so in the most fundamental way. Clothing is inextricably linked with one's personality; 'it has the body's general shape, and it acts in many ways as a second skin, a protective barrier impervious to pain, like hair or toenails, a helpful reinforcement of the body's boundaries'.[73] In antiquity, clothing could raise or reduce someone's personality or status.[74] The soldiers momentarily suspend the drag parody and put Jesus in his place by reminding him that he is not the royal emperor, but a simple victim of their system.

Once the soldiers are satisfied with Jesus' show, they dress him up in his own clothes. Jesus recovers his own clothes/identity, *símbolo de su persona*, 'symbol of his person'.[75] Mark reveals once again that Jesus is not the royal Messiah, the macho man, the *chingón*, but rather the faithful and abject disciple of God. Jesus is not capable of running away naked, as one of his followers had done (Mk 14.51-52), but rather he is docile, waiting to be led out to be crucified, like an abject Messiah. The young man who appeared and disappeared anonymously during Jesus' night of terror—attempting to keep his body intact, inviolable— was punished by Mark by making him anonymous. To be nude it is to be unclassified,[76] and without identity. Contrary to the description of the young man, Mark depicts Jesus with his own clothes/identity, enduring abuse after abuse from the soldiers, exposing his penetrable body as a way to show his personhood. For Butler, one's identity is not imaginable without the permeability of one's border.[77] We have shown how Jesus as an abject body has redefined borders and laws, and now he is experiencing in his own body the permeability and penetrability of the soldier's gaze. He is not walking with *las insignias reales de los gobernantes paganos, que tiranizan a los pueblos* (10.42), 'the royal insignias of the pagan governors who tyrannized the people (10.42)'.[78] But rather, he is walking as a defeated one, a *chingao*, whose penetrable body would reach its climax on the cross.

Then the soldiers 'led him out to crucify him' (Mk 15.20). Walking with his own clothes/identity, bearing the shameful *patibulum* (a heavy wooden bar placed upon his neck) and unable to protect his body: all this is part of the way in which the soldiers establish the political theater of imperial

73. Wilkinson-Duran, *The Power of Disorder*, p. 92.
74. M.E. Vogelzang and W.J. Van Bekkum, 'Meaning and Symbolism of Clothing in Ancient Near East Texts', in H.L.J. Vanstiphout *et al.* (eds.), *Scripta signa vocis* (Groningen: Egbert Forsten, 1986), pp. 265-84 (266).
75. Mateos and Camacho, *Evangelio de Marcos*, p. 668.
76. Wilkinson-Duran, *The Power of Disorder*, p. 92.
77. Butler, *Frames of War*, p. 43.
78. Mateos and Camacho, *Evangelio de Marcos*, p. 668.

triumph. 'The Roman practice of putting its defeated military foes on
parade is well documented (alluded to in the Pauline war of myths, Col.
2.15).'[79] The Romans formed their inferior subjects by exposing them to all
kinds of torture and sexual degradation. Jesus marching with his own identity toward Golgotha reveals his impotence, his total submission. As abject,
he is becoming the 'other' as an outcome of his own suffering, humiliation and death. For Butler, the U.S. empire had produced the 'Arab mind'
through the torture, exposure and shame that the prisoners of Abu Ghraib
and Guantánamo suffered on the basis of their presumptive cultural formation. The U.S. imperial triumph was accomplished when they tortured and
exploited the specific sexual vulnerabilities of these Arab populations. Such
tortures had to do with modesty, taboos on homosexuality and conditions
of public exposure and shame. 'The torture also broke down social codes
of sexual difference, forcing men to wear women's lingerie, and debasing
women through forced nudity.'[80] The Roman soldiers are forming the 'Palestinian mind' with Jesus by exposing him to the gaze of others, breaking social codes and announcing that Jesus' body is capable of penetration. In Greco-Roman society, presenting one's body as a spectacle was
considered to invite not only metaphorical but also physical invasion of
the body.[81] By forcing and exposing Jesus like a *chingao* on his way to
Golgotha, the Roman soldiers promote the triumphalistic propaganda of the
empire. Jesus' public spectacle would conclude with his crucifixion, where
his naked body would be exposed to the gaze of all.

Jesus' Naked and Exposed Body

Scholars usually are somewhat timid in commenting about Jesus' nakedness
during his mockery and also during his crucifixion. When they do provide
a comment regarding Jesus' nakedness, prudence and discretion dominate
their insights and thoughts. They agree that the victims of crucifixion were
scourged and led out naked to be crucified.[82] They probably agree on this
issue because there is no way to ignore the Roman sources, which agree
that people were typically crucified naked.[83] Joel Marcus, after citing some

79. Myers, *Binding the Strong Man*, p. 385.
80. Butler, *Frames of War*, p. 127.
81. Bartsch, *The Mirror of the Self: Sexuality*, p. 155.
82. Stein, *Mark*, p. 708.
83. See Dionysius of Halicarnassus (*Roman Antiquities* 7.69.2), Josephus (*Ant.* 19.270). Artemidorus Daldianus (*Oneirocritica* 2.53) confirms that the Romans usually crucified victims naked. Jerome Neyrey (*Despising the Shame of the Cross*, pp. 113-37) argues that 'The victim's property, normally clothing, was confiscated; hence they were further shamed by being denuded (see Diodorus Siculus 33.15.1).'

examples of people who were led to execution naked, concludes: 'The executions described by these authors, however, took place in Rome; it may be
that in Palestine the Romans avoided nudity, even in condemned prisoners,
out of consideration for Jewish sensibilities.'[84] Other scholars seem to admit
that Jesus indeed was crucified naked, but suggest that he walked wearing his own clothes. 'Jesus' garment will be removed at the cross (v. 24),
but the return of his clothes for the march to Golgotha may have been a
concession to Jewish sensibilities, which found public nakedness offensive
(see *m. Sanh.* 6.3; *Jub.* 3.30-31).'[85] Other more prudish scholars insist that
Jesus neither walked naked nor died naked. 'The victims of crucifixion were
normally hung naked on the cross, and the division of Jesus' clothing suggests this (Melito of Sardis, *On the Pascha* 97), but the fact that Jesus wore
his garments to the place of execution (15.20) may suggest that he was
permitted to wear a loincloth due to Jewish sensibilities (cf. *Acts of Pilate*
10.1).'[86] These scholars seem to draw their insights from Raymond Brown,
who seems to be inclined to favor a 'complete despoliation'. In his own
words, 'I would judge that there is no way to settle the question even if
the evidence favors complete despoliation.'[87] In supporting his argument,
Brown provides several examples in which Jesus is depicted naked. 'In the
late 2d cent. Melito of Sardis (*On the Pasch* 97; SC 123.118) writes of: "his
body naked and not even deemed worthy of a clothing that it might not be
seen. Therefore the heavenly lights turned away and the day darkened in
order that he might be hidden who was denuded upon the cross."'[88] According to Brown, 'Church Fathers like John Chrysostom and Ephraem the Syr-
ian tolerate that view.'[89] If the church fathers were able to 'tolerate' Jesus'
nakedness, who am I to oppose this tradition?

I find it difficult to accept the possibility that the Romans in Palestine
would avoid nudity of the crucified person out of consideration for 'Jewish
sensibilities'.[90] These kinds of interpretations reflect more our dis/pleasure
at gazing upon Jesus' naked body rather than the Romans' ways of showing

84. Marcus, *Mark*, p. 1040.
85. France, *The Gospel of Mark*, 639. Verse 24 does not inform us that Jesus was
naked on the cross. Mark tells us only that they divided his clothes.
86. Stein, *Mark*, p. 712.
87. Brown, *The Death of the Messiah*, 2: 953.
88. Quoted in Brown, *The Death of the Messiah*, 2: 953.
89. Brown, *The Death of the Messiah*, 2: 953. On the same page, Brown states
that there are also a few rare gems from the third and fourth centuries that depict Jesus
naked. Robin M. Jensen ('The Passion in Early Christian Art', p. 56), referring to these
gems, affirms: 'The nudity of Christ may be important in these examples, because it is
otherwise almost unknown in crucifixion iconography.'
90. Roman anti-Semitism has been well documented. In this regard, see J.V.P.D.
Balsdon, *Romans and Aliens* (Chapel Hill: University of North Carolina, 1979). Also,

their mighty power by shaming their victims. Also, these kinds of interpretations seem to suggest that nakedness in public in some way excluded the Jewish people. But unclothing someone in public is still a cause of shame to the one who receives such denigration. For the Roman, 'public nakedness could cause shame (as in Juv. *Sat.* 1.71; Plut. *Roman Questions* 40, *Mor.* 274A)'.[91] Even in the public bath, which was one of the rare sites in which the elite body was disrobed, the vulnerability of being penetrated was a constant threat.[92] Moreover, being exposed to the public gaze of others was a tremendous shame among the Romans. 'There was never a guarantee that one's or another's eyes would not "desoul" one. Toxic shaming occurred any time, any instant, when one sensed that there was not inhabitation in the eye of others, when the eyes of others would violate and consume.'[93] Tacitus tells us that Emperor Tiberius denounced Piso for displaying Germanicus's naked corpse to the public for the crowd to 'handle' or 'violate with their eyes' (*Annales* 3.12).[94] If these observations are correct, why then should the Romans have had some consideration toward the Jews when the Romans did not have any consideration toward their own people? Besides, the Jews themselves did not show any sensibility toward their own people whom they crucified. They even hanged men alive, as if they were things,[95] imitating much of the Romans' practice of crucifixion. In his judicious study about Jewish construction of nakedness in late antiquity, Michael L. Satlow argues that according to the Mishna, 'If the [place of stoning] is further than 4 *amot* from the house of stoning, they give him his garment. They cover a man in front; a woman in both her front and her back. These are the words of Rabbi Yehudah. The sages say: A man is stoned naked, and a woman is not stoned naked (*m. Sanh.* 6.3).'[96] Satlow recognizes that

Molly Whittaker, *Jews & Christians: Greco-Roman Views* (Cambridge: Cambridge University Press, 1984), pp. 3-130, provides full documentation.

91. 'The World Ridicules God's Son'(accessed 4 December 2009); available online at http://www.biblegateway.com/resources/commentaries/IVP-NT/Matt/World-Ridicules-Gods-Son.

92. Bartsch, *The Mirror of the Self: Sexuality*, p. 159.

93. Barton, 'Being in the Eyes', p. 223.

94. Quoted in Bartsch *The Mirror of the Self,* p. 163.

95. Luis Díez Merino ('El suplicio de la cruz en la literatura Judía intertestamental', *Studii Biblici Franciscani Liber Annuus* 26 [1976], pp. 31-120) demonstrated that there is pre-Mishnaic evidence that crucifixion *ante-mortem* was an acceptable penalty for some Jewish groups. He implies that victims were 'hanged' naked.

96. Michael L. Satlow, 'Jewish Construction of Nakedness in Late Antiquity', *JBL* 116 (1997), pp. 429-454 (445). Moreover Josephus (*B.J.* 4.324-25) informs us that when the Idumeans and Zealots took over Jerusalem, they 'displayed' and killed the high priest. Then, they dumped the naked body and prohibited it from being mourned and buried. In Josephus's words, 'Bodies that had lately worn the sacred garment, that had

it is not clear why a man should be stoned naked. 'Of all the four death penalties described in the Mishna, only stoning requires the male culprit to be naked.'[97] What happened to Jewish sensibilities? David W. Chapman, referring to the way in which the Romans shamed their victims, observes, 'A naked man, beaten and ridiculed, hanging for all to see while he slowly dies, his carcass becoming food for birds'.[98] According to Chapman, Jews often imitated these practices. 'Naturally, these perceptions often are mirrored in the Jewish sources.'[99] Moreover, the Romans usually in their territory permitted the crucified to be taken down and buried by their relatives.[100] However, Philo of Alexandria (*In Flaccum* 10 §83) bitterly complains of Flaccus, Roman governor of Egypt, who did not show any sensitivity with respect to the Jews whom he crucified. Flaccus did not allow their relatives to bury the bodies of the crucified persons.

We do not know for sure if Jesus was forced to walk naked from the praetorium to Golgotha. However, in light of the extant literature, it is prudent to conclude that the Roman did not show any special favors to the Jews and that they crucified the abject messiah completely naked, exposed to the gaze of all, as the Gospel of John affirms (Jn 19.23). For Frank J. Matera there is no doubt that 'Jesus dies naked before the view of all'.[101] Xavier Pikaza is more radical when affirming that Jesus dies before the gaze of all, *totalmente desnudo (en rostro y sexo)*, 'totally naked (in face and sex)'.[102] Jesus dies as a *descarado*, exposing not only his face but also his genitalia to gang-banging penetrators. I will follow both Matera's and Pikaza's insight, not because I get any pleasure from gazing upon Jesus' naked body, but rather because it is more plausible that Jesus' nakedness was the way in which the Romans castigated Jesus' unmanly and *descarado* behavior. In Petri Merenlahti's words, 'In terms of the dominant ideology of masculinity, his passion and crucifixion crown his unmanning, as they expose his

presided over cosmic ceremonies and received prostrations from every corner of the globe, were seen naked, thrown out as a carrion for dogs and wild beast.'

97. Satlow, 'Jewish Construction of Nakedness', p. 445. See also Josef Blinzler, 'The Jewish Punishment of Stoning in the New Testament Period', in Ernest Bammel (ed.), *The Trial of Jesus* (Naperville, IL: Alec R. Allenson, 1970), pp. 146-61.

98. David W. Chapman, *Ancient Jewish and Christian Perceptions of Crucifixion* (Tübingen: Mohr Siebeck, 2008), p. 70.

99. Chapman, *Ancient Jewish and Christian Perceptions*, p. 70.

100. Craig A. Evans, 'Jewish Burial Traditions and the Resurrection of Jesus', *JSHJ* 3/2 (2005), pp. 233-48 (241).

101. Frank J. Matera, *Passion Narratives and Gospel Theologies: Interpreting the Synoptics through their Passion Stories* (New York: Paulist Press, 1986), p. 42.

102. Pikaza, *Pan, casa palabra*, p. 408.

inability to protect the boundaries of his body from violation—that is, to keep up his manly status as an "impenetrable penetrator".'[103]

'They brought Jesus to the place called Golgotha (which means the Place of the Skull). Then they offered him wine mixed with myrrh, but he did not take it. And they crucified him. Dividing up his clothes, they cast lots to see what each would get' (Mk 15.22-24). Jesus finally arrived at the place where he would meet his death. He, as an abject body, would die outside the city before everyone's gaze. He was accused of blasphemy (Mk 14.64), and now he would be separated from the house of Israel (Lev. 24.14; Num. 15.35, 36). His body has been cursed, and so he belonged nowhere. Jesus as an abject body dies the shameful death of crucifixion outside the capital city of his people.[104] The public nature of Roman execution shows that one purpose of humiliating the miscreant was to alienate him from his entire social context, so that the spectators, regardless of class, were united in a feeling of moral superiority as they ridiculed the miscreant.[105] So Jesus has been disclaimed by his people and dishonored by the soldiers; he is no longer a Jew or a Roman. Mark has situated him on the border, in the in-between space, *ni de aquí ni de allá*, 'not from here nor from there', but living in the ambiguity of the abjectness. Jesus, who had lived transgressing borders and performing his miracles on the borders, would find his ignominious death outside the city, where abject bodies were relegated.

Mark has been mercilessly accused of being taciturn regarding Jesus' crucifixion. *No se detiene en detalles que sugieran el dolor físico de Jesús*, 'he does not provide any details which might evoke Jesus' physical pain.'[106] Légasse observes that crucifixion is mentioned in the four Gospels without the slightest detail, even in passing, about the one who endured this form of execution. According to him, the 'evangelist felt a horror and disgust'.[107] We as readers hear nothing about the procedure of the crucifixion. 'The story does not say, for instance, whether Jesus was nailed or tied to the cross, and whether his body was fixed to one or two beams.'[108] Ched Myers, after providing us with an intense description of Roman crucifixion, invites

103. Petri Merenlahti, 'Reading Mark for the Pleasure of Fantasy', in J. Harold Ellens and Wayne G. Rollins (eds.), *Psychology and the Bible. A New Way to Read the Scriptures, III* (Westport, CT: Praeger, 2004), pp. 87-104 (98). Cynthia R. Chapman (*The Gendered Language of Warfare in the Israelite-Assyrian Encounter* [Winona Lake, IN: Eisenbrauns, 2004], pp. 26-39) examines in detail representations of nudity in Assyrian reliefs, and she suggests that exposing the enemy was an act of feminization.

104. Matera, *Passion Narrative*, p. 41.

105. K.M. Coleman, 'Fatal Charades: Roman Executions Staged as Mythological Enactments', *Journal of Roman Studies* 80 (1990), pp. 44-73 (47).

106. Mateos and Camacho, *Evangelio de Marcos*, p. 687.

107. Légasse, *The Trial of Jesus*, p. 88.

108. Van Iersel, *Mark*, p. 469.

us 'to appreciate the vivid and terrible image that Mark's simple "and they crucified him" (15.24) would have conjured up for his original audience'.[109] For Marcus it is enough that Mark as well as the other evangelist eschewed the gory particulars of the crucifixion, simply narrating that it occurred and 'leaving the details to the reader's imagination'.[110] Contrary to those opinions, my hermeneutic of *descaramiento* reveals that Mark does not seem to feel 'terror and disgust' by narrating Jesus' crucifixion. Mark has 'overexposed' Jesus' body to all kinds of suffering during the passion narrative, with the result that crucifixion is expected or, as Marcella Althaus-Reid puts it, 'Jesus' life according to Mark is also signed by a multitude of deaths.'[111]

The Crucifixion of a chingao *Messiah*

Cicero argues that 'the very name "cross" should not only be far from the body of the Roman citizen, but also from his thoughts, his eyes, and his ears (*Pro Rabirio* 6.16)'. Mark does not heed Cicero's exhortation. On the contrary, he even seems to take delight and pleasure in overexposing Jesus' penetrable body to our eyes, ears and thoughts without any restrictions whatsoever.[112] For Butler, the photographer who 'captured' the tortured bodies of Abu Ghraib and Guantánamo has the power to build on and augment the events.[113] Mark as a 'photographer' seems to do something similar by naming Jesus' crucifixion twice (Mk 15.24; 15.25) in the same pericope when once would be more than enough. There is no way to omit or ignore the theme of the cross in Mark's passion narrative. As a matter of fact, the pericope of Jesus' crucifixion is marked by the verb crucify, which dominates this scene. Mateos offers us the following chiastic form:

a. v. 24a: *crucifixión de Jesús*/crucifixion of Jesus
   b. v. 24b: *reparto de la ropa de Jesús*/Jesus' clothes are divided
      c. v. 25: *la hora tercia, hora de la crucifixión*/third hour, hour of
         the crucifixion
   b'. v. 26: *la inscripción en la cruz*/the inscription on the cross
a'. v. 27: *crucifixión de dos bandidos*/crucifixion of the two robbers.[114]

---

109. Myers, *Binding the Strong Man*, p. 386.
110. Marcus, *Mark*, p. 1049.
111. Althaus-Reid, *Mark*, p. 520.
112. Merenlahti ('Reading Mark for the Pleasure of Fantasy', p. 91) suggests that the 'manly' Jesus in Mark was created by the community to provide some pleasure and joy. 'In Mark's story, Jesus looks very desirable indeed....'
113. Butler, *Frames of War*, p. 83.
114. Mateos and Camacho, *Evangelio de Marcos*, p. 687.

As we can observe, the verb 'crucify' is found in the beginning, middle and end. Mark does not leave too many details to our imagination.

While Matthew and Luke do not specifically mention the time of Jesus' crucifixion, Mark does indeed note the time of this horrendous crime (Mk 15.25). 'It was the third hour when they crucified him' (Mk 15.25). Mark previously announced Jesus' hour during Jesus' arrest, when he exposed Jesus' body to the gaze of Judas and the mob (Mk 14.41). During the arrest Jesus' enemies were able to inflict violence on Jesus' body because some-how they were protected by the symbolism of the night. They could be 'justified,' he suggests, because they were acting like children of the night. However, Mark moves his audience to a new day, with a new time and with a new hour with the same deadly results. Mark exposes Jesus' body not at night but at day, when everyone who wished might gaze upon Jesus' penetrable body. The time seems to play a pivotal role during Jesus' final spectacle. In Mark's Gospel the third hour was 9:00 A.M. According to John 19.14, 'it was about the sixth hour', that is, noon.[115] Seneca makes it clear that the midday spectacle could be very bloodthirsty: 'I happened to go to one of the lunchtime interludes, expecting there to be some light and witty entertainment, some respite for the purpose of relieving people's eyes of the sight of human blood: far from it' (*Epistulae* 7.3).[116] If John is correct in documenting the time, Jesus' crucifixion would have been witnessed by a great crowd. Perhaps for this reason Mark informs us that 'when the sixth hour had come, darkness fell over the whole land until the ninth hour' (Mk 15.33). Is he attempting to cover Jesus' naked body by the symbolism of the darkness? Anything that we might say about Jesus' time of crucifixion would be merely speculation. The only conclusion that we might draw is that Jesus' body was exposed to the gaze of anyone during the day. Accord-ing to Augustine,

> the Lord was crucified at the third hour by the tongue of the populace, at the sixth hour by the hands of the soldiers. When Pilate took his seat before the tribunal, it was 'about the sixth hour', or early in the sixth hour. When Jesus was nailed to the tree between two thieves, it was the end of the sixth hour. It was between the sixth hour and ninth hour that the sun was obscured and the darkness prevailed, as we have it jointly attested on the authority of the three Evangelist, Matthew, Mark and Luke.[117]

As we can see, all people had plenty of opportunity to gaze and inflict vio-lence on Jesus' body. Seneca informs us, 'In the morning men are thrown to the lions and the bears: but it is to the spectators that they are thrown in

---

115. Evans, *Mark*, p. 503.

116. Quoted in Coleman, 'Fatal Charades', p. 55.

117. Quoted in Oden and Hall, *Ancient Christian Commentary on Scripture: Mark*, p. 233.

the lunch hour' (*Epistulae* 7.4).[118] Mark for some unknown reason is also throwing Jesus' body to the razor sharp eyes of spectators who 'kindly' offered him some wine to relieve his pain.

There are many signs or marks of violence surrounding Jesus' death. For instance, Mark even gives us the two 'cocktail ingredients' that Jesus was offered during his crucifixion. Mark 15.22 reports that Jesus is offered 'wine mixed with myrrh', which Jesus rejects. In Matthew's version, the wine is mixed with gall, but Jesus tasted it and then he refused to drink from it (Mt. 27.34). Again, in Mk 15.26, after Jesus' agonizing scream, someone 'ran, and filled a sponge with wine vinegar'. Scholars agree that these kinds of drinks were given to condemned prisoners in order to reduce the pain of their ordeal.[119] In supporting their arguments, they often quoted Prov. 31.6: 'Give strong drink to the one who is perishing, and wine to those who are bitterly distressed.' The behavior of the Roman soldiers seems to be more in line with the woe of damnation that Habakkuk pronounced against the one who induced the innocent to get drunk in order to gaze upon his naked body. 'Woe to him who gives drink to his neighbors, pouring it from the wineskin till they are drunk, so that he can gaze on their naked bodies' (Hab. 2.15). Recall that I narrated above how Gabino Barreda's friend first got him drunk and then supposedly attempted to penetrate him. Are the soldiers attempting to disinhibit Jesus for their pleasure? Drinking with all its negative connotations might be seen also as a symbol of masculinity and power. Among the Greeks, the Macedonians viewed intemperance as a sign of masculinity and were well known for their drunkenness.[120] The Roman soldiers were also known for their manly practices, which encouraged excessive drinking while playing dice.[121] The effects of drinking might disinhibit drinkers and release their pent-up hostility, leading to verbal and physical attacks. Moreover, the wine might also be used to prepare a person for taking sexual advantage of someone while s/he is intoxicated. However, the Romans soldiers did not need the wine to inflict violence and humiliation on Jesus' body. Nor did Jesus need to be drunk in order to provide a spectacle. He had been totally submissive to the soldiers' gaze, and now he is suspended naked from the cross.

'And they crucified him' (Mk 15.24). Mark situates Jesus' final exposure at Golgotha, whose actual location is a matter of debate.[122] We learned from

118. Quoted in Coleman, 'Fatal Charades', p. 55.

119. Marcus, *Mark*, p. 1049.

120. David J. Hanson, *Preventing Alcohol Abuse: Alcohol, Culture, and Control* (Westport, CT: Praeger, 1995), p. 4.

121. Hanson, *Preventing Alcohol Abuse*, p. 5.

122. See Joan E. Taylor, 'Golgotha: A Reconsideration of the Evidence for the Sites of Jesus' Crucifixion and Burial', *NTS* 44 (1998), pp. 180-203.

the Romans that for exemplary effect crucifixions were held along well-traveled public roadways.[123] This idea is supported by Quintilian's words: 'Whenever we crucify the guilty, the most crowded roads are chosen, where most people can see and be moved by this fear. For penalties relate not so much to retribution as to their exemplary effect.' (*Declamations* 274). Mark seems to be aware of the powerful meaning that a crucified body conveys to his audience and situates Jesus' crucifixion by the road. First he mentions that Simon of Cyrene was 'coming [to the city] from the country' (Mk 15.21). Moreover, Mark informs us that 'those who passed by' hurled insult at Jesus (Mk 15.29). These indications have made some archaeologists conclude that Golgotha was a place to which people had easy access and that it could be seen from afar.[124] Mark needs neither nails to penetrate Jesus nor ropes to hang him from the cross; he needs only viewers to attend the spectacle and take a good look of Jesus' body, which is exposed to everyone's gaze, hanging from or crucified on a tall cross.[125] Some scholars think that the cross of Jesus must also have been higher than the normal cross, because the soldier offered him the sponge soaked in vinegar not by hand but on a reed (Mk 15.36). One can therefore surmise that the feet were at least a yard above the ground. This fact also explains the scornful shouts of the chief priests, 'Let the Christ, the King of Israel, come down now from the cross!' (Mk 15.32).[126] Once Mark leaves Jesus to the gaze of all on a tall cross, he invites all his characters to gaze upon Jesus, whose body is amply exposed in order to provide a great spectacle to all the public.[127]

Here I Am, Gaze at Me

We must be constantly reminded that being for a Roman meant being seen.[128] 'To be at the center of the gaze: at Rome, there was no position more ideologically fraught, more riven with contradictions, more constitutive and

123. Donald G. Kyle, *Spectacle of Death in Ancient Rome* (New York: Routledge, 1998), p. 53.
124. Gibson, *The Final Days of Jesus*, p. 118.
125. For the types of crosses, see John J. Collins, 'The Archeology of the Crucifixion', *CBQ* 1 (1939), pp. 154-59.
126. Blinzler, *The Trial of Jesus*, p. 249.
127. Melito of Sardis (*Peri Pascha* 94), in a sermon given during Easter around the year A.D. 160 and 170, announces that Jesus' death cannot be hidden because it happened in public: 'For if the murder had occurred at night, or if had been slain in a desert place, one might have had recourse to silence. But now, in the middle of the street and in the middle of the city at the middle of the day for all to see, has occurred a just man's unjust murder.' Quoted in Stuart G. Hall, *Melito of Sardis: On Pascha and Fragments* (Oxford: Clarendon Press, 1979), p. 53.
128. Barton, 'Being in the Eyes', p. 220.

destructive of a male civic identity than to be exposed to the power of the eye.'[129] Real men must exhibit themselves without losing their manliness to the 'razor-sharp eyes' of manlier men. This was part of the continuous negotiation that 'real' men must endure day after day in the public space. The stance of honor in Roman art was, as Richard Brilliant has pointed out, the full frontal posture with arm extended. A man made himself as conspicuous, as tender a target as possible, in order to feel the immediacy of his being.[130] Or as Barton put it, 'It was as if the Roman said, "Here I am, come and get me. I am not hiding, go ahead and look . . . if you dare".'[131] Mark seems to be aware of this dynamic and displays his abject Messiah to the razor-sharp eyes of all who want to come and look upon Jesus. Scholars who have studied the role of the public spectacle in Greco-Roman culture have pointed out that the basic requirements for setting a spectacle were 'a person or administrative system to mount the spectacle; a venue equipped with adequate facilities; a supply of persons to be displayed; an approving audience'.[132] Mark, as promoter of his abject Messiah, seems to have the right connections and the right persons to display Jesus' last hour. In the same way that Mark depicted the soldiers as summoning the entire cohort to torture Jesus (Mk 15.16), he is going to bring into his biggest drama all kinds of characters to take a final look at Jesus' penetrable body. Ultimately, the 'act of viewing requires a viewer',[133] and there are some characters who are willing to attend such a morbid spectacle at the cost of Jesus' sexual penetration.

The way in which Jesus would be penetrated is by the mortal weapon of the gaze and the saying of *chingaderas*. Gazing and saying *chingaderas* dominate the entire spectacle of Jesus' death. The first ones who gaze upon Jesus' naked body are the soldiers, who after dividing Jesus' garments sit down to play dice and 'see who gets what'. Some scholars have noticed that there are a few lesser manuscripts of Mark that read, 'and they watched him'. For C.S. Mann this detail certainly makes more sense than the repeated phrase 'they crucified him'. Mann concluded, 'It is tempting to think that originally there was here a statement similar to Matthew's "and they watched him there"'.[134] I had been arguing how Matthew wanted to

129. Bartsch, *The Mirror of the Self: Sexuality*, p. 115.

130. See Richard Brilliant, *Gesture and Rank in Roman Art: The Use of Gestures to Denote Status in Roman Sculpture and Coinage* (New Haven, CT: Academy, 1963).

131. Barton, 'Being in the Eyes', p. 220.

132. Coleman, 'Fatal Charades', pp. 49-50.

133. Alison R. Sharrock, 'Looking at Looking. Can you Resist a Reading?' in David Fredrick (ed.), *The Roman Gaze: Vision, Power, and the Body* (Baltimore: Johns Hopkins University Press, 2002), pp. 265-95 (265).

134. C.S. Mann, *Mark. A New Translation with Introduction and Commentary* (Garden City: Doubleday, 1986), p. 646.

keep the gender roles in their assigned places. However, in this scene, he surprisingly informs us that the soldiers, after dividing Jesus' garments, sat down and 'they kept watch over him there' (Mt. 27.26). Once the soldiers had the distinction and privilege of being the first to gaze upon Jesus' naked body during Jesus' crucifixion, everyone would be welcome to participate in the orgy of the gaze. It is striking that even the robbers who were exposed, sharing Jesus' cruel fate, die in a more honorable way than Jesus.

The robbers participate in a kind of *ménage à trois* sexual encounter, 'one on his right and the other on his left' (Mk 15.27), with Jesus in the middle (Jn 19.18). According to the Mishnah, it was not permissible to execute two criminals on the same day (*m. Sanh.* 6.4), 'but even if this law were binding on the Jews of that time, it definitely did not apply to the Romans'.[135] It is striking that, in Mark's Gospel, Jesus is in some way related to or part of the company of the ambiguous robbers who were not just 'outlaws' but also 'gender outlaws' in the eyes of the manly elite.[136] Mark narrates how people preferred Barabbas, an insurrectionist who had committed murder in the uprising (Mk 15.7) rather than Jesus, the true 'Son of Abba'. He has disposed of his identity, and now he is passing for something that he is not. Moreover, some manuscripts add, probably under the influence of Lk. 23.37, what had been traditionally counted as Mk 15.28, 'And the scripture was fulfilled that says, "And he was counted among the lawless."' But this is not Mark's usual way of referring to scripture, and the best manuscripts do not contain this verse.[137] Craig Evans affirms that the rebels revile Jesus out of 'their fear and anguish',[138] which seems to be obvious because of the dehumanizing death that they are experiencing. However, we are not informed about the robber's trial, mockery, or about the crime that they committed. They had neither been exposed to the public gaze nor flogged as Jesus had been. Mark displays the bandits as being in much better shape than Jesus. These bandits even apparently had the courage and boldness to speak and die as 'real men', not as effeminate ones.

We have argued how speech is a way to prove one's manliness and power. One would perhaps expect a crucified person who has already been reduced to nothingness, who was being deprived of his very humanity, at least to have the opportunity to voice his grievances during his death, a voice to demonstrate that he indeed was dying as a 'hero', as a manly man. Yet even this basic 'human right' was sometimes denied him by cutting out

---

135. Blinzler, *The Trial of Jesus*, p. 253. This corroborates my argument that the Romans did not have any special sensitivity or sensibility toward the Jews in matters of crucifixion.

136. Thurman, 'Looking for a Few Good Men', p. 141.

137. Donahue and Harrington, *The Gospel of Mark*, p. 443.

138. Evans, *Mark 8:27–16:20*, p. 506.

the tongue of a crucified person so that he could no longer utter words or give evidence.[139] Surprisingly, Mark depicts the bandits uttering vociferous complaints against Jesus. The verb that Mark uses in this scene is ὀνειδίζειν, which conveys several meanings such as 'to upbraid, scold, revile, bring reproaches against someone, lay something to a person's charge, raise a complaint against something'.[140] This verb appears also in the inauthentic Markan ending (Mk 16.14), where Jesus reproaches the disciples for their unbelief and hardness of heart. Masculinity was defended even during the crucifixion. Jesus' tongue was not cut out, but his silence indicates that he is incapable of demonstrating his manliness. Jesus' body cannot escape from the robbers' sharp gazes and tongues. They are the ones who even in their 'fear and anguish' utter *chingaderas* toward Jesus. Mark depicts those crucified with Jesus as insulting him (Mk 15.32), and in this way they prove that they are manlier than Jesus, who says nothing. In Mark there is no dialogue between Jesus and the robbers; neither does he promise one of them that he will enter into paradise (Lk. 23.40-43). During the arrest, Jesus attempted to defend his masculinity by refusing to be classified as a robber, but now he is speechless, helpless under the gaze of those lustful bandits who accompany him even to death.

There are other characters who also gaze upon Jesus, such as some who passed by (Mk 15.29), the chief priest and the teachers of the law (Mk 15.31-32), some of those who were near to Jesus (Mk 15.35), and someone who ran and offered Jesus his second cocktail (Mk 15.36). These characters have already appeared during Jesus' trial, accusing him more or less of the same charges (his harsh critique against the Temple and passing for the Messiah). C.G. Montefiore strongly argues that the taunts of the priests and scribes are unhistorical and absurd, because they do not befit the priests and scribes. 'They would hardly have come out on purpose to feast their eyes upon the spectacle of their enemy upon the cross. This kind of thing befits the officers of the Inquisition rather than the members of the Sanhedrin.'[141] We have shown how the religious authorities, the mob and some of Jesus' male disciples have become bound together in a murderous act. All of them must be held accountable in Jesus' death for being incapable of reading the face of Jesus, who uttered, 'You shall not kill.' As Levinas says, 'The face is the other who asks me not to let him die alone, as if to do so were to become

139. Wenhua Shi, *Paul's Message of the Cross and Body Language* (Tübingen: Mohr Siebeck, 2008), p. 31. Cicero (*Pro Cluentio* 187) actually cites a case where a slave by the name of Strato was crucified and his tongue was cut off. While not objecting to the crucifixion itself, Cicero nonetheless objects strongly to the cutting off of a slave's tongue.

140. J. Schneider, 'ὀνειδίζω', *TDNT,* IV, pp. 238-42.

141. Montefiore, *The Synoptic Gospel,* p. 382.

an accomplice in his death.'[142] Once the priest and the scribes became the 'inquisitors', it would be possible for them to 'feast their eyes' on Jesus' naked body. Carlin Barton provocatively informs us that 'The uninhibited gaze did more than violate, it cannibalized'.[143] This concept is corroborated by the wicked Vitellius, who, after killing his enemy, 'was even heard to utter a most brutal speech, in which ... he boasted that he had feasted his eyes on the spectacle of his enemy's death' (Tacitus *Historiae* 3.39).[144] Vitellius's gaze and the joke motif find echoes in the behavior of the priests and the scribes, whose *chingaderas* challenge Jesus' previous words. Yet, the religious authorities were not supposed to greet or engage in any 'theological discussion' with a naked man;[145] the chief priests and the teachers of the law placed themselves in front of Jesus' naked body and challenged him to come down now from the cross so that 'we may see and believe' (Mk 15.32). Through the use of irony Mark is demonstrating that they indeed are blind for behaving and simply imitating Roman practices rather than taking the initiative to cover the nakedness of a fellow Israelite. We saw in Chapter 2 how the male Israelites in (essence) were supposed to be responsible for one another; here, however, they are imitating the behavior of the Gentiles rather than assisting a fellow Israelite who is in great need. By gazing upon Jesus' naked body and taunting *chingaderas* after *chingaderas* they participate in the Romans' macabre fiesta, in which Jesus' broken bread/body has been consummated without any positive results. 'The uninhibited gaze made every Thou an It, something one could consume, something one could destroy with impunity and without regret.'[146]

Mark closes the spectacle by describing the gazing of some women who were watching from a distance (Mk 15.40), and many other women who come up from Jerusalem (Mk 15.41). Mark does not leave out anyone from this public gaze; not even the faithful women are deprived of gazing upon their beloved rabbi. Mark knows that his spectacle needs spectators. We are accustomed to think of men as the active penetrators and women as the passive ones being penetrated, 'but in ancient Rome (as with all cultures that feared the evil eye), women could violate with as much damage to the

---

142. Emmanuel Levinas, "Dialogue with Emmanuel Levinas,' in Richard A. Cohen (ed.), *Face to Face with Levinas* (Albany: State University of New York, 1986), pp. 13-34 (p. 24).

143. Barton, 'Being in the Eyes', p. 225.

144. According to Cicero (*In Verrem* 2.5.26.65), the seafaring Syracusans 'longed to feast their eyes and satisfy their souls' with the torture and execution of Verres' captured pirates.

145. Satlow, 'Jewish Construction of Nakedness', p. 435.

146. Barton, "Being in the Eyes', p. 225.

spirit as men'.[147] Yet in this dramatic scene, the women have other intentions: their gaze is not intended to penetrate Jesus' broken body or to feast their eyes on him, but rather it is a way of being in full solidarity with a *descarado* who has accepted them as a part of his community. The gaze in Greco-Roman culture was not only understood as the penetration or judgment of the other, but as a metaphor for 'our ability to see the divine in ourselves by seeing the divine in others'.[148] These women are also bound by an ethic of *descaramiento,* like Pola *la descarada,* who had seen in Jesus' abject body his divinity. Yet not everyone understands these events in this way. Mark informs us that Jesus' female disciples where gazing from a distance; Robert H. Gundry interprets this as meaning that 'Mark may mention the distance to protect Jesus' ñakedness (cf. v 24b) from close observation by the opposite sex'.[149] Thus, they are not part of this cruel fiesta during which Jesus' body has been consumed and destroyed without any remorse. These faithful women do not share the same space as those who feasted by gazing upon Jesus' genitalia. Furthermore, it is not clear from the text what or who is the object of the women's gaze. So why are they there? Josef Blinzler cites a tradition about respected women of Jerusalem giving a narcotic drink to those condemned to death in order to reduce the pain of the crucified person. Blinzler argues that Jesus was offered this narcotic 'presumably by Jewish women and not by the Romans soldiers for it was, as we have seen, a Jewish custom'.[150] This interpretation somehow resolves the enigmatic presence of the women during Jesus' death. Unfortunately, though, the women are not from Jerusalem, the murderous city; but rather they had followed Jesus from Galilee and cared for his needs. Despite this, Mark does not in fact depict the women as providing the wine mixed with myrrh: the soldiers do so. These women belong to another fiesta, a fiesta in which Jesus' bread/body was freely given for a hungry crowd, not out of pleasure, but rather out of love and compassion.

These women neither approach to take a close look at Jesus' naked body nor utter a single word, and it is possible that they are also victims of the soldiers and religious authorities because of their association with Jesus. The women's powerlessness and silence mirror Jesus' silence and powerless. We have argued that those who are bound by an ethic of *descaramiento* share the same fate and destiny through their bodies. Mark informs us neither that the soldiers forced the women to gaze upon Jesus' naked body nor

147. Barton, 'Being in the Eyes', p. 224. See also Jennifer Glancy, 'The Mistress of the Gaze: Masculinity, Slavery, and Representation', in Alice Bach (ed.), *Biblical Glamour and Hollywood Glitz* (Atlanta: Scholars Press, 1996), pp. 127-45.

148. Bartsch, *The Mirror of Self,* p. 3.

149. Gundry, *Mark,* p. 951.

150. Blinzler, *The Trial of Jesus,* p. 253.

that Jesus was forced to gaze upon the women. However, there is evidence that some victims were forced to witness the crucifixion of their beloved ones, 'but were unable to do anything except to watch helplessly'.[151] We cannot rule out the possibility that these women had been forced to witness and gaze upon Jesus' naked body as a way to inflict terror on Jesus' disciples. Perhaps Mark is using and 'manipulating' what Maud Gleason calls 'the body of pain' to provide a 'spectacle-within-a-spectacle' with the intention of inflicting terror on Jesus' community. Gleason brings to our attention how the Hasmonean king, Alexander Jannaeus, when his authority was challenged during a rebellion, crucified eight hundred Pharisees in the middle of Jerusalem. This incident is reported by Flavius Josephus (*B.J.* 1.97-98), who narrated that before crucifying them, the king forced them to watch the execution of their wives and children while he reclined publicly among his concubines to watch the 'spectacle-within-a spectacle'. This macabre spectacle was so effective that the next night eight thousand more rebels got the message and fled the country.[152] Perhaps for this reason there are not any followers of Jesus there during his crucifixion. Yet, although Jesus, and not the women, is the victim to be crucified, the violation and penetration occurred nonetheless. 'To force another to watch you watching them with soul-withering contempt was a form of violence—of vivisection—as penetrating, as mutilating, as any that one human being could inflict upon another.'[153] The Romans as the *chingones* had killed two birds with one stone; both Jesus and his female friends had been penetrated by the Romans' gaze.

If we were to remove the faithful women from the scene of the crucifixion, we discover that at his execution and death Jesus was surrounded totally by his enemies, represented by the Roman army. As a matter of fact, Jesus' death is sandwiched between the soldiers who crucified him and the centurion who stood in front of Jesus. The centurion's confession, 'Truly this human being was the Son of God', has become a *crux interpretum,* a real *mysterium tremendum* for all the scholars who have attempted to decipher the centurion's words. The crux of the dilemma revolves around whether the centurion's confession is genuine or not. Some would take the centurion's confession as a genuine confession of faith that echoes Mk 1.1 ('Jesus Christ, the Son of God") and that constitutes the climax of the Gospel.[154] Yet

151. Shi, *Paul's Message*, p. 45. See Plato *Gorgias* 473C and Josephus *B.J.* 1.96.

152. Maud Gleason, 'Mutilated Messengers: Body Language in Josephus', in Simon Goldhill (ed.), *Being Greek under Rome: Cultural Identity, the Second Sophistic and the Development of Empire* (Cambridge: Cambridge University Press, 2001), pp. 50-85 (78).

153. Barton, 'Being in the Eyes', p. 224.

154. Donahue and Harrington, *Mark*, p. 449.

others argue that Mark is using irony and that the centurion's confession is of a piece with the actions of the soldiers, the high priests, the scribes, the teachers of the law and of all those who had mocked Jesus as king, prophet, savior and Son of God. 'While it is difficult to determine with precision how Mark does intend the centurion's statement to be understood since it could have had a such wide a range of meanings to Mark's readers, it is likely that in the context of the passion narrative it stands alongside other ironic statements at the foot of the cross about who Jesus is.'[155] I will echo the opinion of those scholars who argue that Mark is using irony. We have seen how ironic the entire passion narrative has been. The trial and mockery of Jesus was a vulgar and cruel parody, between the abject Messiah and his powerful opponents. During Jesus' death and crucifixion the parody would reach its climax. Joel Marcus suggests that 'irony was exactly their intention: this strangely "exalting" mode of execution [meaning the raising of the crucified victim] was designed to mimic, parody, and puncture the pretension of insubordinate transgressors by displaying a deliberately horrible mirror of their self-elevation'.[156] Mark invites us to witness how the sharp eyes of the impenetrable penetrators, represented now in the figure of the centurion, accompanied Jesus to his miserable death. In the end there are only two characters to gaze upon, Jesus, who is on the cross, and the centurion, who 'stands in front of Jesus'.

El chingón y el chingao

Those scholars who have attempted to interpret the story of the centurion as a model of conversion and discipleship often do not pay attention to the ironic elements that the evangelist has left here and there regarding this ambiguous character. Myers observes that Mark sets up the scene with the centurion 'standing over against' Jesus on the cross: 'such spatial tension usually in Mark connotes opposition … not solidarity'.[157] He continues: 'Secondly, this centurion will momentarily reappear to confirm to Pilate that Jesus has indeed died (15.44f.). The fact that the man did not defect from his role as a Roman soldier loyal to Pilate erases the possibility that this is meant by Mark as a *discipleship* story'.[158] Mark is the only one who associated the centurion with Pilate after his 'confession of faith'. On the contrary, in Matthew and Luke, once the centurion testified that Jesus indeed 'was the son of

155. Earl S. Johnson, 'Is Mark 15.39 the Key to Mark's Christology?' *JSNT* 31 (1987), pp. 3-22 (16).

156. Joel Marcus, 'Crucifixion as a Parodic Exaltation', *JBL* 125 (2006), pp. 73-87 (78).

157. Myers, *Binding the Strong Man*, p. 393.

158. Myers, *Binding the Strong Man*, p. 393.

god' both authors remove him from their narratives (Mt. 27.59; Lk. 23.53). The connection of the centurion with Pilate corroborates the fidelity and loyalty that Rome's army had toward the empire; they even took a religious oath to the emperor, praising him as a god or a 'son of god'.[159] In the passion narrative, Mark has been contrasting and confronting two antagonistic powers. On the one hand, we have a crucified messiah who has claimed kinship and has been mocked by all. On the other hand, we are left with the centurion who represents another powerful 'son of god', with power to execute all the emperor's opponents. Butler observes that during the first and second Gulf Wars there were some missiles launched against Iraq on which U.S. soldiers wrote, 'up your ass'. 'In this scenario, the bombing, maiming, and killing of Iraqis is figured through sodomy, one that is supposed to inflict the ostensible shame of sodomy on those who are bombed.'[160] In this context, the U.S. soldiers in their homosexual fantasy became the 'impenetrable penetrators', *los chingones*, and the Iraqis became the 'penetrable penetrated one', or *los chingaos.* In Jesus' time there were not missiles or weapons of mass destruction, but there were terrible crosses through which the Roman soldiers could easily do the equivalent of writing 'up your ass' to ensure that they were indeed the impenetrable penetrators, *los chingones*; and everyone who challenged the mighty empire would become *los hijos de la Chingada,* or terrorists. This is the kind of relationship that Mark depicts between the centurion and Jesus.

Butler, after analyzing some military photos that showed bodies bound together, bodies forced into fellatio, and bodies in poses of dehumanizing degradation, concludes that the field of vision is clear. 'This is torture in plain view . . . The camera itself is ungagged, unbound . . . in showing what the United States can do, as a sign of its military triumphalism, demonstrating its ability to effect a complete degradation of the putative enemy.'[161] Analogically speaking, we continue to see how Mark as a photographer during his passion narrative has ungagged and unbound his 'camera' to show what the centurion can do with the body of Jesus who is in front of him. Mark situates his spectacle and his two main characters facing each other, removing all the characters that might distract us from the gaze, the 'encounter' and penetration that Jesus would suffer at the hands (or eyes) of the manly centurion. *Su atención, como la del lector, está fijada en aquel que ocupa el centro del relato*, 'Mark's intention, as well as that of the reader, is fixed on the one who occupies the center of the narrative'.[162] Mark momentarily suspends the other characters and invites us to fix our attention

159. Johnson, 'Is Mark 15.39 the Key to Mark's Christology?' p. 12.
160. Butler, *Frames of War*, p. 90.
161. Butler, *Frames of War*, p. 84.
162. Pérez Herrero, *Pasión y pascua de Jesús*, p. 313.

on the centurion who was παρεστηκὼς ἐξ ἐναντίας αὐτοῦ, 'standing oppo-site him'. Mark wants to ensure the readers' understanding that the soldier's attention is focused primarily upon Jesus, not elsewhere.[163] The posture of the two characters is sharply different. On the one hand, we have Jesus' corpse or, using Martial's words to describe a crucified criminal, 'His lacer-ated limbs were yet alive, pieces dripping with blood, and in his whole body there was nowhere a body' (Martial *Spectacula* 7.5-6).[164] On the other hand, we have the powerful centurion standing like a manly man watching a body that 'is no longer a body,' in a front-row seat, getting some sexual gratifica-tion by his penetrating gaze. Mark describes the centurion's geographical space with the same Greek verb (παρίστημι) that he had used to locate those who, standing near Jesus, mocked him (Mk 15.35). Thus, it is possible to associate the centurion with Jesus' opponents.

The geographical place or space for watching a spectacle in Greco-Roman culture depended on one's hierarchical status. Not only that. Every category of society was represented and visible, each occupying its own area according to the elaborate seating-divisions imposed by Augustus to reflect his view of the proper social order.[165] There was a strange and bizarre relationship between the victim and the spectator who gained honor and masculinity at the cost of the victim's suffering and death. 'As the victim's world collapses, the spectator's world expands, but not to the same extent

163. Howard M. Jackson, 'The Death of Jesus in Mark and the Miracle from the Cross', *NTS* 33 (1987), pp. 16-37 (19).

164. Quoted in Fredrick, 'Mapping Penetrability', p. 244.

165. Coleman, 'Fatal Charades', p. 72. Suetonius's report regarding how the emperor Augustus regulated the viewing of the game might help to understand how important was the geographical space while attending a spectacle: 'He put a stop by special regula-tions to the disorderly and indiscriminate fashion of viewing the games, through exas-peration at the insult to a senator, to whom no one offered a seat in a crowded house at some largely attended games in Puteoli. In consequence of this the senate decreed that, whenever any public show was given anywhere, the first row of seats should be reserved for senators; and at Rome he would not allow the envoys of the free and allied nations to sit in the orchestra, since he was informed that even freedmen were sometimes appointed. He separated the soldiery from the people. He assigned special seats to the married men of the commons, to boys under age their own section and the adjoining one to their preceptors; and he decreed that no one wearing a dark cloak should sit in the middle of the house. He would not allow women to view even the gladiators except from the upper seats, though it had been the custom for men and women to sit together at such shows. Only the Vestal virgins were assigned a place to themselves, opposite the praetor's tribunal. As for the contests of the athletes, he excluded women from them so strictly, that when a contest between a pair of boxers had been called for at the games in honour of his appointment as pontifex maximus, he postponed it until early the follow-ing day, making proclamation that it was his desire that women should not come to the theatre before the fifth hour' (*Divus Augustus* 40).

or in the same way. In mapping status and gender so carefully, the arena maps penetrability, not only by sexuality and violence, but by a host of other experiences: hunger, fatigue, disease, and pleasure.'[166] Mark seems to be aware of these geographical regulations and has situated the Roman army and its representatives in the first row, and Jesus as a victim in front of the executioners. Mark has informed us how the religious authorities have bound Jesus, led him away and handed him over to Pilate (Mk 15.1), where Jesus' silence dominates the scene. Then, during the crucifixion, the soldiers take their seats in the first row, where they will play dice while watching Jesus' exposed and expendable body (Mk 15.24). Although Mark does not reveal the identity of those who were near to Jesus (Mk 15.35), Gundry suggests that the fetcher of sour wine is a soldier.[167] Finally Mark depicts the centurion who is standing in front of Jesus, in charge of Jesus' execution.[168]

El centurión está situado frente a Jesús o de cara a él; ha podido observar y darse perfecta cuenta de lo sucedido, 'The centurion is situated in front of Jesus or facing to him; and so he was able to observe and notice everything that was happening.'[169] There is an inextricable link between the centurion as the executioner and Jesus as the victim, a link that is accentuated by the centurion's 'visual assassination.'[170] The centurion is in charge of Jesus' execution and represents the mighty army. He is there observing, watching the death of the abject messiah.

> *De este centurión se acentúa de manera especial su relación con el crucificado, señalando su actividad ('viendo') y su posición de atento observador ('estaba frente a él'), todo ello en relación con el modo en que Jesús muere*, This centurion's relation with the Crucified One is emphasized in a special way, pointing out his activity ('gazing') and his position of diligent observer ('he was in front of him'), all in relation to the way in which Jesus died.[171]

A Jesús se lo acaba de llevar la Chingada in front of the centurion who as a *chingón* has seen how a *chingao* breathed his last (Mk 15.39). In Mexico, we always send a person to an 'unknown place' when we say, *vete a la Chingada*, which according to Paz, becomes a distant, vague and indeterminate, place: 'a gray country, immense and empty, that is not located anywhere'.[172] By sending Jesus *a la Chingada*, the centurion is intending to erase Jesus' memory and existence. The centurion confirmed that indeed

---

166. Fredrick, 'Mapping Penetrability', p, 245.
167. Gundry, *Mark*, p. 969.
168. Donahue and Harrington, *The Gospel of Mark*, p. 449.
169. Mateos and Camacho, *Evangelio de Marcos*, p. 730.
170. I am borrowing this phrase from Barton, 'Being in the Eyes', p. 223.
171. Pérez Herrero, *Pasión y pascua de Jesús*, p. 313.
172. Paz, *Labyrinth of Solitude*, p. 79.

Jesus' life and death were *de la Chingada,* and he died as a true *hijo de la Chingada.*

Because we often romanticize and spiritualize the way in which Jesus died,[173] Paul Winter's powerful and vivid description of a crucified person deserves full quotation:

> Nothing could be more horrible than the sight of this living body, breathing, seeing, hearing, still able to feel, and yet reduced to the state of a corpse by forced immobility and absolute helplessness. We cannot even say that the crucified person writhed in agony, for it was impossible for him to move. Stripped of his clothing, unable even to brush away the flies which fell upon his wounded flesh, already lacerated by the preliminary scourging, exposed to the insults and curses of people who can always find some sickening pleasure in the sight of the tortures of others. . . .[174]

The centurion had not lost a single detail surrounding Jesus' death. He is even capable of gazing on how the curtains of the Temple were torn to top to bottom and how Jesus breathed his last.

We have noted how clothes reveal one's identity, and how the symbolism of the clothes is pretty much present throughout Mark's Gospel. 'There is an inordinate amount of attention in Mark to Jesus' clothing. Not only do Jesus' garments suffer the same fate as his body; they seem at times to be an extension of his body.'[175] It is striking that Mark depicts Jesus' garment/body in company of the *chingones* during Jesus' final hours. We have observed how Mark opens his spectacle with the impenetrable penetrators 'playing' and taking off Jesus' garment. 'And they crucified him. Dividing up his clothes, they cast lots to see what each would get' (Mk 15.24). Jesus' garment/identity has become that of a puppy and an object of pleasure, a thing to be used. Mateos and Camacho interpret this text symbolically, arguing that Jesus' garment/body is given for all. They even associate the 'giving' of his garment with Jesus' Eucharistic body.

> *Se descubre aquí una relación con la eucaristía. El reparto de la ropa, que representa la corporalidad de Jesús, corresponde a su primera acción en la Cena: 'Tomad, esto es mi cuerpo'* (14,24), We discover here a relation with the Eucharist. The sharing of the clothes which represent the corporality of Jesus corresponds to his first action during the Last Supper: 'Take it, this is my body' (14.24).[176]

I do not have any problem in identifying Jesus' garments with the Eucharist; my contention is that Mateos and Camacho do not seem to pay enough

173. See the classical book by Martin Hengel, *Crucifixion in the Ancient World and the Folly of the Message of the Cross* (trans. John Bowden; London: SCM Press, 1977).
174. Paul Winter, *On the Trial of Jesus* (Berlin: Walter de Gruyter, 1961), p. 66.
175. Wilkinson-Duran, *The Power of Disorder*, p. 90.
176. Mateos and Camacho, *Evangelio de Marcos*, p. 689.

attention to the fact that the contexts of the Last Supper and Jesus' crucifixion are quite different. They forget that during the Last Supper, Jesus as an abject body freely gives his body/bread to his *descarados/as* friends as a sign of solidarity, inclusivity and respect for life. However, during the crucifixion, Jesus is among the *chingones,* robbed of his identity and humanity, and therefore legitimately liable to cruel treatment and penetration. For Mary Ann Tolbert, the dividing of Jesus' human clothes at his death indicates figuratively his departure from the human world.[177] In a few hours Jesus would have departed this world. Even then, however, his body is still there, naked and exposed to the prying eyes of the *chingones.*

Scholars have often interpreted the tearing of the veil of the Temple as triumphalistic Christian propaganda by which Jesus' death allows us to 'penetrate' into God's holiest place.

> *Efectivamente, con la muerte de Jesús se rompe el velo que impedía penetrar en el santo de los santos, un velo que impedía ver a Dios en el esplendor de su debilidad,* Effectively, with Jesus' death the veil is torn apart which prevents us from penetrating the holy of holies, a veil which prevent us seeing God in the splendor of God's weakness.[178]

My abject interpretation does not wait until Jesus' death to gain access to the God whom Jesus represents. It is in Jesus' broken, penetrable and vulnerable body that God has been operating. Mark has not revealed exactly what curtain was torn at the moment of Jesus' death. Was it the curtain concealing the holy of holies or the curtain between the forecourt and the sanctuary? Likewise the temple curtain is not torn by anyone; it simply tears, spontaneously, at the instant Jesus dies.[179] Mateos and Camacho associated the tearing of the curtains of the Temple with Jesus' own body. *La cortina rasgada en dos es, pues, figura de la humanidad de Jesús rota por la muerte*, 'The curtain torn in two, thus, is the figure of Jesus' humanity which was broken by death.'[180] We showed above how Mark, like a photographer, removed all the characters to focus only on the figure of the *chingón* and *chingao* on the main stage. Here Mark is directing our gaze both to the veil of the Temple and to the Crucified One.

> *Se habla del velo del templo en un relato que no permite desviar la mirada del Gólgota y del crucificado. El velo que se rasga es como si apareciera impreso sobre la cruz,* The veil of the temple is described in a narration which does not allow us to shift our gaze from Golgotha and the Crucified One. The veil that is torn is as if it appeared impressed on the cross.[181]

177. Tolbert, *Sowing the Gospel*, p. 280.
178. Pérez Herrero, *Pásion y pascua de Jesús*, p. 311.
179. Wilkinson-Duran, *The Power of Disorder*, p. 119.
180. Mateos and Camacho, *Evangelio de Marcos*, p. 728.
181. Pérez Herrero, *Pásion y pascua de Jesús*, p. 311

Mark, in an *epiphanic moment,* announces to us that, indeed, the torn veil of the Temple and the crucified share the same fate and destiny: 'both bodies' are capable of penetration. But who might be the sexual predator who would be willing to penetrate 'God's abused child'?[182]

We notice that Mark does not reveal who tore the veil of the temple; he just points out that it was torn from 'top to bottom'. From my hermeneutics *del otro lado* it seems evident that it is the centurion—the impenetrable penetrator—who has both penetrated Jesus' crucified body and Jesus' garment/body from 'top to bottom'. In Greco-Roman culture, penetration between the executor and his victim could be accomplished by proximity. 'This vulnerable self is the true locus of penetrability, not the bare employment of one's anus, vagina, or mouth in copulation. In general, the closer one is to the body in the form of overwhelming sensation, the more penetrable one is.'[183] From this understanding of 'penetrability', it is evident that the centurion is the nearest person to Jesus, who is fully exposed to his avid gaze. Seneca laments concerning the games in the amphitheater that men now kill each other for the sake of spectating alone (*Epistulae* 90.45). If the centurion has Jesus' corpse and garment all for himself, his eyes might be indulging in an orgy of penetration. How did the centurion penetrate Jesus' curtain/body while situated far away from the Temple? Scholars are at pains to try to understand what exactly the centurion saw after Jesus' death. Did he see how the curtains of the Temple were torn from top to bottom? Did he see the way in which Jesus' died? Did he see both events at the same time? These questions have been hotly debated without any agreement being reached. Bas van Iersel asks,

> The Greek verb εἶδον indicates a visual experience, but how is the reader to imagine this? The deep sight is a sound, which can be heard rather than seen. Perhaps because Jesus breathed not just his last but also the Holy Spirit? But how could that have been visible? The only remaining possibility seems to be that the centurion saw the veil of the Temple being torn in two. That possibility has been called into question on the basis of extratextual data.[184]

Marcus argues that it is difficult to imagine the scene physically: 'If the centurion was facing Jesus, who was crucified outside the city walls on Golgotha to the north of the city, he was probably turned away from the Temple, which was on the east end of the city and was orientated eastward; and even if he was turned the right way, and the torn veil was the

---

182. Rita Nakashima Brock (*Journeys by Heart: A Christology of Erotic Power* [New York: Crossroad, 1988]) has denounced as 'divine child abuse' the notion that God the 'Father' welcomes the death of God the 'Son' as payment for our sins.

183. Fredrick, 'Mapping Penetrability', p. 238.

184. Van Iersel, *Mark: A Reader-Response*, p. 480.

outer curtain of the Temple rather than the inner one, *his vision would have had to penetrate intervening objects such as the city wall* [my emphasis].'[185] These geographical challenges that Marcus observes regarding the place of the Golgotha could be resolved if we accept that, symbolically speaking, the impenetrable penetrators were able to 'penetrate intervening objects' through their uninhibited and powerful gaze.

The spies of Tacitus's Tiberius reported to the senate every beating administered, every moan emitted, every humiliation suffered by Tiberius's grandson Drusus while the latter was starving to death in his prison cell in the Palatine dungeon. The senators were amazed and terrified that Tiberius would expose his grandson's humiliation to them, 'just as if the wall had been removed' (Tacitus *Annales* 6.24).[186] According to Philo (*De Abrahamo* 149-55), among the five senses that human beings possess, hearing and seeing have a more prominent place over the other three. He ranked low smell, taste and touch, which have the greatest resemblance to the 'brute beasts' and the 'slaves' and are the 'most greedy and the most strongly inclined to sexual connections'. Moreover, between hearing and seeing, Philo privileges seeing:

> But the sense of hearing inasmuch as that is slow and more effeminate, may be classed in the second rank, and the sense of seeing may be allowed an especial pre-eminence and privilege: for God has made this sense a sort of queen of the rest, placing it above them all, and stationing it as it were on a citadel, and has made it of all the senses in the closest connection with the soul. (*De Abrahamo* 150)

As we can 'see', Philo shares the same idea as the Romans in considering the eye to be the 'manliest' human organ, often linked with force and violence: 'If anger occupies us, then sight becomes more fierce and bloodshot' (*De Abrahamo* 152). Furthermore, for Philo, the eye 'reaches out' and 'acts upon objects', and the light within us 'goes forth towards the thing seen'. Greco-Romans even compare the gaze at a distance to a hand: 'Hipparchus says that the rays from each of the eyes, extended out to their limits as with the touch of the hands, grasp external bodies and return an apprehension of them to the sense of sight.'[187] Thus, the centurion as the impenetrable penetrator does indeed have the power to penetrate intervening objects such as the city walls. Moreover, Gundry reminds us that Mark has not mentioned distance and 'reference to the bottom as well as the top implies that the centurion can see both'.[188]

185. Marcus, *Mark*, p. 1057
186. Quoted in Barton, 'Being in the Eyes', p. 225.
187. Quoted in Bartsch, *The Mirror of the Self*, p. 62.
188. Gundry, *Mark*, p. 970.

The centurion's penetration produced such violence that 'the curtain of the temple was torn in two from top to bottom' (Mk 15.38). In Greco-Roman culture it was believed that a razor-sharp gaze could destroy both the object and the subject of the gaze.[189] The Markan love for duplication has a strong literary effect here: The veil is rent 'from top to bottom' and 'into two' and so will not be reparable.[190] The centurion's penetration has been so powerful that it has 'torn' Jesus' body without any possibility of it being restored or 'revirginized'. Jesus has been 'deflowered' publicly by the impenetrable penetrator who is even capable of hearing Jesus complain to his 'absent Father'.[191] 'Eloi, Eloi, lama sabachthani?'—which means, 'My God, my God, why have you forsaken me?' (Mk 15.34). Scholars do not know what to do about Jesus' last words. For Brown, Jesus is praying, and so he cannot have lost hope: calling God 'My God' implies trust. 'Because he saw how Jesus died, the Marcan centurion confesses that Jesus was God's Son.'[192] I am not very optimistic about this interpretation, because of the fact that Mark has already depicted Jesus' 'praying' with Psalm 22 during his crucifixion—always in relation to his enemies. In Mk 15.24 the evangelist narrates how the soldiers were making a sport of Jesus' body/clothes, alluding to Ps. 22.18, which reads, 'They divide my garments among them and cast lots for my clothing.' Moreover, Mk 15.29, 'those who passed by reviled him', is a clear echo of Ps. 22.7, which states, 'All who see me mock me; they hurl insults, shaking their heads.' Marcus argues that this prayer was interpreted in the Second Temple period as a prophecy of the suffering of the righteous in the end-time.[193] We know that Jesus is the righteous person of God, but the centurion does not. They represent different powers and divinities.

I find very appealing the fact that Mark depicts Jesus using his mother tongue in front of the centurion. Every time that Mark has depicted Jesus talking or saying a single word in Aramaic, his language is surrounded by ambiguity between death and life (Mk 5.41), deafness and hearing (Mk 7.34), blindness and sight (Mk 10.46), rejection and acceptance (Mk 14.36), doubt and confidence (Mk 15.22). People who have been conquered know the effect of being obligated and forced to speak the language of the *conquistadores* and feeling ashamed of their mother tongue. Language and reli-

189. Bartsch, *The Mirror of the Self,* p. 90.

190. Brown, *The Death of the Messiah,* 2: 1102.

191. See William Sanger Campbell, '"Why Did You Abandon Me?" Abandonment Christology in Mark's Gospel', in Geert Van Oyen and Tom Shepherd (eds.), *The Trial and Death of Jesus: Essays on the Passion Narrative* (Leuven: Peeters, 2006), pp. 99-117.

192. Brown, *Death of the Messiah,* 2: 1049.

193. Marcus, *Mark 1–8,* p. 1063.

gions have been shown to be an excellent way to penetrate and dominate
other 'less civilized' cultures. Scholars have observed that Mark uses the
Latin loan word κεντυρίων rather that the Greek forms ἑκατοντάρχης or
ἑκατόνταρχος, which are always used by Matthew and Luke.[194] Mark seems
to compare and contrast both Jesus and the centurion with their respective
tongues, in which one language emerges with power to penetrate, inflict
violence and subjugate, and the other language so to speak becomes penetrated, violated, subjugated and silenced. The first-century rhetorician Quintilian proudly celebrated what he sees as the 'rugged masculinity of Latin',
as compared with the greater facility, 'but dangerous 'effeminate glamour,
of Greek'.[195] Françoise Desbordes, analyzing Quintilian's arguments for the
superiority of Latin over Greek because of 'its' manliness, concluded:

> Les vieux Romains de Quintilien sont, comme le latin, *duri* et *horrid*, et la
> pauvreté leur est vertu, mais ils ont la force, *rubur uiris dignum* (10.1.43).
> Dans l'imaginaire latin, et pas seulement chez Quintilien, la force virile est
> associée comme automatiquement à la rudesse primitive, mal dégrossie,
> mal peignée et sans grace, The old Romans of Quintilian are, like Latin,
> *duri* and *horrid* and their poverty is virtue, but they have force, *rubur uiris
> dignum* (10.1.43). In the Latin imagination, and not only for Quintilian,
> virile force is associated automatically with a primitive roughness, harsh,
> uncombed and without grace.[196]

Moreover, Joy Connolly has shown how for many rhetoricians and histo-
rians from the first century, references to femininity or effeminacy in the
Latin language connote the non-Roman (especially the 'Asiatic' Greek), the
enslaved, and the poor. All these groups, legally, economically and politi-
cally dominated by elite Roman men, are used as a sign of vices that the
manly Romans must avoid.[197] In conclusion, all people who did not speak
the language of the empire were legitimately liable to all kinds of vexations.
    The context in which the centurion pronounced his confession indicates
that he uttered it in Latin. If this were the case, then the association of the
confession with the Roman imperial cult, or the lack thereof, would have
been obvious, because the Latin epithet *divi filius* would immediately direct
one's attention to the Roman imperial cult.[198] The centurion represents the
empire, and Jesus is the defeated insurrectionist who attempts to pass for
a 'king' and 'son of god' when he was indeed a scorned body, betrayed by

194. France, *The Gospel of Mark*, p. 658.
195. Connolly, *Disorderly Women*, p. 73.
196. Françoise Desbordes, 'L'idéal romain dans la rhétorique de Quintilien', *KTÈMA*
= *Civilisations de l'Orient de la Grèce et de Rome antiques* 14 (1989), pp. 273-79 (278).
197. Connolly, 'Virile Tongues: Rhetoric and Masculinity', p. 88.
198. Tae Hun Kim, 'The Anarthrous υἱὸς θεοῦ in Mark 15,39 and the Roman Imperial Cult', *Bib* 79 (1998), pp. 221-41 (224).

his disciples, disowned by his race and abandoned by his 'god'. By using the word κεντυρίων, Mark is acknowledging not just the manliness of the language, but also the power and domination that such language produces in the community. *Como otros términos militares, kentouriôn había penetrado en griego, aunque se usaba raramente*, 'Like other military terms, *kentouriôn* had penetrated into the Greek language, although it was rarely spoken'.[199] Latin suits the largest imperial power of its own day,[200] and the centurion as a representative of the empire is the one who literally has the last word regarding Jesus' death. Mark depicts Jesus uttering a great sound (Mk 15.37), but unfortunately, Jesus' sound is not decipherable; his utterance is lost in translation. 'He dies with a loud, probably wordless cry',[201] in front of the centurion who has the last word. We as readers hear the centurion's confession, talking and reporting to Pilate about Jesus' death (Mk 15.44-45). But we hear nothing about God's voice. The voice that came from heaven and reaffirmed Jesus' sonship during his baptism is totally silent. In Mark's Gospel, Jesus neither commends his spirit into God's hands, as in Lk. 23.46, nor utters 'It is finished', as in Jn 19.30. The empire has succeeded in executing another victim. After all, 'What is the power of this man Jesus as compared to the power of Caesar?... Jesus stands *contra mundum* and is apparently powerless as he faces the world.'[202] Jesus had exclaimed his defeated, muted and effeminate words in front of his executer, the impenetrable penetrator. Once we have seen how Mark has exposed his abject Messiah to the gaze of *los chingones* we can let Jesus die naturally in 'peace'.[203]

Conclusion

We have witnessed how Mark, during Jesus' passion narrative, has exposed Jesus' body to all kinds of violence, vexation and sexual humiliation by his enemies. It remains for us to understand why Mark has exposed Jesus' naked, vulnerable, precarious and penetrable body in the way that he did. What is Mark's intention in describing in such a vivid way Jesus' trial, crucifixion and death? These questions are not easy to answer, and we will not

    199. Mateos and Camacho, *Evangelio de Marcos*, p. 707.
    200. Connolly, *Disorderly Women*, p. 74.
    201. Yarbro Collins, *Mark*, p. 759.
    202. John Pobee, 'The Cry of the Centurion—A Cry of Defeat', in Ernst Bammel (ed.), *The Trial of Jesus* (Naperville, IL: Alec R. Allenson, 1970), pp. 91-102 (94).
    203. This is the conclusion of France (*The Gospel of Mark*, p. 655), who argues, 'The recognition in Jesus of a υἱὸς θεοῦ would follow more naturally from a "noble" or peaceful death than from one in unrelieved depression, which was surely familiar enough to a centurion used to officiating at crucifixions.'

have any conclusive argument. People who have documented methods of torture during times of war have observed that the photographers who capture the pictures, of Abu Ghraib, for example, were not even truly aware of the evil that they were displaying: 'There is no moral confusion here: the photographers don't even seem aware that they are recording a war crime. There is no suggestion that they are documenting anything particularly morally skewed. For the person behind the camera, the aesthetic of pornography protects them from blame.'[204] Is Mark aware of the public exhibition that he has done with Jesus' naked, penetrable body during the passion narrative? Probably by depicting and exposing Jesus to the gaze of all, Mark is moving his audience to identify with some of the characters that he artistically has displayed during Jesus' passion narrative. Mary Ann Tolbert argues that 'the Gospel of Mark was written to do something, to persuade or move people to action. All characters in the Gospel are fashioned to promote this goal, and all of them, regardless of their traditional or historical roots, are also subordinate to this goal.'[205] If Tolbert is correct, then Mark's audience—and we as a part of that audience—are challenged to either become compassionate toward Jesus or to join all those groups who abused him. I ascribe to the opinion of Richard E. DeMaris, who argues that 'Mark would not have dwelt on Jesus' humiliating death had he not seen something positive about it that overshadowed its negative aspects'.[206]

It is up to us as readers to find something positive in Jesus' shameful crucifixion. Wilkinson-Duran asks, 'What difference would it make to understand Jesus as the victim of rape as well as arrest, torture, and execution?' She continues, 'For me it means a different understanding of his powerlessness and his identification with the powerless, and identification with the often invisible, largely African-American prisoners of my country, and a new level of identification with women, who, whether or not they have experienced rape, have lived with its threat as part of their defining daily experience'.[207] Reading and interpreting Jesus' passion narrative from *el otro lado* give me strength to understand that, after all, Jesus' brokenness and penetrability were ways in which God became fully implicated in the lives of those who were at the margin, whose lives did not matter and whose effeminate bodies were not considered to be 'human'. Reading and gazing upon Jesus' body through *otros lados* of interpretation help me to under-

204. Joanne Bourke, 'Torture as Pornography' (accessed 9 December 2009); available online at http://www.guardian.co.uk/world/2004/may/07/gender.uk.

205. Mary Ann Tolbert, 'How the Gospel of Mark Builds Characters', *Interpretation* 47.4 (1993), pp. 347-57 (349).

206. Richard E. DeMaris, *The New Testament in its Ritual World* (New York: Routledge, 2008), p. 95.

207. Wilkinson-Duran, 'Jesus: A Western Perspective,' p. 349.

stand that the Crucified One is indeed the Risen Jesus who challenges us to go back to Galilee and find Good News. It is time to go back to Galilee in hopes of this time, recognizing in Jesus' abject, broken, precarious, penetrable and vulnerable body Good News for all. With this in mind I invite you to see how my reading of *el otro lado* could sustain me in my daily battles, and by extension, perhaps also you.

First Letter of Manuel Villalobos Mendoza to the Markan Community

I, Manuel Villalobos Mendoza, follower and servant of Jesus, the broken, vulnerable, abject and penetrable Son of God, not for my own merits, priest-hood status, legal situation, sexual orientation, or scholar credentials, but rather for God's justice and abundant love. To all the Markan community who live somewhere in the Roman Empire,[1] and to Mark, beloved disciple of Jesus, called to be an apostle and set apart for the gospel of God. Through Jesus and for Jesus' fidelity and passion for the Kingdom of God, we received grace and Good News. Jesus showed us how to live and create an alternative household where bodies *del otro lado* dwell in service. Jesus' scandalous life and association with *descarados/as, hociconas, malcriadas/os,* and effemi-nate bodies as well as his passion for justice for all led him to his death by the Romans, the religious authorities and even by some of his followers. And through Jesus' resurrection, to which Mary Magdalene, Mary the mother of James, Salome, Pola *la descarada*, Rebequita *la malcriada*, and Mark's own mom bore witness: Peace to you from the One who is among us, sitting at the left of those who are *en el otro lado* and believe that *otra interpretación de la Biblia es possible*, 'another interpretation of the Bible is possible'.

First, I thank my God through Jesus Christ and our Mother Ruah for you all, because of your faith, service, perseverance and resistance to the empire, which have been reported all over the world. Your testimony and fidelity to the message of the cross has been accepted with humility and reverence. God is my witness as to how familiar I have become with your gospel since my childhood. In my innocence I even dared to speak to you, beloved Mark. You cannot even imagine how many nights I fantasized about the young man run-ning naked in the middle of the night. Of course I learned later on that you are the only one who reports this *neaniskos* who was the cause of my many nights of insomnia. Your gospel of the cross has been lived out in me and my com-munity, even in our children's games. Indeed we bear in our own bodies the

---

1. Tolbert, *Sowing the Gospel*, p. 304.

mark of the cross. From early times we have become fascinated by the idea of the cross, and the mark of the Crucified One. We even play:

> *Venimos venimos de Veracruz,*
> *Con esta marca y con esta cruz.*
> 'We came, we came from Veracruz
> With this mark and with this cross'.

God is my witness how the cross has marked not just our bodies but also our destinies. The cross of Jesus has sometimes been unbearable, but despite that I am not ashamed of your gospel, because it is the power of God for the salvation of everyone who believes. That gospel gives dignity to every person and that is what sustains and gives me strength to continue working until there is a place for all in Jesus' kingdom.

Who We Are

Perhaps you might ask who we are. This question assumes that there is another before you whom you do not know and cannot fully apprehend or understand. We are beings who are, of necessity, exposed to you in our vulnerability, precariousness, abjectness and singularity of being *del otro lado*. But you also exposed yourself and your gospel long ago, and we have entered into a relationship of mutual recognition, even if you did not want it or expect it. In a certain sense, we know more about you and your community than you know about us. However, we need each other, because without you our own story becomes impossible.[2] For this reason we decided to write you a letter and reveal our identity, struggles, sufferings, dreams and visions of Jesus' kingdom, here and now. The idea of writing to you is not mine. Lupita, a disciple of Jesus, challenged me to write you a letter. I tried to discourage her with many arguments, such as 'this is not an academic way to end a dissertation'. But she is *malcriada y hocicona,* and does not understand those things about PhD dissertations, methods in biblical interpretation, etc. She, as an 'ordinary reader',[3] does not have any 'formal' education: *Las letras no entran cuando se tiene hambre*, 'Words do not come to mind on an empty stomach', she constantly says. But she speaks with a tongue of fire and with wisdom, and frankly all my arguments became nothing when speaking with this daughter of Sofia.

We form part of some biblical groups that week after week gather together in the slums of the south of the city to read, reflect upon and live your holy

---

2. Butler, *Giving an Account*, p. 32.
3. See Gerald O. West, *Biblical Hermeneutics of Liberation* (Maryknoll, NY: Orbis Books, 1995).

gospel. This group is composed of wo/men who are *marimachas, hocico-nas, malcriadas/os* and *del otro lado*. We have intercepted and interpreted 'your' gospel, a gospel that was not written with us primarily in mind. We, as 'accidental readers'[4] have encountered many obstacles to making sense of your gospel, because of the time, the language and the historical situation that separates us. But also we have found life and hope in the way that you have depicted bodies, undoing their gender, crossing boundaries and expos-ing Jesus' exposable, broken and penetrable body to our gaze during Jesus' last hours in Jerusalem. With gratitude and open hearts, we have discovered how Jesus revealed God's justice by accepting all kinds of people, treating them with dignity as humans and therefore as children of God. It is a justice that imitates Jesus by calling us to be compassionate and merciful toward all people, just as it is written, 'Do justice, love mercy, walk humbly with God' (Mic. 6.8). The groups that faithfully read your gospel are composed of many members whose stories and experiences are very similar to some of the characters that you depict in your Gospel. The Ruah has empowered wo/men to challenge the institution, the culture, tradition and religion that for centuries have caged them, silenced them, segregated them, maimed them and killed them—all in the name of God. This is one of the main reasons why I am writing you: to let you know how we have received and interpreted your Gospel in the midst of many signs of death. I am sending you this letter, hoping that you might share it with your entire community. Through this letter you will know who we are, where we are, what is trou-bling us, what we can do, what time it is and for what we hope.

I am writing in the first person singular since lately in biblical interpreta-tion 'we' have resuscitated the more intimate and personal smothered 'I'. I am sure that you understand this perfectly, because it seems that, in the strict sense, you did not write your passion narrative alone, did you? There are some people who even affirm that you essentially invented the genre of the passion narrative by incorporating different stories and traditions into your own passion narrative. Yet with respect to this we are not concerned so much with the question about the *original form*, for no such thing ever existed in oral speech.[5] Moreover, both of us come from cultures where our identity and personality have meaning through being in community. We can easily celebrate our African American sisters' and brothers' saying, 'We are, therefore we exist.' I am sure when you heard all those stories about Jesus' miracles, parables, scandalous meals and his death, many voices

4. See Thomas E. Jenkins, *Intercepted Letters: Epistolary and Narrative in Greek and Roman Literature* (Lanham, MD: Lexington Books, 2006).

5. Werner H. Kelber, *The Oral and the Written Gospel: The Hermeneutics of Speaking and Writing in the Synoptic Tradition, Mark, Paul and Q* (Bloomington: Indi-ana University Press, 1983), p. 45.

were heard and celebrated; and all of them were essential parts in the process of writing your Gospel.

When you wrote your Gospel probably you did not have in front of you many scrolls, great libraries or manuscripts. But certainly you heard stories of people *del otro lado,* subjugated and exploited by *los chingones,* excluded from the religious institutions, confined to an 'unlivable life'; and certainly that helped you to visualize that Jesus' Kingdom of God is for them too. Otherwise, how could you depict Jesus transgressing, crossing and redefining all those kinds of boundaries that separated men from women, insiders from outsiders, pure from impure, masculine from effeminate? Unlike you, I have access to great libraries, journals and have been educated in the center of the empire. But when I write and approach your Gospel, are not the stories of the new Polas *las descaradas,* Rebequitas *las malcriadas y hociconas,* Simones *de los otros lados,* and Nachitos los *machitos* who assumed other faces, other names, other stories and other bodies what helped me to understand your subversive gospel more fully? It is the story of Anita Gonzalez, who has been segregated and marked as a persona non grata by her church because she dared to challenge the authority of her priest. It is the story of Dolores, who was beaten to death by some members of her family because she reported to the police the sexual abuse of her daughter by her own brother. It is the story of Juan, a kid who was beaten with a bat, shot in the stomach, set on fire with gasoline and then dumped in an alley for being in a gang band. It is the story of Maribel, who was killed with the curtains of her bathroom for being a transsexual. It is the story of Pablito, who was asked to leave his religious community because he was too effeminate. It is the story of Gabriel, who was jailed and then deported for being undocumented. It is the story of many children who have been sexually abused by priests. All of these stories have conditioned me in my understanding of your passion narrative and have helped me to find Good News even in the midst of signs of death.

Where We Are

We do not know for sure where you were and where your community was located when you wrote your Gospel. Unlike you, we are located in the center of the empire in Chicago, which, like Nineveh, is an important city that requires more than three days to visit it. Although we live in the center of the empire, we are economically and socially far away from it. We are invisible. Doña Juana, who works hard for Jesus' kingdom, has been living here for almost forty-five years, and she has never been in downtown Chicago or shopped on the 'magnificent mile'. Like many others, she has been deprived of the *Pax Romana,* or the American Dream, as it is known now. The Roman Empire that you knew, has collapsed, and your Gospel indeed has been preached to all nations (Mk 13.10), including nations that did not even exist in your time, such as mine. Jesus, whom I serve with my whole heart by preaching and teaching the gospel of the cross, is my witness to how I remember you in my prayers at all times; and I give you thanks for writing such a radical and subversive gospel. However, since your time, we have witnessed the rise and fall of empire after empire with the same deadly result. Poor people have been exploited, women excluded, people *del otro lado* killed, traditions and memories annihilated. Moreover, some have associated the presence of our Mother Ruah, who since the beginning of creation has accompanied our ancestors, with the name of Ometeotl—the dual God, male and female—with evil powers. As a matter of fact, the new teachers of the law who came not from Jerusalem (Mk 3.22) but from the *otro lado* of the sea accused our ancestors of being possessed not by Beelzebub but by a far more powerful evil spirit. They saw the power of Satan where the Holy Spirit was already working. I am sure that this information must be very shocking to you, but it is also a cause of shame for me, especially when Pope Benedict XVI—whom the church claims to be the representative of Peter on earth—erroneously affirmed that Christianity was not imposed upon our ancestors.

The faith of Jesus our beloved brother and your message of the cross arrived on another Good Friday in 1519, when Hernan Cortez and his men landed in Chalchihuecan in the Gulf of Mexico. They took our land and renamed it *Veracruz* (true cross). Our ancestors soon discovered in their own flesh and souls what the 'true cross' of Jesus meant: Our lands were taken, our women were raped and our gods were 'defeated' by a more powerful God. *Los conquistadores,* or *chingones,* brought the faith of our Lord Jesus Christ together with the sword, with power to kill in the name of God. Faith and the sword, with their respective symbolism and antagonistic forces, have been hunting us ever since. As a way to protest the genocide that our ancestors suffered, we even chanted:

De España nos llegó el Cristo,
pero también el patrón,
y el patrón, igual que a Cristo,
al negro crucificó.

From Spain Christ came,
but with Christ, the conquistador came too,
and the conquistador, imitating the crucifixion of Christ,
crucified the bodies of the African slaves.[6]

6. 'César Calvo'; accessed 5 February 2010; available online at http://cesarcalvo.8m.com/produccion%20musical.htm.

The missionaries promised hope, love and compassion to our ancestors, but the misinterpretation of the Holy Scriptures has brought death, announcing hell and eternal damnation to people *del otro lado* or, as the conquistador called them, sodomites. This was actually the first impression that Cortés as *gran chingón* had about the body of the Indian. In his infamous report to Charles V he declared, 'We have come to know, for certain, that they are all sodomites and practice the abominable sin.'[7] Sadly, one of the earliest misuses of the Bible against the Mexican 'sodomites' is attributed to one apostle of Jesus, named Bernardino de Sahagún, who 'pastorally' recommended what to do with all of those who commit the *pecado contra natura*, 'sin against nature':

> The sodomite is an effeminate, defilement, a corruption, filthy; a taster of filth, revolting, perverse, full of affliction. He deserves laughter, ridicule, mockery; he is detestable, nauseating, disgusting. He makes one acutely sick; Womanish, playing the part of the woman, he merits being committed to the flames, burned, consumed by fire; he burns; he is consumed by fire. He talks like a woman, he takes the part of the woman.[8]

Since then, cardinals, bishops, priests, pastors and other servants of our Lord Jesus Christ, abusing their power, have literally followed Sahagun's advice regarding people like Nachito *el machito* and Simon *el del otro lado*. Through the manipulation of the Bible, *los chingones se han chingao a medio mundo,* apparently without realizing that by doing this they are dehumanizing God's children.

My interpretation of *el otro lado* informs me that your community also included children of *la Chingada.* This bastard breed is evident when the Roman centurion, as a *gran chingón,* penetrated Jesus, and the curtain of the temple was torn in two from top to bottom (Mk 15.38), giving all kinds of cursed bodies access to experience God in a different way. We admired your courage in finding Good News in a *chingao* and a fucked Messiah. We praise the way in which your community took the message of an abject Messiah throughout all the empire, challenging those who demand miraculous signs and those who look for wisdom. We applaud your courage in preaching an abject, vulnerable, penetrable and crucified Messiah—a stumbling block to Jews and foolishness to Gentiles (1 Cor. 1.23). We constantly talk about your faithfulness and boldness in recognizing in the Crucified One the Resurrected One who was moving your community to embrace all kinds of people. However you experienced it, it is not our experience yet. We have not realized fully that in the brokenness and abjection of a *chingao*

7. Garza Carvajal, *Butterflies Will Burn,* p. 138.
8. Francisco Guerra, *The Pre-Columbian Mind* (New York: Seminar Press, 1971), p. 29.

Messiah resides the power of God. We have not yet realized that God is still choosing the foolish things, the lowly of this world, and the despised things to shame *los chingones*, so that no one may boast before the living God (1 Cor. 1.27-29), whose name shall be blessed forever and ever. We as children of *la Chingada* are still searching for our lost identity. We know what it means to be orphans, feeling inferior in front of *los chingones*, rejecting our traditions and values and feeling ashamed of our language. The colonization that people *del otro lado* continue to experience by different kinds of *chingones* has left a severe mark on our bodies and souls. *Los chingones* have done a good job of erasing our historical memory so that we might not bring any further charges against them.

Some people might ask, How did *los chingones* become responsible for the misery and displacement of people *del otro lado*? Should not their corrupt governors and politicians be held responsible for dehumanizing their own people? Are not the Mexican drug cartels responsible for killing thousands of innocent people all over Mexico? Who should be held responsible for the over five hundred young women who have been brutally murdered, most of them sexually assaulted and tortured before being left for dead in cotton fields or in parking lots in Ciudad Juárez? Is it not the war between the two drug cartels of La Familia and Los Zetas that is responsible for all the kidnapping and killing of civilians? Whom should we blame for the marginalization, segregation and exploitation that the Indians have experienced for more than five hundred years? Who is responsible for the thirty-five million Mexicans who live in extreme poverty? I congratulate those people for perceiving that the problems that deny some their dignity to live a livable life are more complex than we thought. In certain ways all of us are responsible for causing suffering to God's vulnerable creation. For all of us have sinned (Rom. 5.12), and through our social sin, destruction, wars, crimes, envy and death have come to God's creation.

As a matter of fact, this *lado* of El Rio Grande with its respective *chingones* is no worse than the other side of the Rio Suchiate—the border of Mexico with Guatemala—with its Mexican *chingones*. Brothers and sisters of South America often experience more violence, aggression, dehumanization and death by the Mexican *chingones* than by the U.S. *chingones*. Very often, no one protests on the streets of Mexico where they meet their deaths. Their deaths do not make headlines in the newspaper. They do not leave a single trace of their existence, because they were never considered humans to begin with; they didn't really have a life, and therefore no murder [or death] has taken place.[9] We have focused so much on the problems that exist on the border with the North that we have forgotten that the border

---

9. Butler, *Precarious Life*, p. 147.

on the South also exists. People from South America often confess that the worst border is not the U.S. border but rather the border between Guatemala and Mexico. I want to scream in outrage and let everyone know that I feel ashamed to be part of a country in which the face of the *other* who speaks our own language, has the same features, and often professes the same faith in our beloved Jesus is received with violence, maiming and death. I beg for forgiveness from the living God, whose name shall be forever praised, for not recognizing in others' agonizing bodies God's voice who utters, 'You shall not kill.' I feel guilty of talking about the dignity, respect and right of the Mexican migrants when we do not grant such rights toward our brothers and sisters of South America. Nonetheless, it is this side of the border where I have lived for over a decade, and it is this mighty empire with its economic practice and Monroe Doctrine 'to leave America for the Americans' that should be held responsible for impoverishing us and forcing us to cross to *el otro lado.*

My dad often told us that we once had 'three yoke of oxen', which from time to time he rented to other people who had more land than we did. According to my dad, the Mexican government forced him to kill his oxen and cattle because of the 'aftosa fever'. When the Mexican government promulgated such an edict, immediately there appeared from nowhere, legions and legions—now we would call them soldiers and marines—in the most remote villages of Mexico, forcing the *campesinos* to sacrifice their animals in order to 'control the disease'. I learned later on that the empire had announced a ' new age', a 'new beginning', that would bring 'civiliza-tion' and 'progress' to all rural areas of Mexico by introducing a sophisti-cated machine called the tractor. This beast coming out of the north even had a name; it was 'John Deere', and it was the cause of admiration and veneration. Because it had power to perform great and miraculous signs, it worked tirelessly and was capable of making agricultural jobs easier with need for only a single worker. The empire needed avid customers to par-ticipate in this dream, so with appealing propaganda and in complicity with the Mexican government, they forced everyone, small and great, rich and poor, free and slaves (Rev. 13.16) to receive a mark of desire in their hearts. Thus, no one could work their land in peace unless they possessed the John Deere tractor, which became the beast of progress. Ninety-five percent of the Mexican *campesinos* were excluded from sharing in this dream, and the sacrifice of their cattle marked the beginning of their eternal nightmare of impoverishment.

This story is neither unique nor isolated from other U.S. interventions in Latin America. The United States has intervened numerous times to dis-place elected governments that threatened American corporate interests. Latin America has indeed been 'for the Americans'—but not for the Ameri-cans who lived across el Rio Grande. We are living in an inverted society that has exchanged the truth of God for a lie (Rom. 1.25). Instead of asking, 'Why do they hate us so much?' they should be asking, 'What we have done to them in the name of progress, peace, security and democracy?' How do we respond to the faces of others that remind us, 'You shall not kill'?

What Is Troubling Us

Beloved Mark, since I have approached your Gospel through *otros lados* of interpretation my body has been deeply distressed and troubled, and my soul is overwhelmed with sorrow to the point of death (Mk 14.33-34), because we often have failed you and have not taken to heart your marks and words exhorting us to go to back to Galilee. You, as an abject writer, following the divine inspiration of our Mother Ruah, and faithful to Jesus' *descarado* behavior, have announced that the Crucified One, now glorified, is to be found not in Jerusalem—in the center—but rather in Galilee—in the margins—in *los otros lados* of exclusion. By sending us back to Galilee, you are showing us once again the path to discover God's presence on the margins, in the borderland, in the abjectness of life. After all, it was in Galilee that Jesus, acting with the power of God, defeated the forces of evil, healed people, fed the crowds and invited wo/men to be part of his group. You, as a vulnerable author, have done your work; your role has been taken over by us now, the vulnerable readers, who must continue it.[10] Although we know that Jesus is to be found in Galilee among *descarados/as, malcriados/as, hocicones/as,* and people *del otro lado*, it seems that we have not been there for a long time. Indeed, a very long time. We as the followers of the abject, precarious and vulnerable messiah have been trapped and seduced into the center, feeling quite comfortable with the way that things are, enjoying the privileges that the empire provides for all its faithful servants.

In our biblical interpretation and discipleship we have often substituted the murderous cities of Jerusalem and Rome for Galilee. We no longer know where Galilee is, nor what kinds of bodies live there. We have become so disconnected from the people that we intend to serve that we do not even realize that we are in the wrong city, with the wrong people, worshipping the wrong god at the wrong time. You might ask, how did we miss the mark, since you explained to us quite clearly and straightforwardly the proper way? I do not know, but somewhere on the way your gospel was lost in translation. Your revolutionary message has been hijacked, protected from erroneous interpretation and blessed with the holy water of orthodoxy. I understand, if you are astonished, that we have been so quickly turning to

10. Geert Van Oyen, 'The Vulnerable Authority of the Author of the Gospel of Mark. Re-Reading the Paradoxes' (paper presented at the annual meeting of the Society of Biblical Literature, New Orleans, Louisiana, 21 November 2009), pp. 1-12.

a different gospel—which is really no gospel at all (Gal. 1.6-7). But the uncontrollable desires of power and domination over God's creation have been more desirable that being servants of all (Mk 10.44).

Not only have we disobeyed your command to go back to Galilee, we have also failed our sisters, such as Pola *la descarada* and Rebequita *la malcriada*. Our divine Savior promised us through your holy Gospel that, 'wherever the gospel is preached throughout the world, what Pola *la descarada* has done will also be told, in memory of her' (Mk 14.9). Such promises, such admonitions, have fallen on deaf ears. The constant fear of being symbolically castrated or emasculated by *otras Polas* who exercise their power in service of the broken ones is still real. We have excluded Pola's body from our tables, and from Holy Orders, for her lack of a penis! We have not learned that after all gender is neither natural nor innate, but rather a social construction through which some bodies have become human and other have been treated as less than human or not human at all. We do not preach enough that we are all children of God through faith in Christ Jesus, and indeed, 'There is neither Jew nor Greek, slave nor free, male nor female, for we are all one in Christ Jesus' (Gal. 3.28). We cannot understand that it is service and the ethic of *descaramiento* that gives testimony to our love of Jesus. The dehumanization that women have suffered for their lack of a penis has put them in mortal peril. They exist in service of the male's interests even if in so doing they find their own death. How many times have I witnessed women from my Bible groups serving like slaves the very ones who abuse them? They even think that by doing these 'services' they are performing a sacred liturgy because 'they are married by the church'. I do not blame them for thinking in this way since in the Mexican tradition the word of God that they heard during their wedding ceremony very often was 1 Tim. 2.9-15,

> A woman should learn in quietness and full submission. I do not permit a woman to teach or to have authority over a man; she must be silent. For Adam was formed first, then Eve. And Adam was not the one deceived; it was the woman who was deceived and became a sinner. But women will be saved through childbearing—if they continue in faith, love and holiness with propriety.

We are so ambiguous in relation to wo/men that often we do not understand this love/hate, acceptance/rejection kind of relationship. I suppose it has something to do with the way in which Mary the mother of Jesus was introduced to us. On the one hand, we promote Mary, the mother of Jesus, as a model for all women. We consider her to be the purest and most immaculate virgin, the one full of grace and virtue, the one who was taken up body and soul into heaven, a model that we insist all 'good' women should strive to imitate. On the other hand, our Mother Mary is expected to be silent and obedient. Please do not ask me how Mary the mother of Jesus became submissive when your friend Luke, the beloved physician (Col. 4.14), depicted her as a *marimacha y hocicona* while announcing that God is in favor of those whose life does not matter (Lk. 1.46-55). I am sure that Mary, the poor *campesina* of Galilee, would not recognize herself in the great basilicas that we have erected in her memory, or in our theology regarding her person, such as *de Maria nunquam satis*, 'Of Mary, one can never say enough.'[11] Ironically, you did not say much about her; and perhaps this lack of information regarding Mary the mother of Jesus has contributed to what we called *marianismo*. This *marianismo* had its roots in the conquest as a result of which we, *los/as hijos/as de la Chingada,* immediately became the children of the Immaculate Conception while accepting the crucified Messiah. We did not have time to process our rape and our colonization. Like a Manichean force, this idea of the whore/virgin or virgin/whore has been impregnated in our bodies. These two realities and forces have shaped our relations and attitudes toward our sisters, mothers and grandmothers.

This *marianismo* has legitimated total subordination of women to men. Women learned early in their lives that *en boca cerrada no entra mosca,* 'flies do not go into closed mouths', and *calladita te ves más bonita,* 'you look better silent'. In our Bible groups when I ask women what they think about your Good News often they look first for their husbands' approval. Even worse, sometimes they say, *Pienso lo mismo que mi esposo,* 'I think the same as my husband.' Women's silence and lack of words have brought upon their bodies enslavement after enslavement without their realizing it. The economic crisis that some people are now experiencing is just one more crisis in the daily struggle for survival for those *del otro lado* who are living in perpetual crisis. Although now both women and men typically work outside the home, when both arrive home after the day's work, women are still the ones who typically prepare the food, clean the house and make sure that everything in the family and household is running smoothly. It is a great shame that even the poorest male often has the privilege and luxury of having a woman as a *criada* to do his cooking, laundry and even bathe him and rub his back.

I am sure that you are surprised that the attitude toward women has not changed much since you wrote your Gospel. But women are not the only ones who have been dehumanized; people like Simón *el del otro lado* and Nachito *el machito* have likewise been segregated, excluded from our communities, our families, and even our tables—in Jesus' name. From time to time, and at key moments, the hierarchical church has used inflammatory language against people who deviate from heteronormative practices, to

11. See Alberto Maggi, *Nuestra señora de los herejes: María y Nazaret* (Cordoba: Editorial el Almendro, 2002).

give the impression that the church remains faithful to its 'constant tradi-tion' in matters of sexuality. Recently, some cardinals have uttered blas-phemous sentences such us, '*En el plan de Dios solo existen hombres y mujeres; no hay otras formas, los homosexuales son mercandería averiada y no están dentro de los planes de Dios,* 'In God's plan there are only men and women; there are no other forms: homosexuals are rotten merchandise, and they are not part of God's plan.'[12] I guess those guardians of the faith have read neither the story of Nachito *el machito* nor of Simon *el del otro lado.* Not only do they tell us that people *del otro lado* are not part of God's plan here on earth, but cardinals want to deprive us even of heaven, which they intimate is reserved for the heterosexual population. At least that is what Mexican cardinal Javier Lozano Barragán seems to be imparting when he says: 'Transsexuals and homosexuals will never enter the kingdom of heaven and it is not me who says this, but Saint Paul.'[13]

Now, as those cardinals, guardians of the truth, bring to memory Paul, the great apostle of the Gentiles, let me ask you how he is doing: Do you still accompany him in his missionary travels? Did you get along with him after the dispute that you caused? (Acts 15.36-41). If you meet him in some part of the empire, please inform him that we have used two words—*mala-kos* and *arsenokoitai*— of his vice list (1 Cor. 6.9-10) as a 'clobber text' to deprive people *del otro lado* of access to God's kingdom. Please tell him that we have obsessively and compulsively preached and condemned 'homosexual' persons, and that we have consciously and intentionally for-gotten (although they are mentioned in the same vice list) the injustices of the fornicators, thieves, misers, drunkards, slanderers and robbers. Please let him know that his two ambiguous terms *malakos* and *arsenokoitai* have been maligned and erroneously translated by the New American Bible as 'boy prostitutes' and 'practicing homosexuals'. Tell him that I want to scream in outrage because these two words, which were written more than two thousand years ago and used then in perhaps quite a different way than we use them now, undergird the official teachings of the church regarding homosexuality! *¡Hazme el chingao favor!* Mark, I beg you to intercede for us before Paul, because I am sure that he would lose his temper if he knew that there are people who still boast more of the works of the law than of faith in Jesus, the abject and penetrable Messiah. By acting in arrogance

12. These words were pronounced by the Peruvian cardinal Juan Luis Cipriani dur-ing a homily. See Beto Ortiz, 'Perú y el fantasma de la homofobia'; accessed 6 March 2010; available online at http://www.ar.terra.com/terramagazine/interna/0,,OI1946644-EI10363,00.html.

13. Michael Krebs, 'Cardinal: Homosexuals "Will Never Enter the Kingdom of Heaven"'; accessed 6 March 2010; available online at http://www.digitaljournal.com/article/283080.

and by claiming wisdom and privilege to judge and condemn people *del otro lado,* by denying them their humanity and condemning them to live the unlivable life, they show they have become blind.

We people *del otro lado* have been obliged to bargain away our humanity since the time of the colonization. For many *chingones,* the 'Indians' were perceived as not being really human. The *chingones* therefore felt justified in committing the worst genocide in human history; yet the Indians raised no complaint and did not move groups to seek some economic compensation for annihilating those bodies. Colonization has forced us to bargain away our humanity, because the discourses, the laws, religion, and even history find us unintelligible; and we are still in a perpetual process of attaining the status of humanness. In order to be able to legitimate ourselves as human beings, we have taken a foreign *logos* for ourselves. That borrowed *logos* is the Western *logos.*[14] Probably you experienced something similar in your community, since being human is not something to be taken for granted, but rather something that must be negotiated every single day. We are on many fronts less than human, inhuman, not human at all. What kind of humanity can the Mendoza family have if the four of them are living in a small apartment with a tiny kitchen, feeding their two kids on their meager income and also sending some money from their miserable salary back home to Mexico? What kind of humanity does Rosita have if she hasn't even a remote chance of going to university because she is poor, because there are four brothers ahead of her, and because her dad does not believe in educating women? What kind of humanity does Sergio have when he is unemployed and must pay the *coyote* who brought him to Chicago? What kind of humanity does Alejandro have when he needs dialysis three times a week, and does not have medical insurance or any kind of help because he is undocumented? What kind of humanity does Coni have when her dad is in jail awaiting deportation? What kind of humanity does Antonio have, if, though being against the war, he has decided to join the Armed Forces and go to Iraq in hopes that this way he can some day afford to attend university? Despite all of these struggles, sufferings and miseries that I witness in my community, reading your gospel has helped me to find my own voice. That, at least, is something that I can do.

What We Can Do

I never cease to give you thanks for depicting some wo/men as *malcriadas y hociconas.* Your characters have been celebrated and appropriated in unimaginable ways. As a matter of fact, Rebequita's personality has helped me

14. Leopoldo Zea, *Filosofía Americana como filosofía sin más* (Mexico City: Siglo XXI, 1969), pp. 9-31.

to find my own voice in my biblical interpretation. I must confess to you that the process of recovering my own voice has been painful and difficult. It is not easy to be *del otro lado en tierra de machos* without losing some privileges. There is always a price to pay for being opinionated and angry about the church, but the Spirit of the Crucified One challenges me to overcome both my fear and the fear that is used against people who have found life through your Gospel. A couple of years ago when I was teaching in a major seminary in Ciudad Juárez (on the border with the United States), the bishop questioned my credentials and accused me of teaching *como en el otro lado, como protestante/*'as if I were on the other side, as if I were protestant'. When I confessed to him that I was not just teaching *como en el otro lado* but in fact was *del otro lado*, he expelled me from his diocese because my teachings were contrary to 'sound doctrine and tradition'. I crossed to the United States and started the painful process of finding not only my voice but embracing my *otros lados* through interpreting the Bible. Now, it is obvious that being constantly situated *en el otro lado*, I must interpret the Bible *del otro lado* and write *del otro lado*, because for centuries I and people like me have been deliberately excluded from biblical interpretation. I cannot think, read or write 'straight' into the biblical text, because I had embraced and celebrated *el otro lado*.

Unfortunately, many biblical scholars are often not willing to recognize my interpretation of the Bible as valid, because they find my body and discourse 'impossible, illegible, unrealizable, unreal and illegitimate',[15] because I am a *joto*. In the winter of 2004 I was invited to the *Asociación Bíblica Mexicana* to talk about the 'Bible and homosexuality'. I knew that the audience, composed almost entirely of priests, would not easily listen to what I had to say. As soon as I presented myself as someone *del otro lado*, all their questions challenged my credentials rather than engaged my arguments. Finally, an irritated priest yelled at me, *¿Quién quiere escuchar tus joterías?*, 'Who wants to listen to your *joterías* anyway?' He unceremoniously reduced my interpretation of the Bible to worthless *joterías*, insisting that my hermeneutics did not follow the rigor of the historical-critical method. Mark, please do not think that this particular priest was acting out of his zeal and devotion to the Word of God. His harangue revealed his fear and anxiety toward my sexual orientation more than it did his commitment to the truth. The priest told me, 'Your hermeneutics could be accepted in el *otro lado*, but not here. Your interpretation and conclusion are contrary to common sense.' To my surprise, I could not get a word in edgewise to reply, so hotly were some of the participants debating among themselves. If I had been able to, I might have said, 'Many quite nefarious ideologies

---

15. Butler, *Gender Trouble*, p. viii.

pass for common sense. For decades of American history, it was "common sense" in some quarters for white people to own slaves and for women not to vote.'[16] Beloved Mark, it is 'common sense' in Mexico that people *del otro lado* deserve to die. It is 'common sense' that they like to be beaten, as indeed my own father thought. It is 'common sense' that they ought to be expelled from their family and school. It is 'common sense' that their fate is to burn in hell.

In Mexico as well as in the United States, a *joto* is regarded with suspicion, and his/her *joterías* are difficult to accept, even among other *jotos*. When my *jotos* friends find out that I am primarily interested in issues of gender and masculinity in your passion narrative, they often accuse me of 'seeing *joterías*' where they are not. They only half-jokingly conclude, 'You should be incinerated or at least jailed for using the Bible for your own convenience.' Ironically, our Mexican word *joto* was coined in a Mexican jail called *El Palacio Negro de Lecumberri*. This jail operated from 1900 until 1976 and was divided into sections, each section identified by a letter of the alphabet. All those bodies that were crossing, transgressing and undoing their genders were confined to section 'J' [pronounced *hota*]. When the inmates of section J were noisy, the guard would say something like, *Callen a los del área J*, 'Shut up, inmates in area J.' Eventually that became, *Callen a los jotos,* 'Shut up, *jotos.*' Since then, the desire to shut up the *joto* and his/her *joterías* seems to be part of the Mexican psyche as well as that of (hetero)sexual biblical scholars. I hope that I have been able to demonstrate in my dissertation that I am not interpreting the Bible for my own convenience.

In the history of biblical interpretation, Anglo as well as some Latino (hetero)sexuals have let their voices be heard in order to legitimate their voice as something sacred, valuable and worthy of transmitting life and hope. Yet, the voices and interpretations of other minority groups have been left out of the biblical discourse. I am glad that you did not fantasize while talking about your community, as your friend Luke did, while affirming that all believers were together and had everything in common (Acts 2.44). I love your dysfunctional community, because it is more in tune with my experience. There is still some brokenness and division among minority biblical scholars. We view one another with suspicion and do not trust one another. A few minority biblical scholars have been assimilated by the empire; in my humble opinion, they no longer represent the struggles of their communities. In Chapter 1, most excellent Mark, I explained why I crossed to *el Norte*. However, I did not reveal that in Mexico a *joto* like me is not allowed to interpret the Bible because 'I have my own agenda', as I

16. Judith Butler, 'A "Bad Writer" Bites Back', *New York Times*, 20 March 1999, p. 15.

am often told, meaning that my word is illegitimate, incapable of producing any 'real meaning' in my biblical interpretation. 'He is a bastard who speaks nonsense', they say of me, whereas their discourse and interpretation are classified and validated on the basis of their superior 'social location'. In this context, my body and my *joterías* have become homeless and borderless, even though I have not even left my own country. Nonetheless, now that you have depicted Jesus' crossing borders, announcing liberation to all people, I am attempting to find life in the ambiguity of the borderland.

Being exposed to *otros lados* here in the United States has helped me to embrace my own body and challenge the 'official' and 'heteronormative' interpretation of the Bible. Reading your passion narrative through *del otro lado* has helped me to see things differently and interpret the Bible in a more liberating way. I have already experienced and suffered enough because of the official and orthodox interpretation of the Bible. As one *del otro lado* I have been voiceless, searching always for my *in xóchitl in cuícatl—flor y canto*, [17] which might help me in understanding my own life and reality, in seeking the truth and beauty in all of creation, as our ancestors believed. Like other minority groups that live in *otros lados* and that see in the Word of God a call to freedom, I also turned to the Bible in hopes that the reading would reveal my *in ixtli in yóllot—rostro y corazón*, [18] which is the only way to be human. It is the encounter with the face and heart of the other that consecrates God's *kairos*, 'a time in between', [19] a moment when the stranger becomes a friend, the outsider becomes an insider, the sojourner becomes a citizen, and bodies *del otro lado* fall in a trance and find hope in the ambiguity of Nepantla.

What Time Is It?

I have been writing to you about all of these struggles and despairs that we people *del otro lado* have patiently endured on the Lord's Day, when I fell into a trance. And behold! I saw the heavens open and a multitude of men and women *del otro lado* worshipping the creator saying, 'Hallelujah! For our Lord God the Almighty reigns. Let us rejoice and be glad and give God glory!' (Rev. 19.6-7). I was absorbed in my heavenly vision, thinking to

17. The idiomatic expression *in xóchitl in cuícatl*, which literally means 'flower and song', has a metaphorical sense of poem, poetry, artistic expression, in a word, symbolism. For the Aztec's philosophers or Tlamatinimes, *in xóchitl in cuícatl* was a way to know truth on earth.

18. The idiomatic expression *in ixtli in yóllot*, which literally means 'face and heart', was the way in which one became a person.

19. To understand the notion of *kairos* as a time in-between, see Phillip Sipiora and James S. Baumlin, *Rhetoric and Kairos: Essays in History, Theory, and Praxis* (Albany: State University of New York Press, 2002).

myself, how could they sing that God reigns when there are wars, hunger, poverty, earthquakes, disease and sin, with its crude reality, that reign in all creation? I was trying to understand the problem of evil in the world, when the angel of inspiration approached me and asked me, 'Child of the new humanity, who lives *en el otro lado,* why do you complain so bitterly, like those that do not have faith? Why you do not realize that Mark, the servant of Jesus, through his Gospel has announced and proclaimed a new beginning, a new era, a new time? He reproached me by saying, 'You have been overlooked in denouncing what is wrong but have not paid attention to Mark's ἀρχή. This ἀρχή,' the angel of revelation continues, 'always signifies primacy, whether in time—beginning, *principium*—or in rank—power, dominion, office.[20] How could you forget that God reigns and that God is in control of the entire creation? Why did you not pay attention to Mark's message that declares that the time is fulfilled and the kingdom of God is at hand (Mk 1.15)? Why did you not believe that God is doing everything new, as it is written, "See, I am doing a new thing! Now it springs up; do you not perceive it? I am making a way in the desert and streams in the wasteland" (Isa. 43.19). Why do you not believe in what you have already written that God's power resides in Jesus the abject Messiah?' As soon as the angel of inspiration pronounced the last word, I burst into tears for my lack of faith.

After this I looked up and, behold, a door on the south was opened. From the south door, a black angel full of radiance and beauty appeared before me. His head and hair were black as the night, his teeth were beautiful as an ivory tower, and his eyes were like emeralds. His feet were like bronze glowing in a furnace, and his voice was like the sound of a sweet melody (Rev. 14-15). In his left hand he held the Book of Life, which was decorated with a red star. As soon as the black angel pronounced my name, I fell in love, and I praised the living God. Immediately, the black angel said to me: 'Manuel! Your prayers, concerns, and tears have come up as a memorial offering before God who has been always on your side' (Acts 10.4). Then the black angel—whose image is still pretty much in my mind— gave me the Book of Life with the following instructions: 'Write on it, some of your dreams, visions, and hopes that you have learned by reading the holy Gospel of Mark, our beloved disciple.' As soon as he pronounced the last word, I woke up, in fear, wondering what kind of vision this might be.

For What We Hope

Blessed be God who through Mark, the beloved disciple, has announced hope for all of us who dared to go back to Galilee. Mark, I want to take

---

20. Gerhard Delling, 'ἀρχή', *TDNT,* I: 479.

your invitation seriously. I would like to go back to Galilee in order to follow Jesus' steps, to become part of his movement, to enter into an ethic of *descaramiento* with all those vulnerable and precarious bodies in order to experience that the abject and penetrable Messiah is indeed the Resurrected One. We hope that this time we are not going to confuse, change, or substitute Galilee for Jerusalem, Rome, Chicago, or Mexico City, knowing that usually the Good News does not emerge from the center, but rather from the margins and the borderlands, where Jesus with the power of God is offering a livable life.

My hermeneutics in favor of a livable life must help me to declare that it is not enough merely to survive, as we often say in our daily language. It is not enough to live in a state of suspension between life and death.[21] It is not enough to sing: *No vale nada la vida*, 'Life is worth nothing,' and behave and act if *La vida no vale nada.* By returning to Galilee, I hope to be a witness to the fact that Jesus, the vulnerable and precarious Messiah has defeated the forces of death and the evil ideologies that legitimate someone to be human and deem millions and millions to be inhuman. Therefore, we hope for a life *for all*—with no exceptions. My hermeneutics in favor of life must denounce that we cannot speak out in defense of unborn life while ignoring the fact that humanity is valued and perceived differently by many depending on its race, gender, sexual orientation, legal status, and economic situation. We cannot claim to be protectors and defenders of life when the humanity of people *del otro lado* is a stake. The 'cheapest thing in Iraq is a human being, a human life. It is cheaper than an animal, than a pair of used-up batteries you buy on the street. Especially people like us.'[22] By returning to Galilee, we hope to understand that all life—as precarious as it might be—is sacred, because we are followers of God who protects Life. We hope to worship and follow Jesus whose life was in full solidarity with those who did not count and did not matter. We hope to enter into an ethic of *descaramiento* with all people. We hope to realize that we as human beings are tied to one another, even and especially in our loss and vulnerability. We hope to realize that it is the face of the other, the vulnerability of the other, the precariousness of their body that demands an ethical response from us. We hope to understand that the dignity and respect for all kinds of life neither comes from philosophical arguments nor theological discourse, constitutions nor religious discourse, but rather that it emerges from God who is the God of life.

We hope to find Good News for *all* through your gospel. Indeed, if the Gospel is neither Good nor News for *all* people, *all* cultures, *all* races, *all* God's creation, then let it be a curse on those idolatrous interpretations!

21. Butler, *Precarious Life,* p. 36.
22. Human Rights Watch, '*They Want Us Exterminated*', p. 1.

God's creation and people *del otro lado* have already suffered tremendously from all kinds of bibliolatry. I hope for a hermeneutics capable of transgressing borders, of subverting gender, and of debunking identities to bring comfort to people who live *en el otro lado*. I hope to share the Good News with other minority groups that are in *otros lados* of exclusion, whose lives are threatened by the forces of death. I hope that my brothers and sisters will understand that my hermeneutic *del otro lado* does not want *to replace* any of their insights, methods or hermeneutical approaches, but rather to *displace* them to the margins, to Galilee, where Jesus is to be found. I hope that they will forgive me for denouncing that often we are not engaged in an ethic of *descaramiento* anymore with the people that we intend to serve. I hope for a deep dialogue among other minority groups, a dialogue in which the Spirit of Truth guides us to foster and create the new family of God.

I hope for a more radical and inclusive idea of family that is more in tune with your own understanding of household. I hope to announce that our idea about family and so-called Christian family values often have little to do with Jesus' vision of household. I have lately been wondering why you have depicted Jesus as being quite 'anti-family' for demanding of all his followers that they leave home—mother, father, brothers, sister and fields for the sake of the gospel (Mk 10.29). Are not these requirements contrary to the values of the household and family that the Greco-Roman and Palestinian culture demanded and promoted? Please do not get me wrong. I am not complaining by asking these questions. On the contrary, for people 'like us', who belong nowhere, the idea that Jesus displaced his household to *otros lados* during his passion narrative has been a motif of celebration. It is in this context that I hope to share that Jesus' new family is not restricted to so-called Christian family values but that it is more radical in its demands. I hope to share that Jesus' new family is open to everyone, regardless of race, gender, sexual orientation, and economic and legal situation. It is Jesus' provocative idea of family that allows me to reclaim a place in the new household of God for all those bodies that have been intentionally forgotten, excluded from God's table. It is Jesus' willingness to eat with all kinds of people that moves me to denounce the idea of the happy heterosexual, white, middle-class family as being the only way to form God's family. I ask God for wisdom and strength to support all those bodies that have decided to celebrate God's diverse family in the midst of hearing day after day that they are destroying God's creation. I hope that one day we might understand that the true family of God should be rooted in service, compassion and solidarity to vulnerable and precarious people rather than in one's sexual orientation.

Reading your Gospel *del otro lado* has forced me to hope not only for Good News for God's human family, but also for our Pachamama—Mother Earth—which is still experiencing the suffering and subjugation that Adam's sin brought upon her (Rom. 8.19-22). We have sinned not just against God, our brothers and sisters, but also against our Pachamama for ignoring her cries and laments. I know that through your Gospel you announce a new beginning and have depicted Jesus with the wild animals (Mk 1.12), perhaps symbolizing a new creation in which both humans and the rest of God's creation coexist and cohabit the earth in harmony until God's final manifestation. I hope to learn to read the signs of the time and defend the land, the air, the trees, and the birds in order to celebrate God's bountiful creation. My hermeneutic *del otro lado* cannot ignore the language of our Pachamama, such as climate change, earthquakes, tsunamis, genetically modified seeds and the denuded soil that proclaim our brokenness and our failure to protect God's habitat. I would like to hope for a community that is fully involved in defending God's creations, defending them not just by their writings but also by living in ways that do not hurt our Pachamama. I would like to add my voice to the voice of my brothers and sisters from Chiapas while demanding, *Queremos un mundo donde quepan muchos mundos en armonía con la naturaleza*, 'We want a world where many worlds fit in harmony with nature.' I hope that once we become the guardians of creation, we will be able to share God's bountiful economy with our brothers and sisters who live on both *lados* of the Rio Grande.

I was busy writing you all my hopes in the Book of Life, when the black angel, the one who is like the Morning Star, appeared to me in my dreams. And look! He showed me el Rio Grande of the water of life (for a few) and death (for millions), as clear as crystal (for this side) and muddy as excrement (on the other side), flowing from the thrones of God and of the Lamb down the middle of the great and hateful borderline. On each side of the river and border stood the Tree of Life, bearing twelve crops of fruit, yielding its fruit every month. And the leaves of the tree are for the healing of the nations (Rev. 22.1-3). After this heavenly vision, the black angel woke me up and said to me: 'Manuel, in an act of justice, reclaim the fruits of the Tree of Life, which are for the entire creation, and not just for a few *chingones*.' He continued, 'Warn them that the Roi—the God Who Sees—has once again heard the cry of the migrants and has seen how the line is intended to secure and protect God's Tree of Life for the benefit of *los chingones*. Tell them, he continued, that no matter how many laws and patrols are positioned to stop the immigration, the influx of boundary-crossers will never stop, because they are reclaiming a slice of life in restitution for being disposed and displaced.[23] I asked him, 'How can I do that since I can barely

---

23. Leticia Guardiola, 'Borderless Women and Borderless Texts: A Cultural Reading of Matthew 15:21-28', in Phyllis A. Bird (ed.), *Reading the Bible as Women: Perspectives from Africa, Asia, and Latin America* (Atlanta: Scholars Press, 1997), pp. 69-81 (73).

speak and write?' He replied to me, 'Fear not, because you are not alone. Do not forget that you have been baptized and sealed as Manuel—God with us—and God has indeed revealed all those things to you.' Immediately, the black angel put words in my mouth and forced me to write: 'God's children *del otro lado* are not asking for charity, but rather they demand restitution for their economy that they might be healed and live in peace on the other side of the river.' As soon as the black angel pronounced this sentence against *los chingones*, I woke up. I felt comforted knowing that God is the only owner of the Tree of Life, and that at harvest time God sends people to collect the fruits of the Tree of Life that are capable of feeding God's creation.

I have chosen to conclude this letter, beloved Mark, by recalling your parable of the wicked and rapacious tenants, who, instead of giving back the fruits of the vineyard to the servants of God, became murderous. However, the richness of this provocative parable and the economic aspect involved in the death of Jesus the beloved Son I leave for another letter. I am happy to see how this parable somehow encapsulates some of the concerns, struggles and challenges that we have to endure every day for lack of opportunity to live a livable life. Living *en el otro lado* we realize that 'some humans take their humanness for granted, while others struggle to gain access to it'.[24] We people *del otro lado*, who have been dehumanized, seized, beaten to death and killed for transgressing borders and reclaiming the fruit of the vineyard, have learned how to negotiate our existence among signs of death. With sadness and tears in my eyes, I have found that God's words have been taken in vain and have been used to cause suffering and pain to people *del otro lado*. Moreover, some tenants of God's vineyard, claiming legitimacy to administer the earth, to watch for democracy in others' countries, and to protect us from terrorist attacks, often have become murderers and robbers of God's creation. However, the sins of ambition, power and control are not exclusive to this side of the river. We often live as enemies of the cross, and our god indeed is our stomach, and our glory is in our shame (Phil. 3.18-19). But now we have experienced new theophanies, and your holy gospel has announced a new era, a new beginning that enables us to hear the Good News for all. We are experiencing here and there God's kairotic moment, a moment that calls us to celebrate life and hope for a new heaven and a new earth. My community of *el otro lado* gives you thanks and praises you for challenging us to go back to Galilee and experience Jesus' resurrection through the experience of the abject, precarious and penetrable Messiah. We admire you because the experience of your community regarding Jesus' resurrection is not a *mysterium tremendum*, but rather a real revelation, a manifestation of God in favor of life, in solidarity with people whose lives do not matter.

---

24. Butler, *Frames of War*, p. 76.

Personal Greetings

I commend to you our sister Mila Diaz, an apostle of Jesus. She has been chosen among the saints of God to be responsible in reading our letter to you. We have sent you the best that we have, to make sure that all your community knows about the struggles, sufferings and hopes that we experience in *el otro lado*. She will speak to you not only through her mind, but also through her heart, because she bears in her entire body the marks of the cross of Jesus. She will explain to you with great detail—even in your own language—how the Holy Ruah is at work in our Bible groups. I beg you to receive her in the Lord in a way worthy of the saints and to give her any help she may need from you, for she has been a great help to many people *del otro lado*, including me (Rom. 16.12-13).

Carl, my fellow worker, sends his greetings to you, as do Gerardo, and all the priests of Our Lady of Guadalupe.

I, Manuel Villalobos Mendoza, who wrote down this letter, greet you in the name of Jesus, the abject and penetrable Messiah.

Dr Barbara Reid, Dr Barbara Bowe and Dr Carolyn Osiek, who have taught me how to read the Bible through feminist eyes, send you their greetings.

Dr Osvaldo Vena, a servant of Jesus since his childhood, who has accompanied me and encouraged me to embrace *el otro lado*, greet you in Jesus' name.

Dr Lallene Rector, a beloved child of Sofia, who has worked hard to understand our connectedness as human beings with our creator, greets you and wishes you peace.

Dr Ken Stone, a prophet of YHWH, who has shared his wisdom and insights with me, and has lived *en otros lados* of exclusion, greets you with the kiss of peace.

Tim, Antonieta and Tony, a real family to me here in Chicago, greet you.

Joanne Rodríguez greets you, and so do Ángela Schoepf, María Kennedy and all the brothers and sisters of the Hispanic Theological Initiative.

Ulrike Guthrie, who has edited this letter, greets you.

Ricardo, Laura, Ricardito, Marianita and 'la Gogol', whose hospitality I and the whole church here enjoy, send you their greetings.

Arturo and Ana, who are the creators of *Centro de Trabajadores Unidos* and vigilantly watch over the dignity of the migrants, greet you in the name of the God of justice.

Victor, Joe and little Joe, who, despite being segregated for supposedly destroying Christian family values, remain faithful to the service of God, greet you.

Ana Valtierra and all those that gathered in her household to worship God greet you.

Yolanda Pantoja—my beloved friend—and Alex and Gaby send you their greetings.

All the brothers and sisters who live *en el otro lado* send you greetings.

Greet one another with a holy kiss.

The peace of the God of justice, whose power was manifested in Jesus, the abject, precarious, vulnerable and penetrable Messiah, be with you all. Blessed be the one who reads Mark's Gospel from *otros lados*, and blessed are those who hear it and take to heart what is written in it, because the time is near (Rev. 1.3). The ones who gave testimony speak: Amen. Come, abject Messiah!

BIBLIOGRAPHY

Aberbach, M. 'The Relation between Master and Disciple in the Talmudic Age'. Pages 1-24 in *Essays Presented to Chief Rabbi Israel Brodie on the Occasion of his Seventieth Birthday*. Edited by H.J. Zimmels, J. Rabinnowitz and I. Finestein. London: Soncino Press, 1967.

Adams, J.N. *The Latin Sexual Vocabulary*. Baltimore: John Hopkins University Press, 1982.

Aland, Kurt. *Synopsis quattuor Evangeliorum: Locis parallelis Evangeliorum Apocryphorum et Patrum adhibitis edidit*. Stuttgart: Deutsche Bibelgesellschaft, 1996.

Albright, W.F., and C.S. Mann. *Matthew: Introduction, Translation and Notes*. New York: Doubleday, 1971.

Allen, W.C. *The Gospel according to Saint Mark: With Introduction, Notes and Map*. London: Rivingtons, 1915.

Allison, Dale C. 'The Eye Is the Lamp of the Body (Matthew 6.22-23=Luke 11.34-36)'. *New Testament Studies* 33 (1987), pp. 61-83.

Althaus-Reid, Marcella. 'Mark'. Pp. 517-25 in *The Queer Bible Commentary*. Edited by Deryn Guest, Robert Goss, Mona West and Thomas Bohache. London: SCM Press, 2006.

Amsel, Nachum. 'Homosexuality in Orthodox Judaism'. Accessed 13 May 2009. Online at http://www.lookstein.org/resources/homo sexuality_amsel.pdf

Anguiano Alberto. Email correspondence, 10 May 2009.

Anzaldúa, Gloria. *Borderland/La Frontera: The New Mestiza*. San Francisco: Spinster/Aunt Lute, 3rd edn, 2007.

—'Interviews with Gloria Anzaldúa by Karin Ikas'. Accessed 19 July 2009. Online at http://www.auntlute.com/www.auntlute.com/auntlute.com/GloriaAnzalduaInterview.html.

Armour, Ellen T., and Susan M. St. Ville, eds. *Bodily Citations: Religion and Judith Butler*. New York: Columbia University Press, 2006.

Austin, J.L. *How to Do Things with Words*. Cambridge, MA: Harvard University Press, 1975.

Bachelard, Gaston. *The Psychoanalysis of Fire*. Translated by Alan C.M. Ross. Preface by Northrop Frye. Boston: Beacon Press, 1964.

Balsdon, J.V.P.D. *Romans and Aliens*. Chapel Hill: University of North Carolina Press, 1979.

Barclay, Henry Swete. *Commentary on Mark*. Grand Rapids: Kregel Publications, 1977.

Bartlet, J. Vernon. *St. Mark*. New Century Bible. Edinburgh: T. & T. Clark, 1925.

Barton, Carlin. 'Being in the Eyes. Shame and Sight in Ancient Rome'. Pages 216-35 in *The Roman Gaze: Vision, Power, and the Body*. Edited by David Fredrick. Baltimore, MD: Johns Hopkins University Press, 2002.

Bartsch, Shadi. *The Mirror of the Self: Sexuality, Self Knowledge, and the Gaze in the Early Roman Empire*. Chicago: University of Chicago Press, 2006.

Belo, Fernando. *A Materialist Reading of the Gospel of Mark*. Translated by Matthew J. O'Connell. Maryknoll, NY: Orbis Books, 1981.

Berkovits, Eliezer. *Jewish Women in Time and Torah*. New Jersey: Ktav, 1990.

Berquist, Jon L. *Controlling Corporeality: The Body and the Household in Ancient Israel*. London: Rutgers University Press, 2002.

Best, Ernest. 'Role of the Disciples in Mark'. *New Testament Studies* 23 (1977), pp. 377-401.

Blair, E.P. 'Simon'. In *The Interpreter's Dictionary of the Bible*. Edited by G.A. Buttrick. 4 vols. Nashville: Abingdon. 1976.

'Blindman's Buff'. *Encyclopedia Britannica*. Accessed 3 November 2009. Online at http://www.britannica.com/EBchecked/topic/69380/blindmans-buff.

Blinzler, Josef. *The Trial of Jesus*. Translated by Isabel and Florence McHug. Westminster, MD: Newman Press, 1959.

—'The Jewish Punishment of Stoning in the New Testament Period'. Pages 146-61 in *The Trial of Jesus*. Edited by Ernest Bammel. Naperville, IL: Alec R. Allenson, 1970.

Boring, M. Eugene. *Mark: A Commentary*. Louisville, KY: Westminster John Knox Press, 2006.

Borrell, Agustín. *The Good News of Peter's Denial: A Narrative and Rhetorical Reading of Mark 14:54.66-72*. Translated by Sean Conlon. Atlanta: Scholars Press, 1998.

Bovon, François. *The Last Days of Jesus*. Translated by Kristin Hennessy. Louisville, KY: Westminster John Knox Press, 2006.

Bourke, Joanne. 'Torture as Pornography'. Accessed 9 December 2009. Online at http://www.guardian.co.uk/world/2004/may/07/gender.uk.

Boyarin, Daniel, 'Are There Any Jews in "The History of Sexuality"'. *Journal of the History of Sexuality* 5 (1995), pp. 333-55.

—*A Radical Jew: Paul and the Politics of Identity*. Berkeley: University of California Press, 1994.

Bravo, Carlos. *Jesús, hombre en conflicto: El relato de Marcos en América Latina*. México: Centro de Reflexión Teológica, 1986.

—*Galilea Año 30: Para leer el Evangelio de Marcos*. Córdoba: Ediciones el Almendro, 1991.

Braun, Willi. *Feasting and Social Rhetoric in Luke 14*. New York: Cambridge University Press, 1995.

Brilliant, Richard. *Gesture and Rank in Roman Art: The Use of Gestures to Denote Status in Roman Sculpture and Coinage*. New Haven: The Academy, 1963.

Brown, Raymond. *The Death of the Messiah: From Gethsemane to the Grave, I*. New York: Doubleday, 1994.

Broadhead, Edwin K. *Mark*. Sheffield: Sheffield Academic Press. 2001.

Büchsel, F. 'βαστάζω'. In *Theological Dictionary of the New Testament*. Edited by G. Kittel and G. Friedrich. Translated by G.W. Bromiley. 10 vols. Grand Rapids: Eerdmans, 1964-1976.

Bultmann, Rudolf. *The History of the Synoptic Tradition*. Translated by John Marsh. New York: Harper & Row, 1963.

Butler, Judith. 'Gendering the Body: Beauvoir's Philosophical Contribution'. Pp. 253-62 in *Women, Knowledge, and Reality: Explorations in Feminist Philosophy*. Edited by Ann Garry and Marilyn Pearsall. Boston: Unwin Hyman, 1989.

—*Gender Trouble: Feminism and the Subversion of Identity*. New York: Routledge, 1990; anniversary edition 1999.
—*Bodies That Matter: On the Discursive Limits of Sex*. New York: Routledge, 1993.
—'Imitation and Gender Insubordination'. Pages 307-20 in *The Lesbian and Gay Studies Reader*. Edited by Henry Abelove, Michèle Aina Barale and David M. Halperin. New York: Routledge, 1993.
—*Excitable Speech: A Politics of the Performative*. New York: Routledge, 1997.
—*The Psychic Life of Power*. Stanford, CA: Stanford University Press, 1997.
—'How Bodies Come to Matter: An Interview with Judith Butler'. *Signs: Journal for Women in Culture and Society* 23 (1998), pp. 275-86.
—'Subject of Sex/Gender/Desire'. Pages 273-291 in *Feminism & Politics*. Edited by Anne Phillips. New York: Oxford University Press, 1998.
—'A Bad Writer Bites Back'. *New York Times* (March 20, 1999).
—*Subjects of Desire: Hegelian Reflection in Twentieth-Century France*. New York: Columbia University Press, 1999.
—*Precarious Life: The Power of Mourning and Violence*. New York: Verso, 2004.
—*Undoing Gender*. New York: Routledge, 2004.
—*Giving an Account of Oneself*. New York: Fordham University Press, 2005.
—'Afterword'. Pages 276-91 in *Bodily Citations: Religion and Judith Butler*. Edited by Ellen T. Armour and Susan M. St. Ville. New York: Columbia University Press, 2006.
—*Frames of War. When Is Life Grievable?* New York: Verso, 2009.
Byrne, Brendan. 'The Scariest Gospel'. Accessed 29 September 2009. Online at http://www.americamagazine.org/content/article.cfm?article_id=4816.
—*A Costly Freedom: Theological Reading of Mark's Gospel*. Collegeville, MN: Liturgical Press, 2008.
Camery-Hoggatt, Jerry. *Irony in Mark's Gospel: Text and Subtext*. Cambridge: Cambridge University Press, 1992.
Campbell, William Sanger. 'Engagement, Disengagement and Obstruction: Jesus' Defense Strategies in Mark's Trial and Executions Scenes (14.53-64; 15.1-39)'. *Journal for the Study of the New Testament* 26 (2004), pp. 283-300. Capel Anderson, Janice, and Jeffrey L. Staley, eds. *Taking It Personally: Autobiographical Biblical Criticism*. Atlanta: Scholar Press, 1995.
—'"Why Did You Abandon Me?" Abandonment Christology in Mark's Gospel'. Pages 99-117 in *The Trial and Death of Jesus: Essays on the Passion Narrative in Mark*. Edited by Geert Van Oyen and Tom Shepherd. Leuven: Peeters, 2006.
Carrillo, Héctor. *The Night Is Young: Sexuality in Mexico in the Time of AIDS*. Chicago: University of Chicago, 2002.
'César Calvo'. Accessed 5 February 2010. Online at http://cesarcalvo.8m.com/produccion%20musical.htm.
Chambers, Samuel A., and Terrell Carver. *Judith Butler and Political Theory: Troubling Politics*. New York: Routledge, 2008.
Chapman, Cynthia R. *The Gendered Language of Warfare in the Israelite-Assyrian Encounter*. Winona Lake, IN: Eisenbrauns, 2004.
Chapman, David W. *Ancient Jewish and Christian Perceptions of Crucifixion*. Tübingen: Mohr Siebeck, 2008.
Chau, Manu. *Clandestino*. CD. Release date: 6 October 1998.
Clark, K.W. 'Bethany'. In *The Interpreter's Dictionary of the Bible*. Edited by G.A. Buttrick. 4 vols. Nashville, TN: Abingdon, 1976.

Clements, R.E. '*zākhār*'. In *Theological Dictionary of the Old Testament*. Edited by G.J. Botterweck and H. Ringgren. Translated by J.T. Willis, G. W. Bromiley and D.E. Green. 8 vols. Grand Rapids: Eerdmans, 1974.

Coleman, K.M. 'Fatal Charades: Roman Executions Staged as Mythological Enactments'. *Journal of Roman Studies* 80 (1990), pp. 44-73.

Collins, John. J. 'The Archeology of the Crucifixion'. *Catholic Biblical Quarterly* 1 (1939), pp. 154-59.

Connolly, Joy. 'Virile Tongues: Rhetoric and Masculinity'. Pages 83-97 in *A Companion to Roman Rhetoric*. Edited by William Dominik and Jon Hall. Oxford: Blackwell, 2007.

Connolly, Michele A. *Disorderly Women and the Order of God: An Australian Feminist Reading of the Gospel of Mark*. PhD diss., Graduate Theological Union, 2008.

Conway, Colleen M. *Behold the Man: Jesus and Greco-Roman Masculinity*. Oxford: Oxford University Press, 2008.

Corbeill, Anthony. 'Political Movement. Walking and Ideology in Republican Rome'. Pages 182-215 in *The Roman Gaze: Vision, Power, and the Body*. Edited by David Fredrick. Baltimore, MD: Johns Hopkins University Press, 2002.

Counihand, Carole and Penny Van Esterik. 'Introduction'. Pages 1-7 in *Food and Culture: A Reader*. Edited by Carole Counihan and Penny Van Esterik. London: Routledge, 1997.

Crossan, John Dominic. *The Historical Jesus: The Life of a Mediterranean Jewish Peasant*. New York: HarperSanFrancisco, 1991.

Croy, N. Clayton. *The Mutilation of Mark's Gospel*. Nashville, TN: Abingdon, 2003.

Cuervo, Rufino José. *Diccionario de construcción y régimen de la lengua Castellana, Tomo II*. Santafé de Bogotá: Instituto Caro y Cuervo, 1994.

Culbertson, Phillip. 1998. 'Designing Men: Reading the Male Body as a Text'. *Journal of the Society for Textual Reasoning* 7 (1998). Accessed 13 November 2009. Online at http://etext.virginia.edu/journals/tr/archive/volume7/Culbertson1.html.

Culpepper, Alan. *Mark*. Macon, GA: Smyth & Helwys, 2007.

Danker, Frederick William, *A Greek-English Lexicon of the New Testament and Other Early Christian Literature*. Chicago: University of Chicago Press, 2000.

Danove, Paul L. *The Rhetoric of Characterization of God, Jesus, and Jesus' Disciple in the Gospel of Mark*. New York: T. & T. Clark International, 2005.

Dannemann, Irene. 'The Slave Woman's Challenge to Peter'. Pages 53-57 in *Transgressors: Toward a Feminist Biblical Theology*. Edited by Claudia Janssen, Ute Ochtendung and Beate When. Translated by Linda M. Maloney. Collegeville, MN: Liturgical Press, 2002.

De la Torre, Miguel A., and Edwin David Aponte, eds. *Introducing Latino/a Theologies*. Maryknoll, NY: Orbis Books, 2001.

—*Reading the Bible from the Margins*. Maryknoll, NY: Orbis Books, 2002.

DeMaris, Richard E. *The New Testament in its Ritual World*. New York: Routledge, 2008.

Derrett, J. Duncan M. *Law in the New Testament*. London: Darton, Longman & Todd, 1970.

Desbordes, Françoise. 'L'idéal romain dans la rhétorique de Quintilien'. *KTEMA = Civilisations de l'Orient de la Grèce et de Rome antiques* 14 (1989), pp. 273-79.

Díez Merino, Luis. 'El suplico de la cruz en la literatura judía intertestamental'. *Studii Biblici Franciscani Liber Annuus* 26 (1976), pp. 31-120.

Donahue, John R., and Daniel J. Harrington. *The Gospel of Mark.* Collegeville, MN: Liturgical Press, 2002.

Douglas, Mary. 'Deciphering a Meal'. Pages 36-54 in *Food and Culture: A Reader.* Edited by Carole Counihan and Penny Van Esterik. London: Routledge, 1997.

—*Purity and Danger: An Analysis of the Concepts of Pollution and Taboo.* London: Routledge, 2004.

Dowd, Sharyn, and Elizabeth Struthers Malbon. 'The Significance of Jesus' Death in Mark: Narrative Context and Authorial Audience'. *Journal of Biblical Literature* 125 (2006), pp. 271-97.

Duke, Paul D. *Irony in the Fourth Gospel.* Atlanta: John Knox Press, 1985.

Edwards, James R. *The Gospel according to Mark.* Grand Rapids: Eerdmans, 2002.

Ernout, A. 'Vis-vires-vis'. *Revue de philologie, de littérature et d'histoire anciennes* 28 (1954), pp. 165-97.

Evans, Craig A. *Mark 8:27–16:20.* Nashville, TN: Thomas Nelson Publishers, 2001.

—'Jewish Burial Traditions and the Resurrection of Jesus'. *Journal for the Study of the Historical Jesus* 3 (2005), pp. 233-48.

Eve, Eric. 'Spit on your Eye: The Blind Man of Bethsaida and the Blind Man of Alexandria'. *New Testament Studies* 54 (2008), pp. 1-17.

Flores, Fernando. '101 formas de llamar a un homosexual'. Accessed 1 June 2009. Online at http://anodis.com/nota/4092.asp.

Foucault, Michel. *Power/Knowledge: Selected Interviews and Other Writings, 1972–1977.* New York: Pantheon, 1972.

—*Discipline and Punishment.* London: Tavistock, 1977.

—*History of Sexuality, I.* Translated by Robert Hurley. London: Penguin, 1990.

—*The Politics of Truth.* Edited by Sylvère Lotringer. Introduction by John Rajchman. Translated by Lysa Hochroth and Catherine Porter. Los Angeles: Semiotext(e), 1997.

—'Sex, Power and the Politics of Identity'. Pages 163-73 in *Ethics: Subjectivity and Truth.* Translated by R. Hurley. Edited by Paul Rabinow. New York: New York Press, 1997.

France, R.T. *The Gospel of Mark: A Commentary on the Greek Text.* Grand Rapids: Eerdmans, 2002.

Fredrick, David. 'Introduction'. Pages 1-30 in *The Roman Gaze: Vision, Power and the Body.* Edited by David Fredrick. Baltimore, MD: Johns Hopkins University Press, 2002.

—'Mapping Penetrability in Late Republican and Early Imperial Rome'. Pages 236-64 in *The Roman Gaze: Vision, Power and the Body.* Edited by David Fredrick. Baltimore, MD: Johns Hopkins University Press, 2002.

Fuentes, Carlos. *The Death of Artemio Cruz.* Translated by Sam Hileman. New York: Farrar, Straus & Giroux, 1964.

Garza Carvajal, Federico. *Butterflies Will Burn: Prosecuting Sodomites in Early Modern Spain and Mexico.* Austin: University of Texas Press, 2003.

Gibson, Shimon. *The Final Days of Jesus: The Archeological Evidence.* New York: Harper One, 2009.

Gilmore, David D. *Manhood in the Making: Cultural Concepts of Masculinity.* New Haven: Yale University Press, 1990.

Glancy, Jennifer. 'The Mistress of the Gaze: Masculinity, Slavery, and Representation'. Pages 127-45 in *Biblical Glamour and Hollywood Glitz.* Edited by Alice Bach. Atlanta: Scholars Press, 1996.

Gleason, Maud. 'Mutilated Messengers: Body Language in Josephus'. Pages 50-85 in *Being Greek under Rome: Cultural Identity, the Second Sophistic and the Development of Empire*. Edited by Simon Goldhill. Cambridge: Cambridge University Press, 2001.

Good, Edwin M. *Irony in the Old Testament*. Philadelphia: Westminster Press, 1965.

Goodspeed, Edgar J. 'The Original Conclusion of the Gospel of Mark'. *American Journal of Theology* 9 (1905), pp. 484-90.

Guardiola, Leticia. 'Borderless Women and Borderless Texts: A Cultural Reading of Matthew 15:21-28'. Pages 69-81 in *Reading the Bible as Women: Perspectives from Africa, Asia, and Latin America*. Edited by Phyllis A. Bird, Atlanta: Scholars Press, 1997.

Gubar, Susan. *Judas: A Biography*. New York: W.W. Norton, 2009.

Gundry, Judith M. 'Children in the Gospel of Mark, with Special Attention to Jesus' Blessing of the Children (Mark 10:13-16) and the Purpose of Mark'. Pages 143-76 in *The Child in the Bible*. Edited by Marcia J. Bunge. Grand Rapids: Eerdmans, 2008.

Gundry, Robert H. *Mark: A Commentary on his Apology for the Cross*. Grand Rapids: Eerdmans, 1993.

Guerra, Francisco. *The Pre-Columbian Mind*. New York: Seminar Press, 1971.

Hall, Stuart G. *Melito of Sardis: On Pascha and Fragments*. Oxford: Clarendon Press, 1979.

Hanson, David J. *Preventing Alcohol Abuse: Alcohol, Culture, and Control*. Westport: Praeger, 1995.

Harrill, Albert, J. 'Cannibalistic Language in the Fourth Gospel and Greco-Roman Polemics of Factionalism (John 6:52-66)'. *Journal of Biblical Literature* 127 (2008), pp. 133-58.

Hegel, G.W.F. *Phenomenology of Spirit*. Translated by A.V. Miller. Oxford: Oxford University Press, 1979.

Hekster, Olivier. 'Captured in the Gaze of Power, Visibility, Games and Roman Imperial Representation'. Pages 156-76 in *Imaginary Kings: Royal Images in the Ancient Near East, Greece and Rome*. Edited by Olivier Hekster and Richard Fowler. Stuttgart: Steiner, 2005.

Henderson, Jeffrey. 'Greek Attitudes toward Sex'. Pages 1249-63 in *Civilization of the Ancient Mediterranean: Greece and Rome, II*. Edited by Michael Grant and Rachael Kitzinger. New York: Charles Scribner's Sons, 1988.

Hengel, Martin. *Crucifixion in the Ancient World and the Folly of the Message of the Cross*. Translated by John Bowden. London: SCM Press, 1977.

Hentrich, Thomas. 'Masculinity and Disability in the Bible'. Pages 73-87 in *This Abled Body: Rethinking Disabilities in Biblical Studies*. Edited by Hector Avalos, Sarah J. Melcher and Jeremy Schipper. Atlanta: Society of Biblical Literature, 2007.

Hester, David, 'Eunuchs and the Postgender Jesus: Matthew 19.12 and Transgressive Sexualities'. *Journal for the Study of the New Testament* 28 (2005), pp. 13-40.

Hornsby, Teresa J. 'The Annoying Woman: Biblical Scholarship after Judith Butler'. Pages 71-89 in *Bodily Citations: Religion and Judith Butler*. Edited by Ellen T. Armour and Susan M. St. Ville, New York: Columbia University Press, 2006.

Human Rights Watch. *They Want Us Exterminated: Murder, Torture, Sexual Orientation and Gender in Iraq*. New York: Human Rights Watch, 2009.

Hun Kim, Tae. 'The Anarthrous υἱὸς θεοῦ in Mark 15,39 and the Roman Imperial Cult'. *Biblica* 79 (1998), pp. 221-41.

Iersel, Bas M.F. van, *Mark: A Reader-Response Commentary*. Translated by W.H. Biss-cheroux, Sheffield: Sheffield Academic Press, 1998.

Iverson, Kelly R. *Gentiles in the Gospel of Mark: 'Even the Dogs under the Table Eat the Children's Crumbs'*. New York: T. & T. Clark International, 2007.

Jackson, Howard M. 'The Death of Jesus in Mark and The Miracle from the Cross'. *New Testament Studies* 33 (1987), pp. 16-37.

Jagger, Gill. *Judith Butler: Sexual Politics, Social Change and the Power of the Perfor-mative*. New York: Routledge, 2008.

Jenkins, Thomas E. *Intercepted Letters: Epistolary and Narrative in Greek and Roman Literature*. Lanham, MD: Lexington Books, 2006.

Jennings, Theodore W. *The Insurrection of the Crucified: The 'Gospel of Mark' as Theo-logical Manifesto*. Chicago: Exploration Press, 2003.

—*The Man Jesus Loved: Homoerotic Narratives from the New Testament*. Cleveland, OH: Pilgrim Press, 2003.

Jensen, Robin M. 'The Passion in Early Christian Art'. Pages 53-84 in *Perspectives on the Passion: Encountering the Bible through the Arts*. Edited by Christine E. Jones. New York: T. & T. Clark International, 2007.

Jeremias, Joachim. *The Eucharistic Words of Jesus*. Translated by Norman Perrin. New York: Charles Scribner's Sons, 1966.

Jobling, David, Tina Pippin and Ronald Schleifer, eds. *The Postmodern Bible Reader*. Oxford: Blackwell, 2001.

Johnson, Earl S. 'Is Mark 15.39 the Key to Mark's Christology?' *Journal for the Study of New Testament* 31 (1987), pp. 3-22.

Karris, Robert J. *Luke: Artist and Theologian*. New York: Paulist Press, 1985.

Kelber, Werner H. *The Oral and the Written Gospel: The Hermeneutics of Speaking and Writing in the Synoptic Tradition, Mark, Paul and Q*. Bloomington: Indiana University Press, 1983.

Kiley, Bernadette. 'The Servant Girl in the Markan Passion Narrative: An Alternative Feminist Reading'. *Lutheran Theological Journal* 41 (2007), pp. 48-57.

Kingsbury, Jack Dean. *Conflict in Mark*. Minneapolis: Fortress Press, 1992.

Kinukawa, Hisako. *Women and Jesus in Mark: A Japanese Feminist Perspective*. Maryknoll, NY: Orbis Books, 1994.

Kirschner, Robert. 'Halakhah and Homosexuality: A Reappraisal'. *Judaism* 37 (1988), pp. 450-58.

Kitzberger, Ingrid Rosa, ed. *The Personal Voice in Biblical Interpretation*. New York: Routledge, 1999.

—'Pre-Liminaries'. Pages 1-11 in *Autobiographical Biblical Criticism: Learning to Read. Between Text and Self*. Edited by Ingrid Rosa Kitzberger. Leiden: Deo, 2003.

Klosinski, Lee E. *The Meals in Mark*. PhD diss., Claremont: Claremont Graduate School, 1988.

Krebs, Michael. 'Cardinal: Homosexuals "Will Never Enter the Kingdom of Heaven"'. Accessed 6 March 2010. Online at http://www.digitaljournal.com/article/283080.

Kristeva, Julia. *Powers of Horror: An Essay on Abjection*. Translated by Leon S. Roudiez. New York: Columbia University Press, 1982.

Kuefler, Matthew. *The Manly Eunuch: Masculinity, Gender Ambiguity, and Christian Ideology in Late Antiquity*. Chicago: University of Chicago Press, 2001.

Kyle, Donald G. *Spectacle of Death in Ancient Rome*. New York: Routledge, 1998.

Lacan, Jacques. *Feminine Sexuality: Jacques Lacan and the École Freudienne.* Edited by Juliet Mitchell and Jacqueline Rose. Translated by Jacqueline Rose. New York: Norton, 1982.

Lamas, Marta. 'By Night, a Street Night, "Public" Women of the Night on the Streets of Mexico City'. Pages 237-54 in *Gender Places: Feminist Anthropologies of Latin America.* Edited by Rosario Montoya, Lessie Jo Frazier and Janise Hurtig. New York: Palgrave Macmillan, 2002.

Légasse, Simone. *The Trial of Jesus.* Translated by John Bowden. London: SCM Press, 1997.

Levinas, Emanuel. 'Dialogue with Emmanuel Levinas'. Pages 13-34 in *Face to Face with Levinas.* Edited by Richard A. Cohen. Albany: State University of New York, 1986.

—*Difficult Freedom: Essays on Judaism.* Translated by Seán Hand. Baltimore, MD: Johns Hopkins University Press, 1990.

Ley de acceso de las mujeres a una vida libre de violencia del Distrito Federal. Accessed 14 November 2009. Online at http://www.asambleadf.gob.mx/al/pdf/010803000083.pdf.

Leyerle, Blake. 'John Chrysostom on the Gaze'. *Journal of Christian Studies* 1 (1993), pp. 159-74.

Liew, Tat-siong Benny. 'Re-Mark-able Masculinities: Jesus, the Son of Man, and the (Sad) Sum of Manhood?' Pages 93-135 in *New Testaments Masculinities.* Edited by Stephen D. Moore and Janice Capel Anderson. Atlanta: Society of Biblical Literature, 2003.

Lloyd, Moya. 'Performativity, Parody, Politics'. *Theory Culture and Society* 16.2 (1999), pp. 195-213.

—*Judith Butler: From Norms to Politics.* Cambridge: Polity Press, 2007.

Luz, Ulrich. *Matthew 21–28.* Minneapolis: Fortress Press, 2005.

Macdonald, Dennis R. *The Homeric Epics and the Gospel of Mark.* New Haven: Yale University, 2000.

Maggi, Alberto. *Nuestra Señora de los Herejes: María y Nazaret.* Cordoba: Editorial el Almendro, 2002.

Malbon, Elizabeth Struthers. *In the Company of Jesus: Characters in Mark's Gospel.* Louisville, KY: Westminster John Knox Press, 2000.

Manlio, Simonetti, ed. *Ancient Christian Commentary on Scripture: Matthew 14–28.* Downers Grove, IL: InterVarsity Press, 2002.

Mann, C.S. *Mark: A New Translation with Introduction and Commentary.* Garden City: Doubleday, 1986.

Marcus, Joel. 'Crucifixion as a Parodic Exaltation'. *Journal of Biblical Literature* 125 (2006), pp. 73-87.

—*Mark 8–16.* New Haven: Yale University Press, 2009.

Martinez-Vazquez, Hjamil A. 'Dis-covering the Silences. A Postcolonial Critique of U.S. Religious Historiography'. Pages 50-78 in *New Horizons in Hispanic/Latino(a) Theology.* Edited by Benjamin Valentin. Cleveland, OH: Pilgrim Press, 2003.

Mateos Juan and Fernando Camacho. *El Evangelio de Marcos: Análisis lingüístico y comentario exegético, III.* Córdoba: Ediciones el Almendro, 2008.

Matera, Frank J. *Passion Narratives and Gospel Theologies: Interpreting the Synoptics through their Passion Stories.* New York: Paulist Press, 1986.

Matsuda, Mari J., Charles R. Lawrence III, Richard Delgado and Kimberlè Williams Crenshaw, eds. *Words That Wound: Critical Race Theory, Assaultive Speech, and the First-Amendment.* Boulder, CO: Westview Press, 1993.

Mayordomo Marin, Moisés. 'Construction of Masculinity in Antiquity and Early Christianity'. In *Lectio Difficilior.* Accessed 9 August 2009. Online at http://www.lectio.unibe.ch/06_2/marin_construction.htm.

McRuer, Robert. *The Queer Renaissance: Contemporary American Literature and the Reinvention of Lesbian and Gay Identities.* New York: New York University Press, 1997.

Meekosha, Helen. 'The Meaning of Gender'. Pages 764-69 in *Encyclopedia of Disability, 2.* Edited by Gary L. Albrecht, Thousand Oaks, CA: Sage Publications, 2006.

Merenlahti, Petri. 'Reading Mark for the Pleasure of Fantasy'. Pages 87-104 in *Psychology and the Bible: A New Way to Read the Scriptures, III.* Edited by J. Harold Ellens and Wayne G. Rollins.Westport, CT: Praeger, 2004.

Michaelis. W. 'κρατέω'. In *Theological Dictionary of the New Testament.* Edited by G. Kittel and G. Friedrich. Translated by G.W. Bromiley. 10 vols. Grand Rapids: Eerdmans, 1964-1976.

Messinger Cypess, Sandra. *La Malinche in Mexican Literature: From History to Myth.* Austin: University of Texas Press, 1991.

Miller, Susan. *Women in Mark's Gospel.* New York: T. & T. Clark International, 2004.

Miquel, Esther. 'Historicidad en los realatos evangélicos de las unciones de Jesús. Semejanzas entre la praxis de Jesús y la de algunos grupos filosóficos contraculturales de la época Helenístico-Romana'. *Estudios Bíblicos* 62 (2004), pp. 3-26.

Moloney, Francis J. *The Gospel of Mark.* Peabody, MA: Hendrickson Publishers, 2006.

Montefiore, Claude Goldsmid. *The Synoptic Gospel, I.* London: Macmillan, 1927.

Moxnes, Halvor. *Putting Jesus in his Place: A Radical Vision of Household and Kingdom.* Louisville, KY: Westminster John Knox Press, 2003.

—'Jesus in Gender Trouble'. *Cross Currents* 54 (2004), pp. 31-46.

Myers, Ched. *Binding the Strong Man: A Political Reading of Mark's Story of Jesus.* Maryknoll, NY: Orbis Books, 1988.

Nakashima Brock, Rita. *Journeys by Heart: A Christology of Erotic Power.* New York: Crossroad, 1988.

Nancy, Jean-Luc. 'La existencia exiliada'. *Archipiélago: Cuadernos de Crítica de la Cultura* 26-27 (1996), pp. 34-40.

Nasrallah, Elkin. 'La muerte de Celedonio Martinez'. Unpublished poems. Email correspondence, 1 June 2009.

Nesbitt, Charles F. 'The Bethany Tradition in the Gospel Narrative'. *Journal of the American Academy of Religion* 19 (1961), pp. 119-24.

Neufeld, Dietmar. 'Jesus' Eating Transgressions and Social Impropriety in the Gospel of Mark: A Social Scientific Approach'. *Biblical Theology Bulletin* 30 (2000), pp. 15-26.

Neyrey, Jerome. 'The Idea of Purity in Mark's Gospel. *Semeia* 35 (1986), pp. 91-128.

—'Despising the Shame of the Cross: Honor and Shame in the Johannine Passion Narrative'. *Semeia* 69 (1996), pp. 113-37.

—'Jesus, Gender, and the Gospel of Matthew'. Pages 43-66 in *New Testament Masculinities.* Edited by Stephen D. Moore and Janice Capel Anderson. Atlanta: Society of Biblical Literature, 2003.

Nickoloff, James B. 'Sexuality: A Queer Omission in U.S. Latino/a Theology'. *Journal of Hispanic Latino Theology* 10 (2003), pp. 31-51.

Nineham, D.E. *The Gospel of Saint Mark.* Baltimore, MD: Penguin Books, 1963.

Nolland, John. *The Gospel of Matthew: A Commentary on the Greek Text.* Grand Rapids: Eerdmans, 2005.

North, J.L. 'Marcos ho kolobodaktylos: Hippolytus Elenchus vii.30'. *Journal of Theo-logical Studies* 28 (1977), pp. 498-507.

Nussbaum, Martha C. 'The Professor of Parody: The Hip Defeatism of Judith Butler'. *The New Republic* 220.4 (1999), pp. 38-45.

Oden, Thomas C. and Christopher A. Hall. *Ancient Christian Commentary on Scripture: Mark.* Downers Grove, IL: InterVarsity Press, 1998.

—*The African Memory of Mark: Reassessing Early Church Tradition.* Downers Grove, IL: InterVarsity Press, 2011.

Ortiz, Beto. 'Perú y el fantasma de la homofobia'. Accessed 6 March 2010. Online at http://www.ar.terra.com/terramagazine/interna/0,,OI1946644-EI10363,00.html.

Oyen, Geert Van, 'The Vulnerable Authority of the Author of the Gospel of Mark. Re-Reading the Paradoxes'. Paper presented at the annual meeting of the SBL. New Orleans, LA, 21 November 2009.

Paz, Octavio. *The Labyrinth of Solitude: Life and Thought in Mexico.* Translated by Lysander Kemp. New York: Grove Press, 1961.

Peláez, Jesús. 'La praxis curativa de Jesús en el Evangelio de Marcos. Una salvación que se brinda a todos'. *Éxodo* 56 (2000), pp. 37-42.

Pérez-Álvarez, Eliseo. 2007. *Marcos.* Minneapolis: Augsburg Fortress.

Pérez Herrero, Francisco. *Pasión y pascua de Jesús según san Marcos. Del texto a la vida.* Burgos: Imprenta Santos, 2001.

Pikaza, Xavier, *Pan, casa palabra: La iglesia en Marcos.* Salamanca: Ediciones Sígueme, 1998.

Pilch, John J. 'Death with Honor: The Mediterranean Style Death of Jesus in Mark'. *Biblical Theology Bulletin* 25 (1995), pp. 65-70.

Pobee, John. 'The Cry of the Centurion—A Cry of Defeat'. Pages 91-102 in *The Trial of Jesus.* Edited by Ernest Bammel. Naperville, IL: Alec R. Allenson, 1970.

Rhodes, David. *Reading Mark: Engaging the Gospel.* Minneapolis: Fortress Press, 2004.

Rivera Pagán, Luís N. 'El SIDA: Desafío a la conciencia cristiana'. Pages 53-68 in *Los sueños del ciervo: Perspectivas teológicas desde el Caribe.* Quito: Ediciones CLAI, 1995

Robbins, Vernon K. *New Boundaries in Old Territory: Form and Social Rhetoric in Mark.* New York: Peter Lang, 1994.

Roland Guzman, Carla E. 'Sexuality'. Pages 257-64 in *Handbook of Latina/o Theolo-gies.* Edited by Edwin David Aponte and Miguel A. De la Torre. Saint Louis: Chalice Press, 2006.

Rousselle, Aline. 1988. *Porneia: On Desire and the Body in Antiquity.* New York: Basil Blackwell.

Rubin, Gayle. 2006. 'The Traffic in Women: Notes on the "Political Economy" of Sex'. Pages 87-106 in *Feminist Anthropology:A Reader.* Edited by Ellen Lewin. Mal-den, MA: Blackwell.

Salih, Sara. *Judith Butler.* New York: Routledge, 2002.

Samuel, Simon. *A Postcolonial Reading of Mark's Story of Jesus.* New York: T. & T. Clark, 2007.

Sanders, J.N. 'Those Whom Jesus Loved (John IX.5)'. *New Testament Studies* 1 (1954), pp. 29-41.

Santos, Narry F. *Slave of All: The Paradox of Authority and Servanthood in the Gospel of Mark.* Sheffield: Sheffield Academic Press, 2003.

Santos Pachecho, Salvador. Email correspondence, 10 January 2010.

Satlow, Michael L. 'Jewish Construction of Nakedness in Late Antiquity'. *Journal of Biblical Literature* 116 (1997), pp. 429-54.

Scarry, Elaine. *The Body in Pain: The Making and Unmaking of the World*. New York: Oxford University Press, 1985.

Schildgen, Brenda Deen. *Power and Prejudice: The Reception of the Gospel of Mark.* Detroit, MI: Wayne State University Press, 1999.

Schmidt, T.E. 'Mark 15:16-32: The Crucifixion Narrative and the Roman Triumphal Procession'. *New Testament Studies* 41 (1995), pp. 1-18.

Schneider, J. 'ὀνειδίζω'. In *Theological Dictionary of the New Testament*. Edited by G. Kittel and G. Friedrich. Translated by G.W. Bromiley. 10 vols. Grand Rapids: Eerdmans, 1964–1976.

Schottroff, Luise. *Lydia's Impatient Sister:A Feminist Social History of Early Christianity.* Translated by Barbara and Martin Rumscheidt. Louisville, KY: Westminster John Knox Press, 1995.

Schüssler Fiorenza, Elisabeth. *Jesus: Miriam's Child, Sophia's Prophet: Critical Issues in Feminist Christology.* New York: Continuum, 1994.

Segovia, Fernando. 'Toward Latino/a American Biblical Criticism: Latin(o/a)ness as Problematic'. Pages 193-223 in *They Were in One Place? Toward Minority Biblical Criticism.* Edited by Randall C. Bailey, Tat-siong Benny Liew and Fernando Segovia. Leiden: Brill, 2009.

Senior, Donald. *The Passion of Jesus in the Gospel of Mark.* Collegeville, MD: Liturgical Press, 1984.

Severus of Al'Ashmunein. *History of the Patriarchs of the Coptic Church of Alexandria.* Edited, translated and annotated by B. Evett. Paris: Firmin-Didot, 1948.

Sharp, Carolyn J. *Irony and Meaning in the Hebrew Bible*. Bloomington: Indiana University Press, 2009.

Sharrock, Alison R. 'Looking at Looking. Can you Resist a Reading?' Pages 265-95 in *The Roman Gaze: Vision, Power, and the Body.* Edited by David Fredrick. Baltimore, MD: Johns Hopkins University Press, 2002.

Shi, Wenhua. *Paul's Message of the Cross and Body Language*. Tübingen: Mohr Siebeck, 2008.

Sipiora, Phillip and James S. Baumlin, eds. *Rhetoric and Kairos: Essays in History, Theory, and Praxis.* Albany: State University of New York Press, 2002.

Sloyan, Gerard S. *Jesus on Trial: A Study on the Gospels.* Minneapolis: Fortress Press, 2006.

Smith, Morton. *The Secret Gospel: The Discovery and Interpretation of the Secret Gospel according to Mark.* New York: Harper & Row, 1973.

Staley, Jeffrey L. 'What Is Critical about Autobiographical (Biblical) Criticism?' Pages 12-33 in *Autobiographical Biblical Criticism: Between Text and Self.* Edited by Ingrid Rosa Kitzberger. Leiden: Deo, 2002.

Stein, Robert H. *Mark.* Grand Rapids: Baker Academic, 2008.

Stone, Ken. 'Bibles That Matter: Biblical Theology and Queer Performativity'. *Biblical Theology Bulletin* 38 (2008), pp. 1-20.

Streeter, B.H. *The Four Gospels: A Study of Origins.* New York: Macmillan, 1925.

Sugawara, Yuji. 'The Minor Characters in Mark's Gospel: Their Role and Functions'. *Annual of the Japanese Biblical Institute* 24 (1998), pp. 66-82.

Swancutt, Diana M. 2003. 'The Disease of Effemination: The Charge of Effeminacy and the Verdict of God (Romans 1:18–2:16)'. Pages 193-234 in *New Testament*

Masculinities. Edited by Stephen D. Moore and Janice Capel Anderson. Atlanta: Society of Biblical Literature.

Tamez, Elsa. 'Epístola de Priscila a los Hermanos y Hermanas Reunidos en Sâo Paulo Brasil'. Paper presented at Conferencia Sobre Cristianismo en América Latina y el Caribe: Trayectorias, Diagnóstico y Perspectivas. Sâo Paulo, Brasil, 29 July, 2003.

Taylor, Joan E. 'Golgotha: A Reconsideration of the Evidence for the Sites of Jesus' Crucifixion and Burial'. *New Testament Studies* 44 (1998), pp. 180-203.

Taylor, Vincent. *The Gospel According to St. Mark. The Greek Text with Introduction. Notes, and Indexes.* London: Macmillan & Co. Ltd., 1953.

'The World Ridicules God's Son'. Accessed 4 December 2009. Online at http://www. biblegateway.com/resources/commentaries/IVP-NT/Matt/World-Ridicules-Gods-Son.

Thurman, Eric. 'Looking for a Few Good Men: Mark and Masculinity'. Pages 137-61 in *New Testament Masculinities*. Edited by Stephen D. Moore and Janice Capel Anderson. Atlanta: Society of Biblical Literature, 2003.

—*Writing the Nation/Reading the Men: Postcolonial Masculinities in Mark's Gospel and the Ancient Novel.* PhD diss., Drew University, 2010.

Tijerina Revilla, Anita. 'Muxerista Pedagogy: Raza Womyn Teaching Social Justice through Student Activism'. *The High School Journal* 87.4 (2004), pp. 80-94.

Tolbert, Mary Ann. *Sowing the Gospel: Mark's World in Literary-Historical Perspective.* Minneapolis: Fortress Press, 1989.

—'How the Gospel of Mark Builds Characters'. *Interpretation* 47 (1993), pp. 347-57.

—'Mark'. Pages 350-62 in *Women's Bible Commentary*. Edited by Carol A. Newsom and Sharon H. Ringe. Louisville, KY: Westminster John Knox Press, 1998.

Tombs, David. 'Crucifixion, State Terror, and Sexual Abuse'. *Union Seminary Quarterly Review* 53 (1999), pp. 89-109.

—'He Is Not Here'. Disappearance, Death and Denial. Pages 194-210 in *Truth and Memory: The Church and Human Rights in El Salvador and Guatemala*. Edited by Michael A. Hayes and David Tombs. Leominster: Gracewing, 2001.

Trible, Phyllis. *Texts of Terror: Literary-Feminist Readings of Biblical Narratives.* Philadelphia: Fortress Press, 1984.

Trimble Alliaume, Karen. *Re(as)sembling Christ: Feminist Christology, Identity Politics, and the Imagination of Christian Community.* PhD diss., Duke University, 1999.

Vaage, Leif E. 'En otra casa: El discipulado en Marcos como ascetismo doméstico'. *Estudios Bíblicos* 63 (2005), pp. 21-42.

Vena, Osvaldo. *Evangelio de Marcos.* Miami, FL: Sociedades Bíblicas Unidas, 2008.

Vine, Michael E. 'The "Trial Scene" Chronotope in Mark and Jewish Novel'. Pages 189-203 in *The Trial and Death of Jesus: Essays on the Passion Narrative in Mark*. Edited by Geert Van Oyen and Tom Shepherd. Leuven: Peeters, 2006.

Villalobos Mendoza, Manuel. 'Bodies *del otro lado* Finding Life and Hope in the Borderland: Gloria Anzaldúa, The Ethiopian Eunuch of Acts 8:26-40, *y Yo*'. Pages 191-221 in *Bible Trouble: Queer Reading at the Boundaries of Biblical Scholarship*. Edited by Teresa J. Hornsby and Ken Stone. Atlanta: Society of Biblical Literature, 2011.

Vogelzang, M.E. and W.J. Van Bekkum. 'Meaning and Symbolism of Clothing in Ancient Near East Texts'. Pages 265-84 in *Scripta signa vocis*. Edited by H.L.J.

Vanstiphout, K. Jongeling, F. Leembuis and G.J. Reinink. Groningen: Egbert For-
    sten, 1986.
Waetjen, Herman C. *A Reordering of Power: A Socio-Political Reading of Mark's Gos-
    pel.* Minneapolis: Fortress Press, 1989.
Walter, Jonathan. 'Invading the Roman Body: Manliness and Impenetrability in Roman
    Thought'. Pages 29-43 in *Roman Sexualities.* Edited by Judith P. Hallett and
    Marilyn B. Skinner. Princeton: Princeton University Press, 1997.
Webb, Geoff R. *Mark at the Threshold: Applying Bakhtinian Categories to Markan
    Characterization.* Leiden: Brill, 2008.
West, Gerald O. *Biblical Hermeneutics of Liberation.* Maryknoll, NY: Orbis Books,
    1995.
Whittaker, Molly. *Jews and Christians: Greco-Roman Views.* Cambridge: Cambridge
    University Press, 1984.
Wilkinson-Duran. Nicole. 'Jesus: A Western Perspective'. Pages 246-349 in *Global
    Bible Commentary.* Edited by Daniel Patte *et al.* Nashville, TN: Abingdon, 2004.
—*The Power of Disorder: Ritual Elements in Mark's Passion Narrative.* London: T. &
    T. Clark, 2008.
Williams, Joel F. *Other Followers of Jesus: Minor Characters as Major Figures in
    Mark's Gospel.* Sheffield: JSOT Press, 1994.
Winter, Paul. *On the Trial of Jesus.* Berlin: Walter de Gruyter, 1961.
Yarbro Collins, Adela. *Mark: A Commentary.* Minneapolis: Fortress Press, 2007.
Zea, Leopoldo. *Filosofía americana como filosofía sin más.* México: Siglo XXI, 1969.

Primary Sources: Greco-Roman

Artemidorus Daldianus. *The Interpretation of Dreams.* Edited by Maria Mavroude.
    Athens: Histos, 2002.
Cicero. *On Duties.* Edited by M.T. Griffin and E.M. Atkins. New York: Cambridge Uni-
    versity Press, 1991.
—*Orations.* Loeb Classical Library, 198. Edited by H. Grose Hodge. Cambridge, MA,
    and London: Harvard University Press, 2002.
—*The Verrine Orations.* Loeb Classical Library, 293. Edited by L.H.G. Greenwood.
    Cambridge, MA: Harvard University Press, 1928.
Dionysius of Halicarnassus. *Roman Antiquities.* Loeb Classical Library, 319. Edited by
    Earnest Cary. Cambridge, MA, and London: Harvard University Press and Wil-
    liam Heinemann, 1937.
Homer. *The Odyssey: Books 1–12.* Loeb Classical Library, 104-105. Edited by A.T.
    Murray. Cambridge, MA: Harvard University Press, 1998.
Juvenal. *Satires.* Loeb Classical Library, 91. Edited by Susanna Morton Braund. Cam-
    bridge, MA and London: Harvard University Press, 2004.
Martial. *Epigrams.* Loeb Classical Library, 94-95, 480. Edited by D.R. Shackleton
    Bailey. Cambridge, MA, and London: Harvard University Press, 1993.
Plato. *Gorgias.* Loeb Classical Library, 166. Edited by W.R.M. Lamb. London and Cam-
    bridge, MA: William Heinemann and Harvard University Press, 1925.
Plutarch. *Artaxerxes. Moralia IV.* Loeb Classical Library, 305. Edited by Bernadotte Per-
    rin. Cambridge, MA, and London: Harvard University Press and William Hein-
    emann, 1926.

Quintilian. *The Lesser Declamation.* Loeb Classical Library, 500-501. Edited by D.R. Shackleton Bailey. Cambridge, MA: Harvard University Press, 2006.

Seneca. *Epistles.* Loeb Classical Library, 75-77. Edited by Richard M. Gummere. Cambridge, MA, and London: Harvard University Press and William Heinemann, 1917–1925.

Suetonius. *Augustus.* Loeb Classical Library, 31. Edited by J. C. Rolfe. London and New York: William Heinemann and Macmillan, 1914.

Tacitus. *The Annals.* Loeb Classical Library, 249, 312, 322. Edited by Clifford H. Moore and John Jackson. Cambridge, MA: Harvard University Press, 1931–1937.

—*The Histories.* Loeb Classical Library, 111, 249. Edited by Clifford H. Moore and John Jackson. Cambridge, MA, and London: Harvard University Press and William Heinemann, 1925–1931.

Primary Sources: Jewish

Josephus. Translated by H. St. J. Thackeray *et al.* 10 vols. Loeb Classical Library. Cambridge, MA: Harvard University Press, 1926-1965.

Philo. *On Abraham.* Loeb Classical Library, 289. Edited by F.H. Colson. Cambridge, MA, and London: Harvard University Press and William Heinemann, 1935.

—*Flaccus.* Loeb Classical Library, 363. Edited by F.H. Colson. Cambridge, MA, and London: Harvard University Press and William Heinemann, 1935.

INDEX OF PASSAGES

Index of Authors

CPSIA information can be obtained
at www.ICGtesting.com
Printed in the USA
LVHW051744050721
691876LV00004B/354

9 781910 928